Union Organizing and Staying Organized

Ken Gagala

Reston Publishing Company, Inc.
Reston, Virginia

Library of Congress Cataloging in Publication Data

Gagala, Kenneth L.
Union organizing and staying organized.

Includes index.
1. Trade-unions—United States—Organizing.
I. Title.
HD6490.072U643 1983   331.89'12'0973   82–25047
ISBN 0–8359–8064–2
ISBN 0–8359–8063–4 (pbk.)

10   9   8   7   6   5   4   3   2   1

Printed in the United States of America

Contents

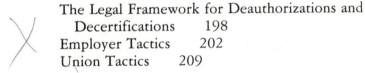

Exhibits

Preface

My interest in union organizing was sparked as a child by the men and women of my family who endured the degradation of the "open shop" and participated in the tumultuous CIO organizing drives of the 1930's around Hamtramck and Detroit. Yet it was not until 1977 that I proceeded from the labor history books and the oral tradition of a family of Polish workers in America to an examination of contemporary union organizing. Part of my job at the time was to develop courses for the Cornell University Labor Studies Program, and the union activists participating in the program expressed a strong desire for a course on organizing, which accordingly would be for college credit and would need the sanction of academicians outside the confines of the program—no easy task, because it would be without precedent or even the availability of a contemporary book on organizing from a union perspective. Also, it might challenge the "neutrality" and "objectivity" which universities prescribe, often inconsistently.

With the assistance of Teamster organizer Vicki Sapporta, I contacted Walt Englebert of the Teamsters' Western Conference, who had taught organizing classes for the union. Walt quickly comprehended the situation and applied his considerable organizing talent to the problem. He suggested that he team-teach the course in point-counterpoint fashion with John Bodilly of Southern Oregon

State College, an extraordinary professor of management with over 30 years of corporate labor relations experience, including the negotiation of the first contract on behalf of Gallo Wineries with the United Farm Workers. In July 1979, John Bodilly and Walt Englebert taught what presumably was the first college credit course on union organizing.

Shortly afterward I came to the University of Minnesota's Labor Education Service, all the while continuing to gather information on organizing and expanding my investigation to include its counterpart, preventing decertification. In the Spring of 1981 I introduced a course on organizing and staying organized in the University's Union Leadership Academy, with the very capable assistance of two experienced organizers, John Robertas of the Teamsters and Marcus Widenor, formerly of the Ladies Garment Workers. Concurrently, I began work with individual unions on strengthening their external and internal organizing efforts.

The objective of this book is to improve the odds for unions in meeting the major challenge confronting them today: organizing and staying organized. It is a compilation and interpretation of information provided by union organizers, union activists, labor lawyers, union avoidance consultants, personnel administrators, NLRB representatives, and labor educators. While I alone bear responsibility for the errors of omission and commission, thanks are due to the following people in addition to the aforementioned: Joe Adler, Ray Bliss, Bob Bonacorda, Bill Bonifer, Bob Bouten, Floyd Child, Tom Coffey, Gene Daniels, Nancy Daniels, Tony De Angelis, Jeff Fiedler, Leo Gagala, Tom Hall, Bob Harbrant, Ann Herson, Pete Ingram, Art Jelinski, Sam Kaynard, John Kestler, Steve Klonouski, Les Krause, Bill Mackey, Karl Meller, Donna Mobley, Dan Parkhurst, Renas Parkhurst, Jan Radle, Dick Ross, Eddie Selden, Ann Thompson, Ellie Woller, and Joe Zymanski.

Special thanks are due to my wife, Pat, who typed the manuscript and provided valuable criticisms.

What's Wrong Today?

In 1945, at the end of World War II, about one out of every three American workers belonged to a labor union. Just ten years later, at the time of the AFL-CIO merger, the proportion had slipped to one out of four workers. And in 1978, only one out of five American workers belonged to a union.

While in 1955 unions won two out of three union authorization elections conducted by the National Labor Relations Board (NLRB), they lost more elections than they won between 1975 and 1980. Between 1968 and 1978, a 200 percent increase occurred in the number of NLRB-conducted decertification elections in which organized workers decide whether or not to continue union representation. In 1978, unions lost 74 percent of the decertification elections conducted.

The names John L. Lewis, Jimmy Hoffa, and George Meany are synonymous to most people with the concept of a "labor movement." However, the unions they once headed no longer dominate their respective industries.

In 1974, 70 percent of the nation's coal was produced by members of the United Mine Workers of America. During World War II, John L. Lewis could stop the production of war material by pulling the miners out of the pits. In 1982, only 44 percent of U.S. coal production came from union-organized mines and the proportion is dropping fast.

The International Brotherhood of Teamsters, for many years the nation's largest labor organization, has experienced a drop of 400,000 members and the union is struggling to maintain its domination of the interstate trucking industry established by Jimmy Hoffa.

For twenty-five years after the AFL-CIO merger, George Meany, a former plumber from the Bronx, served as labor's spokesman. Meany had a particular affinity for the seventeen building trade unions in the federation. In 1973, about 30 percent of the nonresidential construction in the country was non-union while in 1982 60 percent was non-union. The June 1979 cover of *Fortune* magazine hailed the development with the headline "How the Contractors Broke the Union's Grip."

What happened?

THE "RIGHT-TO-WORK" EFFECT

Union membership, where is it? Seventy-five percent is concentrated in ten states. New York has more union members than eleven Southern states including Texas. Population and jobs are moving to the South and the West—the "Sun Belt"—and most Sun Belt states have so-called "right-to-work" laws which prohibit unions from negotiating "union shop" clauses in contracts. Union shop clauses require workers represented by unions to maintain union membership and, consequently, to pay for the services rendered by unions through dues and initiation fees.

The effect of "right-to-work" laws on the financial ability of unions to conduct drives to organize new members is substantial. In 1977, 21.5 million workers were covered by collective bargaining agreements, while only 19.3 million workers belonged to unions. This translates into one out of every ten workers enjoying the benefits of union representation without contributing to the cost of operating unions.

States with low proportions of union membership encourage the exodus from states where the bulk of the union members live with advertising slogans like "Virginia Is Not Only a Right-to-Work State, It's a Want-to-Work State." Virginia Governor John Dalton called the law prohibiting the union shop "the single most beneficial statute in bringing in new industry to the state." "Right-to-work" is more than a law that prohibits mandatory union membership, because it keeps unions small, weak, and disorganized. Hourly industrial wages in Virginia, for example, rank 17 percent below the national average—a very crucial problem, because twenty states have "right-to-work" laws.[1]

Political power is also shifting to the Sun Belt. As a result of the 1980 census, most of the heavily unionized states lost seats in the U.S. House of Representatives, while states with low proportions of unionization gained seats.

CHANGING JOB STRUCTURE

In addition to jobs shifting to the Sun Belt, the types of jobs in the U.S. economy are changing. Manufacturing jobs in industries such as automobiles, steel, rubber, and electrical appliances are declining. These traditionally unionized industries are being adversely affected by automation and foreign competition. In contrast, growth is occurring in service industries such as medical care, food service, banking, and insurance.

Between 1959 and 1979, the number of white-collar workers increased by 20 million, while the blue-collar work force increased by only 10 million. There are about 49 million white-collar employees, yet only a little over 7 million are organized. If they are to grow, unions must adapt to the changing structure of the economy.

BREAKING AND STRETCHING THE LAW TO PREVENT UNION ORGANIZATION

Congress passed the National Labor Relations Act in 1935 with the intent of stopping the violence surrounding union organizing campaigns by granting workers the opportunity to choose whether or not to be represented by unions through secret ballot elections conducted by the National Labor Relations Board. Employers are not to discharge or otherwise discriminate against workers desiring union representation. The intent of the law, however, can be subverted by employers who want to prevent union organization of their employees.

A blueprint for dodging unionization is outlined by a management consultant specializing in the construction industry: If an election is likely to occur, the employer should attempt to delay the election. "If it is near the tail end of a (construction) job, and you are not going to be in the area again, there will be no election."

After the NLRB certifies a union as the bargaining agent for a group of workers, the employer is required by law to "bargain in good faith" with the union. For the consultant, this is no obstacle; "It doesn't mean you sign an agreement." An employer can make inadequate offers until a strike occurs; "You goad them into a strike." If a strike occurs, the employer is advised to bring in strikebreakers.[2]

There is strong evidence that significant numbers of employers are following the blueprint for avoiding unionization and that the plan works. If an employer and union agree to have the NLRB conduct an election as a "consent" election, balloting occurs rather quickly. But if the employer files objections to the election, balloting is delayed. In 1962, 46 percent of all NLRB elections were conducted as consent elections, but in 1977, only 9 percent were consent elections. In 1962, 11 percent of all NLRB elections were completed in the same month that the union requested the election and 59 percent in the month that followed, but in 1977, only 2 percent occurred in the month of filing and only 40 percent during the following month. Delays mean election losses for unions. When the election occurs in the same month as the request, unions win 59 percent of the elections. When the election is delayed six months, unions win only 46.5 percent of the elections. Winning the election does not mean that employer resistance stops. There is a 20 percent chance (one out of five) that the union will never secure a collective bargaining agreement with the employer![3]

In 1979, unions filed over three times as many unfair labor practice charges (alleged violations of the laws governing labor relations) against employers as they did in 1968, while the number of NLRB elections increased by only 10 percent. The charge most frequently filed is unlawful dismissal of an employee for union activity. By firing union activists, employers can succeed in frightening other workers into avoiding the union. If found guilty of unlawful discharge, the penalties imposed by the law (usually reinstatement with back pay) are not likely to deter employers determined to avoid unionization and, more importantly, are unlikely to reduce the level of fear among workers at unorganized workplaces, because final settlement of discharge for union activity cases can be dragged through the courts for years. Unscrupulous employers view the penalties as the cost of a license to kill unions.

An example of how the law operates or, more properly, fails to operate is the twenty-four year struggle between the Textile Workers Union and Milliken and Company. In 1956, the company closed a textile mill in South Carolina to avoid unionization. The NLRB and the U.S. Supreme Court found the employer guilty of dismissing workers for union activity in order to discourage unionization at its other plants. Finally in 1980, the union, employer, and NLRB agreed that $5 million should be divided among 427 workers who lost their jobs and the survivors of 126 workers who have died since 1956. The approximate $10,000 per worker settlement is little consolation to workers who were too old or otherwise unable to get another job since 1956. For Milliken, the $5 million settlement is a wrist slap; its annual sales are an estimated $2 billion.[4]

Between 1963 and 1976, J. P. Stevens Company was forced to pay $1.3 million in back wages to workers illegally fired for union activity. This is less than 25 percent of what the company would have had to pay if the union had been successful at organizing and had negotiated a one cent per hour wage increase for all Stevens employees.[5]

Violating the law pays dividends with no relief in sight for unions. In 1980, the NLRB awarded $33 million in back pay to discharged workers, double the previous highest year.

BREAKING AND STRETCHING THE LAW TO DECERTIFY UNIONS

Under the law, an organized employer is not to promote a union decertification. However, the intent of the law can be dodged. A management consultant, tells how: "The decertification campaign is as wide as your imagination. Here are a few do's and don'ts. You can't write an anti-union speech, but you can tell a 'loyal' employee how to write one. Don't tell such an employee, 'I want you to file' a decertification petition. Tell him he has a right to file. Don't tell him you will pay for his going to the NLRB, but 'wink' at him so that he knows you will 'make it up.' "[6]

The idea is to plant the seed for decertification and to nurture it. Lloyd Laudermilch, a member of the Operating Engineer's union, testified before the House Subcommittee on Labor-Management how he received an anonymous call from the "Lone Ranger" advising him to organize a union decertification. The "masked man" turned out to be the director of employee relations for Humana, Inc., Laudermilch's employer.[7]

Another union decertification technique is to take a hard-line stance in collective bargaining and force the union into a strike. With union members on strike, the employer then hires strikebreakers and encourages "loyal" employees to cross picket lines. Then, the workers replacing the strikers petition the NLRB for a decertification election.

This scenario was recently followed in Clinton, Iowa, between Clinton Corn Processing Company and Grain Millers Union, Local 6. On August 1, 1979, union members voted overwhelmingly to strike because of an impasse in collective bargaining. The next day the company began to hire strikebreakers. Ten and a half months later, the 750-member Grain Millers Union, Local 6, was decertified.

According to Michael Krajnovich, Local 6 Business Representative, there was a dramatic change in labor relations at Clinton Corn beginning in 1975. "They brought in a personnel man who believes in a union-free environment." Prior to 1975 there had been only fifteen arbitration cases in the Local's history. But from 1975 to August 1, 1979, there were twenty-two cases. Local 6 won eighteen of the twenty-two cases, but its treasury was being drained. Krajnovich describes the company's offer in the negotiations leading to the strike as "pretty much a slap in the face," particularly its refusal to budge on safety language, although it had just been cited by OSHA for twenty-six violations.[8]

While an increase in the number of arbitration cases does not necessarily mean that employers are more hostile to unions than in the past (unions may simply be choosing to go to arbitration more frequently), there is no question that the labor relations environment is much different from what it was in 1970. Between 1971 and 1980 the number of requests for arbitrators from the American Arbitration Association nearly tripled from 6,658 to 17,062. The same was true of requests to the Federal Mediation and Conciliation Service; they increased from 8,479 in 1969 to 27,189 in 1979.[9]

THE DEFEAT OF LABOR LAW REFORM

The Province of Ontario, Canada, with a history and political ideology similar to that of the United States and Canada's most industrialized and populated province, has labor laws that limit the ability of employers to subvert unionization. Unions are certified as bargaining agents as soon as more than half of the workers sign cards expressing a desire to join. Unlike the United States, secret-ballot elections are not held. Employers who refuse to bargain can be sued for damages or have contracts imposed on them by provincial labor boards. Also employers have only a limited right to ask courts to review such decisions.

The political process exerts a great deal of influence on the ability of unions to organize in the United States. In 1977 and 1978, an effort was made to change the laws regulating organizing. In 1976, 50 percent of all elections were delayed 246 days or more. The "Labor Law Reform" bill would have set a maximum of seventy-five days between the request for election and actual balloting. Employers would have been required to pay unlawfully discharged employees twice as much as their lost wages, and it would have prevented cases like Milliken from dragging on for years. Also, employers who violate the law could have been barred from receiving federal government contracts for up to three years.

Employers lobbied hard and were able to defeat the bill through a Senate filibuster. Some international union presidents believed that the executives of large corporations had come to view organized labor as a "partner" rather than an adversary. However, the role of major corporations, many of them organized since the 1930s, in defeating "Labor Law Reform" altered their view.[10] The battle lines between labor and management are still drawn, because employers evidently believe overwhelmingly that unions do more harm than good.[11]

SOPHISTICATED MANAGEMENT TECHNIQUES

Prior to the 1940s, many employers substantial enough to have anything called a "personnel department" had a few clerks to take care of the payroll and a legion of armed guards to protect the property from theft and takeover by the workers. Foremen did the hiring and firing and used motivational techniques dating back to the building of the pyramids in Egypt to get production out of workers and to keep them out of unions. Employers unable to afford a permanent security force could, when the need arose, engage spies, thugs, strike-breakers, and other "consultants" who traveled from employer to employer rendering their services.

Workers desiring to organize conducted strikes and attempted to overpower the security forces of employers. Force met force with the outcome often depending on whose behalf the police or national guard intervened.

The era of violent physical confrontation waned with the Supreme Court's upholding the constitutionality of the Wagner Act in 1937, U.S. immersion in World War II, which brought a no-strike pledge from unions and acquiescence regarding union recognition from management, and passage of the Taft-Hartley Act in 1947 which restricted organizational strikes and sympathy strikes for union recognition. The NLRB election conducted under "laboratory conditions" became the focus of the union organizing process.

With the passage of the era of violent confrontation, flak jackets and billyclubs were traded for business suits and sharpened pencils, more appropriate for work in the "laboratory." The personnel office for many employers changed from a minor clerical function and paramilitary command post to a relatively sophisticated managerial operation. The power to hire and fire shifted from the foreman to the personnel department. While the carrot and stick still prevail as the method for motivating employees, they are used more subtly and less harshly than in the past so as to, in the management dictum, "make unions unnecessary." Granting the personnel office power to reprimand supervisors for their treatment of employees and their failure to adequately implement union avoidance policies is not uncommon. The personnel department has daily access to employees, thereby giving it the potential to conduct union avoidance activities on a continuous basis.

Employers desiring to train their supervisory personnel in union avoidance techniques need not look far. Universities and management education organizations offer courses on the subject. Employers unable to afford full-time union avoidance activities can hire consultants on a per diem basis when the need arises. *Business Week* magazine estimates that there are at least 10,000 labor lawyers and hundreds of consultants who advise employers on union avoidance.[12]

We have seen that under the law, unions operate at a disadvantage. Unscrupulous employers can and do violate the law because the punishment for their actions is so meager. However, illegal actions are only part of the reason why unions are failing to organize. Management has developed sophisticated rhetorical, psychological, and organizational techniques to retard unionization.

Union avoidance activities can be divided into two categories. Long-term activities occur without any indication of a union organizing effort and can be likened to preventive maintenance of capital equipment. Examples are designing workplaces so that employees have limited contact with one another, i.e., little opportunity to pursue union organization among themselves, training foremen and other first-line supervisors to regularly communicate with employees on the advantages of working non-union, and copying certain provisions of union contracts such as grievance procedures.

Short-term activities are triggered by the initiation of union organizing activities and are likened by management to emergency repairs of broken equipment. Examples are intensified discussions between supervisors and employees on the disadvantages of unionization, communication with the families of employees on the projected impact of union representation, and films, slide shows, and speeches directed at large groups of employees on company time.

OBSTACLES TO ORGANIZING IN THE HOUSE OF LABOR

Some critics lay the responsibility for the declining proportion of the labor force belonging to unions directly on organized labor itself. A usual starting point is an interview with George Meany, late president of the AFL-CIO, which appeared in the February 21, 1972, issue of *U.S. News and World Report*.[13] In the interview, Mr. Meany is quoted as saying that he is unconcerned about organized labor's declining representation, because American unions, unlike European unions, have always represented a minority of workers and have done quite well despite their smaller numbers.

Because the AFL-CIO president is viewed as the official spokesman for the labor movement, it may be that organized labor at the

leadership level is not concerned about declining union representation of the labor force. Historically, the AFL was very slow at
attempting to organize semi-skilled industrial workers and in some
cases actually obstructed their organization. Some observers feel that
despite the merger of the AFL unions which represented primarily
skilled craftsmen, and the CIO unions which represented primarily
semi-skilled industrial workers, the passive approach to organizing
of the old AFL dominates the merged organization. George Meany's
statement can be viewed as a confirmation of this opinion.

At the local level, business agents and other full-time union
officers sometimes express privately an opposition to organizing new
members. The local union's workload increases because of the additional services required by new members, while the number of
union staff members often does not increase accordingly. Likewise,
an increase in membership does not always result in increases in the
salaries of union staff members.

Rank and file union members sometimes resist increased organizing efforts by the union if the organizing is to be financed by
a dues increase, because they apparently see little direct benefit for
themselves. Also, some union members view organizing as a liability
even if no dues increase is involved. When the union increases its
organizing efforts, the result may be a decline in the quality of service
received during contract negotiations and in the processing of grievances. A greater share of dues being spent on organizing may mean
the inability to process grievances through to arbitration.

In 1945, 62 percent of the union members surveyed by the
Opinion Research Corporation wanted the union movement to grow
larger. In 1950, the proportion desiring union growth fell to 50
percent. In 1962, only 46 percent of union members surveyed wanted
the labor movement to grow. The proportion declined even further
to 38 percent in 1966.[14] One must conclude that corresponding with
the decline in the proportion of union members in the labor force,
there has been a decline in the desire of union members to have
unions grow. Because unions are essentially democratic organizations, an important explanation of the declining unionized proportion
of the labor force may be that as unions grow, the incentive to spend
union funds on organizing new members decreases, while the incentive to finance services to the existing membership increases.[15]

In private, some union organizers are very critical of their unions'
organizing policies. Because organizers are not as accountable to the

union membership as union staff who service and negotiate contracts, cronies of union leaders are allegedly put out to pasture as organizers to await retirement or, more likely, death. New members of the organizing staff allegedly receive little or no training—certainly much less than the management personnel, labor lawyers, and union avoidance consultants they confront. Sour grapes or valid criticisms?

In addition to these alleged internal obstacles, the image organized labor conveys to the public through the media is often cited as an obstacle to organizing. During the 1930s when unions experienced their fastest rate of growth, unions were viewed as downtrodden underdogs fighting for a new and better world. Today, the public image is far different. Strikes, particularly in the public sector by teachers, sanitation workers, transit workers, police, and fire fighters, have soured some people. Racial and sex discrimination, corruption, and violence in a small minority of unions have projected a tarnished image on all unions. AFL-CIO support of U.S. involvement in the Vietnam War and its failure to endorse George McGovern's presidential candidacy in 1972 despite an AFL-CIO-COPE rating far more favorable than that of Richard Nixon disillusioned many, particularly young people. In 1972, the Opinion Research Corporation reported that 50 percent of the public surveyed thought that unions are too powerful and two thirds thought that strikes and other labor actions seriously hurt the country.[16]

The placement of relatives in union positions has brought charges of nepotism and abuse of power against union leaders. A recent study by the University of Michigan's Survey Research Center disclosed that two thirds of the *union members* surveyed thought that labor leaders served their own interests rather than those of the rank and file.[17]

CONCLUSIONS

Obviously, there are some factors contributing to the decline of union membership that unions cannot change—and others that they can affect.

Unions have railed and rallied against "right-to-work" since the passage of Taft-Hartley in 1947 to no avail. These efforts have failed despite presumably more favorable political climates in Washington during periods when larger proportions of the labor force belonged to unions.

Unions cannot in the near future stop the decline of the heavily unionized Northeast and Midwest and the movement of jobs to the low-wage and energy-rich Sun Belt. In a country like Sweden, such drastic regional disallocations would not be tolerated. Organized labor in the United States does not have the political power to temper the change. Unions can, however, intensify their efforts to organize workers in the Sun Belt.

Unions cannot slow down the growth of white-collar and service industries and the relative decline of heavily unionized blue-collar, manufacturing industries. But unions can intensify their efforts to organize the growing, unorganized sectors of the economy.

Despite the really inhumane deficiencies in the laws regulating the organization and decertification of unions, there is little that unions can do to change the laws. If changes did not occur in 1948 or even 1977, they will not occur today. The political calculus is against organized labor. Unions can, however, improve the way they operate under existing laws despite the clear advantages enjoyed by employers.

Unions cannot change the sophisticated techniques used by management to avert unionization. However, unions can study the techniques used by management, adapt them to serve their needs, and develop a counteroffensive.

FOOTNOTES

[1] Glenn Frankel. "Virginia Law Creates Haven for Business," *The Minneapolis Star*, October 14, 1980.

[2] "Taking Aim at Union Busters," *Business Week*, November 12, 1979, p. 99.

[3] Richard Prosten. "The Rise in NLRB Election Delays: Measuring Business' New Resistance." *Monthly Labor Review*, February 1979, pp. 38–39.

[4] "The NLRB Settles Its Most Notorious Case," *Business Week,* December 15, 1980.

[5] *The American Lawyer*, April 1980, p. 18.

[6] "Labor-Management Climate," *AFL-CIO American Federationist,* March 1982, p. 22

[7] "Like It? He *Revels* in It." Memo from COPE, October 29, 1979.

[8] David Prosten. "House Hears Sordid Tales of Union-Busting Experts," *Washington Teamster*, November 2, 1979.

[9] "Grainmillers Local Decertified after 10-1/2 Month Strike," *Labor Notes*, July 22, 1980, p. 13.

[10] A. H. Raskin. "Big Labor Strives to Break Out of Its Rut," *Fortune,* August 27, 1979.

[11] Frank Allen. "Bosses Say Unions Do More Bad Than Good," *Wall Street Journal*, December 11, 1980.

[12] "Taking Aim at 'Union Busters,'" *Business Week*, November 12, 1979, p. 98.

[13] "Interview with George Meany," *U.S. News & World Report,* February 21, 1972.

[14] Derek Bok and John Dunlop. *Labor and the American Community.* (New York: Simon and Schuster, 1970), p. 15. Since 1966, the Opinion Research Corporation has not surveyed union members on this issue, nor have Gallup, Harris, and Roper.

[15] Richard N. Block, "A Theory of the Supply of Union Representation and the Allocation of Resources." In Myron Roomkin and Hervey Juris, "The Changing Character of Unionism in Traditionally Organized Sectors," *Monthly Labor Review*, February 1979, pp. 37–38.

[16] Wilfrid Sheed. "Whatever Happened to the Labor Movement?" *Atlantic Monthly*, July 1973.

[17] Raskin, "Big Labor Strives."

2

Making the Law Work Better for Unions

Sixteen years ago, I received my first practical exposure to organizing law when my uncle was fired from his job as an insurance agent. He had been employed by the company for nineteen years, and for the last twelve of those years, he had been the local union's president, chief negotiator, and strike leader. His employer told the NLRB that he was fired simply for not meeting his sales quotas to counter my uncle's charge that he had been set up for the discharge by having his sales territory cut and that the real reason was his union activity.

After two months of deliberations, the employer offered my uncle a cash settlement, if he would agree to drop his request for reinstatement to his job. Unemployed with bills accumulating, he accepted the offer. My uncle never fully recovered from this incident. He held a succession of jobs and never regained the spark that had made him an award-winning insurance salesman and a capable and dedicated local union leader.

I will never know whether my uncle was set up for the discharge and fired for union activity. But I do know that if the law had not presumed that he was guilty until proven innocent by allowing the employer to cut off his means of livelihood while the case proceeded, he would have been less inclined to accept the compromise and may have ultimately been reinstated.

As a twenty-three year old college graduate at the time with courses in labor relations and labor law to my credit, I was astonished.

The law does not operate as smoothly as portrayed in the textbooks. Further investigation disclosed that my uncle's case was not unique; thousands of workers find themselves in similar situations each year, because discharge and other discipline for union activity are seldom clear-cut matters.

With the prospects dim for changes in union-organizing law, it is important that unions develop strategies to make the law work better to their advantage. This chapter attempts to accomplish those objectives.

A concise overview of the law regulating union organizing is provided. It is not intended to replace the services of labor lawyers nor the comprehensive labor law books on the subject. Instead, it is the framework within which suggestions for improving the performance of unions are made.

JURISDICTION OF THE LABOR MANAGEMENT RELATIONS ACT

In 1935, the passage of the National Labor Relations Act (NLRA) or Wagner Act gave workers in the private sector the right to organize into unions and established the National Labor Relations Board (NLRB) to administer the law. NLRA was amended in 1947 by the Labor Management Relations Act (LMRA), also called the Taft-Hartley Act.

LMRA regulates union organizing in the private sector. State and federal government agencies (except for the U.S. Postal Service) are not covered by LMRA but by other statutes. The Railway Labor Act of 1926 regulates the organizing of railroad and airline employees. While this chapter examines only the provisions of LMRA, it should be instructive to those interested in organizing in the state, federal, railroad, and airline sectors because of the close parallel between laws, particularly in regard to unfair labor practices committed by employers and unions.

With the exception of agricultural workers, domestic workers in private homes, independent contractors, and supervisors, all private sector employees have the right to organize under LMRA. This does not mean, for example, that supervisors cannot form unions, only that they do not receive the protection of the law. An employer would, for example, be allowed to discharge supervisors for attempting to form a union, while it would be prohibited by LMRA from firing its nonsupervisory employees for union activity. By not including certain workers under the law's protection, however, their ability to organize is remote.

I once had a job delivering soft drinks to retail outlets. As a man ages, that job can become very difficult. Years of bouncing around in a truck take their toll on the back and kidneys. Lifting 300 cases of soda weighing sixty to seventy-five pounds apiece every day can become unbearable as a man approaches age sixty-five. Accordingly, as workers aged their productivity tended to decline. For years, the company and the union had an informal agreement that long-term employees would be transferred to either lighter duty bottling plant jobs in the bargaining unit or field supervisor jobs out of the bargaining unit when they could no longer work as delivery men.

Then, a change in managers occurred. Six new field supervisor jobs were created and older workers were "promoted" into them. Within three months, four of the six new supervisors were fired. This occurred before the passage of ERISA, so the workers lost their pension benefits as well. Because the workers were out of the bargaining unit, the union could not seek their reinstatement. The discharged employees had not been particularly active in the union, so the action cannot be classified definitely as an effort to break the union. During union-organizing drives, however, some employers have "promoted" union supporters out of the potential bargaining unit and fired them expressly for their union support.[1]

The federal government is empowered to regulate interstate commerce; therefore, LMRA applies to employers whose business involves sales and purchases with consumers and businesses in other states. While nearly all private sector employers are covered by the broad umbrella of "affecting interstate commerce," the organizer should be aware that a very small number of employers are not covered.

In order to reduce its workload, the National Labor Relations Board has set dollar values on the sales or gross receipts of businesses below which it will not assert jurisdiction. A non-retail business must either sell $50,000 worth of product or have purchases of at least $50,000 from other states. A retail business and hotels and taxi cab companies must have at least $500,000 of sales or gross receipts. Public utilities and local transportation companies must have $250,000; interstate transportation companies need $50,000 to be covered.

Newspapers require $200,000. Other communication companies need sales or gross receipts of $100,000, while health care institutions must do at least $250,000 worth of business. Defense contractors affecting interstate commerce regardless of sales come under the NLRB's jurisdiction.

Before initiating an organizing campaign under LMRA procedures, the organizer should be reasonably assured that the employer comes within the NLRB's jurisdiction. In chapter 4, methods for determining the financial condition of employers who are potential targets for organizing campaigns will be examined. If after completing such an analysis, questions of jurisdiction still exist, the organizer should not hesitate to contact the Board prior to starting a campaign.

UNFAIR LABOR PRACTICES

The NLRB attempts to maintain "laboratory conditions" around the union authorization process. By sheltering workers from certain activities of employers and unions, the Board attempts to give workers the opportunity to make as reasonable a choice as possible and as is practical in a situation of intense competition between unions and employers. Violations of the requirements for laboratory conditions are classified as "unfair labor practices":

Threats   Unions are not to threaten workers or the property of workers who do not support the union. Likewise, it is an unfair labor practice for a union to threaten to persuade an employer to punish workers who do not support the union. For example, an organizer would violate the law by telling a worker that he or she will have a rough time after the union is authorized if the worker does not demonstrate his or her support for the union during the campaign preceding the election.

Since the passage of the Wagner Act, employers have been prohibited from making any threat to fire, demote, deny promotion, change shifts or jobs, withdraw benefits, or close down the plant if workers support unionization. However, between 1935 and 1947, the NLRB viewed virtually any statement by an employer as a threat or promise with the result that statements and actions of employers which the Board would find to be unfair labor practices were easily recognizable by union organizers. The so-called "freedom of speech" for employers provision of Taft-Hartley changed the situation so that the Board now attempts to distinguish between threats and honest expressions of opinion by employers. Often, the line between the two is very narrow and very difficult to distinguish.

Certainly, an outright threat to close the plant if the union is authorized is easy to recognize as an unfair labor practice. But the employer can cast the same fear in workers and correspond to NLRB regulations by making statements that shift the responsibility for the action to another party. For example, the employer can predict that customers might be lost because of unionization if customers fear that strikes might make the company an unreliable source of supply. The potential loss of customers could result in layoffs and even a plant closing. Here, the deciding factor to the Board seems to be whether or not the employer has control over the outcome of what might occur if the union is recognized as bargaining agent.[2]

Employers can also convey the message that unionization will bring adverse consequences by softening their approach. By stating that while the firm has *no intention* of moving, it may be forced to *consider* moving if its costs increase due to unionization, the Board may find that the employer is merely exercising its right of free speech, particularly if the employer has not been found to have committed other unfair labor practices. Because of the fine line between permissible and nonpermissible behavior, union avoidance consultants insist that managers stick to the prepared texts of speeches and not interject their personal interpretations.

The employer has the right to state that the union cannot guarantee certain benefits such as pensions and medical and dental plans, which often are cited by unions as benefits of organizing. The employer can also state that in collective bargaining, unions must sometimes give up benefits. However, the employer is prohibited from stating that if the union wins, it will not bargain until a court forces it to do so. Nor can the employer tell workers that when the union comes in, "bargaining starts from scratch," because in fact bargaining starts with the wages and benefits that exist when the union is authorized.

Due to the fine line between free speech and threats, the organizer should file unfair labor practice charges whenever statements that could be construed as threats occur. The procedures for filing unfair labor practice charges are discussed in a later section of this chapter.

Threats often are conveyed by planting rumors so that the source of the threat is difficult to identify. A supervisor approaches a worker in his department and says "I overheard two guys from another department talking at the coffee machine this morning. Do you know if it's true that the last three places this organizer got hold of closed down and moved out of state?" At the outset of a campaign and periodically thereafter, workers must be warned about rumors. Some organizers establish a "rumor control center" and widely publicize its telephone number. As difficult as it is, in-plant organizing committee members should attempt to trace rumors back to their source so that unfair labor charges can be filed with the NLRB.

An implicit threat that is nearly impossible to combat occurs when an employer establishes a policy of maintaining some non-union facilities. One giant manufacturing company is reputed to have a policy of maintaining at least one non-union plant capable of producing each of its product lines. The non-union facility may be located in the United States or in another country. In the event of a strike, production is shifted to a non-union plant and the union's collective bargaining power is reduced accordingly. Unorganized employees soon become aware of this corporate strategy.

During organizing campaigns, employers are prohibited from creating an atmosphere that can be construed as threatening. An example of a threatening atmosphere would be inordinate increases in the number of plant security guards and searches of employees as they enter and leave the workplace.

Employers can make anti-union buttons and stickers available to workers. Employees, however, can neither be forced to wear them nor can they be asked to wear them. The act of asking by itself is viewed as threatening by the NLRB. Unions, however, can ask workers to display pro-union insignia.

Granting and Promising Benefits   A union can waive the initiation fees and/or dues until a contract is signed for all workers in a unit it is attempting to organize. However, a union cannot offer to waive these expenses for only those workers supporting unionization prior to an election, because the Board views this action as an effort to bribe workers into supporting organization.

Unions and employers can give prizes of small monetary value and hold raffles to induce workers to attend meetings and to vote in NLRB-conducted elections. Also, they can purchase food and drinks and hold parties for workers.

Employers cannot promise benefits to workers if they choose not to form a union. Also, an employer cannot hold meetings with workers and ask them why they might choose to be represented by a union, because this implies that the employer will improve conditions if the union loses. The Board may also find that an employer is implying that wages, benefits, and working conditions will be improved even if it only asks workers about these matters during an organizing campaign. Again, the line between permissible and unpermissible behavior is very fine. When in doubt, the organizer should not hesitate to file an unfair labor practice charge with the NLRB.

During an organizing campaign, an employer cannot increase wages or benefits unless the increase was planned or regularly scheduled. Also, an employer cannot cancel a planned or regularly scheduled wage increase during an organizing drive. That is punishment for union activity.

A union avoidance consultant describes how the law can be averted in regard to unscheduled wage increases during a union organizing campaign:

> What happens if you haven't . . . any consistent pattern of increases? Now we don't have anybody from the board here, do we?
>
> What you do is backdate about six memorandums prior to when union activity started and you set your target date for your entries, backdating the memorandum . . . afterwards telling the regular Personnel Manager. And you are the Plant Manager, you write your Personnel Director a letter you backdated about 15 months before the union activity started. You directed him to survey the facilities in the area so we can bear a wage increase on January 15 _____. The survey finds the following rates and this is what I recommend on January 15, and then on January 15 _____. There is no way the board can touch it . . . you have a tremendous advantage over the union when you go to a hearing.[3]

Sometimes, organizers find themselves in the difficult position of having an employer announce an unscheduled wage or benefit increase during a campaign without making any effort to disguise the action as an attempt to dissuade workers from forming a union. By filing an unfair labor practice charge and halting the increase, the organizer faces the likelihood that some workers will be alienated toward the union. By ignoring the employer's action, some workers may believe that they have no need for a union or, more likely, that they can resurrect the threat to form a union whenever the employer is slow to adjust wages and benefits in the future.

The usual practice is to refrain from filing an unfair labor practice charge and, thereby, to allow the wage or benefit increase to be enacted. However, the organizer must explain the legality of the situation to workers, emphasizing that his or her union and other unions will not be used to accommodate future threats to extract wage and benefit increases. The organizer should not be reluctant to explain that union organizing is very expensive relative to the financial resources of unions and that other unions will be advised to avoid future organizing drives if workers are merely interested in the threat of unionization.

Libel   Unions and employers are not to make libelous statements about each other. A libelous statement is not truthful and injures a person's reputation. In addition to being an unfair labor practice, libel is subject to state laws and can result in expensive law suits. Accusing the employer of criminal acts, sexual deviancy, treason, lying, and cheating is very dangerous. Attacking the employer's character and personal life can backfire, even if the statement is truthful, because the attack may arouse sympathy for the employer among workers.

A case in point: An organizer distributed a leaflet showing the employer's large house with two expensive cars parked in front. The employer countered with a letter describing how hard he and his wife worked to build the business and hoping that his personal life would not be attacked any further by the union. The organizer felt a chill coming over the campaign after the exchange and ultimately lost the election.

"Captive Audience Speeches" and the "Twenty-Four Hour Rule"   The NLRB allows employers to gather large groups of employees together on company time for speeches, slide-shows, films, and other presentations urging them not to support the union. Under the Board's "twenty-four hour rule," captive audience speeches cannot be conducted within twenty-four hours of an election. All other campaign tactics (leafletting, individual conversations, *voluntary* mass meetings, telephone calls, letters, house calls, etc.) are not affected by the twenty-four hour rule.

Normally, outside organizers are not present at captive audience speeches. It is an unfair labor practice for them and union supporters among the election unit to disrupt captive audience speeches so as to prevent the employer from speaking. Furthermore, employees can be fired under Board rules for preventing the employer from speaking.

Some organizers instruct union supporters to sit toward the front of the audience. At the conclusion of the speech, union supporters raise their hands and shout "Questions!" Employers are often instructed by union avoidance consultants not to answer questions. The union has demonstrated that it does not agree with the employer's position and that the employer is either afraid to debate the union or is acting in a strong-armed manner, if it will not answer questions. If questions are allowed, union supporters can rebut the employer's position.

Substantial Misrepresentations in Campaign Statements

While the Board attempts to maintain laboratory conditions, it gives employers and unions the right to exaggerate their positions. The Board feels that workers who are to make the choice between union and no union can usually recognize campaign statements for what they are, because workers are familiar with the exaggerated claims of television advertisers and politicians during political campaigns. Until recently, the Board would set aside elections if campaign statements violated *all three* of the following guidelines:

1. The statement is a substantial misrepresentation of the truth. If a union leaflet said that average wages at unionized plants in the industry are $10 per hour when in fact they are $9.90, the Board probably would not consider this to be a substantial misrepresentation. However, if they are in fact $8.80 per hour, this statement would probably be considered a serious misrepresentation of the truth, even if the union did not mean to lie.

2. The statement must be about an important fact which might cause workers to change their support. Let us suppose that a union leaflet claims that the union was formed in 1870 when

in fact it was formed in 1930. The difference of sixty years is a substantial misrepresentation. But while this difference is important to labor historians, it is not likely to influence workers regarding support for the union.

3.   The other side must have sufficient time to correct the error. The NLRB has no firm rule on what constitutes sufficient time. A serious misstatement made to a unit of twenty-five employees working a single shift in one location where they must walk along a public sidewalk in order to go to and from work might be able to be corrected within forty-eight hours of an NLRB election. However, two weeks time might be insufficient for a larger unit scattered among several locations over a broad geographic area. What constitutes sufficiency of time to respond depends upon circumstances surrounding the election.

In August 1982, the Board ruled that it would no longer follow these guidelines.[4] Because the Board has been inconsistent, even when in doubt file an unfair labor practice charge.

Unreasonable Restrictions on the Union's Right to Solicit and Distribute Literature

Union organizers can distribute leaflets and authorization cards and can converse with workers they are attempting to organize on public property such as at plant gates, public sidewalks, and driveways. This right of free speech is guaranteed by the U.S. Constitution. However, the organizer's right to communicate with workers and to distribute literature on the private property of employers is restricted. Only in very rare situations where the union can demonstrate that access to employees is impossible because of the location of the plant, the dispersion of workers' homes over a large area, and the lack of a single newspaper, radio, or television station capable of reaching all of the workers, will organizers be allowed on the employer's property.

In the film *Norma Rae,* the organizer is shown entering the targeted employer's plant. Organizers did have access to J. P. Stevens Company plants after a court ruled that access was necessary in an attempt to counterbalance the labor law violations committed by the employer. Because this film is about the only exposure the public has had to the union-organizing process, it is unfortunate that the impression was conveyed that organizing is a bit easier than it really is, because organizers rarely have access to workers at the workplace.

Also, they seldom have access to company bulletin boards as depicted in the film.

Courts have ruled that shopping centers are not public property. Therefore, organizers must confine their activities to the public property surrounding shopping centers. This is an extreme disadvantage, because shopping centers tend to be located along roads with heavy automobile traffic traveling at fairly high speeds. Inducing workers to stop their cars so the organizers can speak with them or distribute union literature is not only difficult, it is a potential source of serious traffic accidents. As a consequence, organizers find themselves in the position of violating the law in order to gain access to workers. Likewise, organizers are often forced to violate the law when employers situate workplaces down long private roads. A long-time union organizer told me that he does not know of an organizer who has not been arrested for trespassing.

Obviously, contacting workers off the job is much more difficult than contacting them on the job. Therefore, it is extremely important for the organizer to develop effective in-plant organizing committees, because employees can converse with other employees about joining the union and can distribute union literature at the workplace during nonwork times. More will be said about in-plant organizing committees in later chapters.

It is an unfair labor practice for an employer to impose a broad rule against talking union and distributing union literature and to penalize and threaten to penalize workers for violating the rule. In general, workers can talk union on their free time (lunch and rest breaks) in work areas and nonwork areas and union authorization cards can be distributed in work and nonwork areas. However, the employer can restrict the distribution of other union literature to nonwork areas (lavatories, locker rooms, cafeterias, parking lots, and vending machine areas) because of the potential litter problem.

An employer may have a rule against distribution of political literature, merchandising material, charitable solicitations, and any other material even in nonwork areas. This rule is legal as long as it is not applied against union literature. Workers may wear union buttons, T-shirts, or other union insignia as long as the union apparel does not adversely affect production or safety. Workers who come in contact with the public, particularly retail sales personnel, can be restricted from wearing obtrusive union insignia and can be confined to talking union in nonwork areas.

Blacklists   Prior to 1935, workers discharged for union activity found it very difficult to obtain employment elsewhere, because employers conspired against them by circulating lists with the names and descriptions of known union activists. In the early 1930s, my grandparents' neighbor was blacklisted by Detroit's auto industry. An able-bodied man, he was never able to be hired for more than casual labor jobs. He knew that he was blacklisted because some employers told him so. While NLRA made blacklisting an unfair labor practice, it still occurs, but in different, more subtle forms.

Some union avoidance consultants advise employers to screen job applicants who have been union members. Whether the worker is "pro-union" or "anti-union" is often not viewed as important. Instead, the mere fact of previous union membership is viewed as enough to make the applicant a poor risk in regard to unionization. The employer does not ask the applicant whether he or she was a union member but merely checks whether the applicant's previous employers are organized.

Another way of identifying potential union supporters is through the administration of psychological tests and structured interviews. Applicants are not asked directly about unions. Instead, they are asked about group action as a way of achieving progress and various social issues. Group action-oriented "liberals" are viewed as poor risks for the maintenance of a union-free workplace.

One consultant has gone on to say:

> Blacks tend to be more prone to unionization than whites . . .
> if you can keep them at a minimum you are better off. . . . I feel
> the same way about Indians that I do about Blacks . . . stay the
> hell away from Puerto Ricans. Mexicans are OK if they feel that
> their first-line supervisor is their friend . . . Cubans are great.
> They are all Hispanic surnames, so you can stick with one and
> still keep your EEOC limits.[5]

Proving that an employer discriminates against potential union supporters is extremely difficult. Naturally, an employer is not going to admit discrimination and a union cannot get action from the NLRB on a mere suspicion of discrimination. Where a union has targeted an employer who appears to be engaging in discrimination, the union should consider conducting a controlled experiment to demonstrate the employer's discriminatory pattern. Gather a group of workers with similar characteristics—age, race, sex, education, and experience. Have half the group demonstrate "pro-union" traits and the other half "anti-union" traits when applying for employment. If the test demonstrates discrimination, action by the NLRB might be expected.

Spying Employers are prohibited from spying on the union or conveying the impression to workers that they are spying on union activities. Unlawful spying includes taking pictures of union-organizing activities, observing who attends union meetings, asking workers if they plan to attend or attended union meetings, tapping telephones, using electronic devices to eavesdrop on union meetings, and sending agents to meetings for the purpose of reporting on what occurred.

Rocci Pettigrew, an agent of the West Coast Detective Agency, testified recently before a House Labor-Management subcommittee investigating union avoidance consultants that he posed as an employee of the Anja Engineering Company in Monrovia, California, during a union-organizing drive. Employees who indicated any pro-union sentiments were reported to the employer. As many as twenty-four agents worked at the company during the union-organizing drive and "would find ways to set them (union supporters) up, get them fired or arrested (for theft)." Pettigrew said he was involved in having forty-six pro-union employees fired.[6]

The organizer should warn union supporters to be wary of individuals who urge them to commit illegal actions and actions that violate employer work rules. The annals of labor union history are replete with accounts of agent provocateurs breaking up unions. Apparently, this insidious practice still occurs.

Employers are also prohibited from interrogating employees about union activities except in limited situations where the questioning is directly relevant to gathering information on an unfair labor practice case. The interrogation cannot be a fishing trip by the employer; it must be directly related to the unfair labor practice case.

Selection and Domination of the Union Employers are prohibited from forming "company unions" dominated by and dedicated to advancing the interests of employers. During the 1920s, company unions were probably the dominant form of "union" in the country. Today, employers sometimes establish and support employee organizations intended primarily to promote social activities like ski trips and bowling leagues; these are legal as long as they do not purport to engage in activities normally considered to be within the scope of collective bargaining.

While "company unions" as such do not appear to be propagated widely by employers today, during union-organizing drives employers sometimes promote "vote-no" committees which are of shorter duration than "company unions" but have the same purpose of subverting legitimate unions. "Vote-no" committees enjoy a particular advantage under the law. While the employer and its agents—foremen and other management personnel—can be cited for committing unfair labor practices with statements—that the plant will close if a union is authorized, for example—the "vote-no" committee can make the same statements without committing unfair labor practices. In the section on "third party conduct," we will see that "vote-no" committees do have certain restrictions placed upon them by the NLRB.

From the outset of an organizing campaign, the union must be alert to any employer support of a "vote-no" committee, because if the employer lends support to the committee, it is viewed as "employer dominated" and, therefore, in violation of NLRB provisions regulating "company unions." Support comes in many forms. Look for "vote-no" committee members leaving their work stations at times when other employees are working, committee members approaching other workers "on the clock," committee members using the employer's typewriters and duplicating equipment, and inordinate numbers of meetings between committee members and management personnel. These incidents should be documented in preparation for the filing of unfair labor practice charges.

If two or more legitimate unions are attempting to organize a group of workers, the employer has the right to give workers its opinion on which union it prefers. However, the employer cannot assist in any way the union that it prefers to win the NLRB-conducted election.

Discharge and Other Punishments for Union Activity

Employers are prohibited from discharging, harassing, denying promotions, reducing wages and fringe benefits, demoting workers to less favorable jobs, and punishing workers in any other way for union activity. These are the most vile anti-union actions available to employers who are determined to avoid unionization. Discharge and other forms of punishment are the tactics most likely to literally scare workers out of their union support.

Naturally, employers will not admit that they have punished workers for union activity; instead they will claim that the punishment was rendered for some other reason. Accordingly, the union must prove to the satisfaction of the Board that the employee was actually disciplined for union activity in order for the Board to impose a remedy which will reinstate the worker to his or her previous position and, if applicable, grant the worker back pay. Discipline for union activity cases become more complicated when employers attempt to smokescreen the real reason for the discipline by taking similar action against workers who are not union activists.

Another form of punishment for union support is the isolation of union supporters from other workers so that they cannot talk union. Usually, this takes the form of assignment to parts of the workplace where only a few other employees work. Fred Bowler, a maintenance worker at a hospital where he had earned supervisory commendations for his excellent work, felt the wrath of his employer when his union support was discovered. Fred was assigned to the basement "doing useless, stupid things like dusting storage spaces." This was not the end of Fred Bowler's harassment for union activity. "An order from his head supervisor to clean twenty-five porter's sinks and closets was repeatedly frustrated by his immediate boss who assigned him as many as five new jobs a day. Later when Bowler was taken to task for 'dragging his feet' on the first job, he tried to reason with them saying he had been hopelessly detoured by other assignments."

When he was unable to "cite dates and times he said his immediate supervisor walked away laughing. Next came an official reprimand for failing to complete one of the multitude of conflicting job assignments."[7]

That's right, dates and times! The supervisor was apparently setting Fred Bowler up for a discharge. If Fred could not be specific as to the punishments for union activity, his rights under LMRA would be diminished.

Less subtle incidents of punishment for union support are described by International Brotherhood of Electrical Workers President Charles Pillard before recent House Labor-Management Sub-committee hearings:

> During that campaign the company reassigned the leading employee organizer. He received a cut in pay. The company assigned him an 8-foot square area in the shipping department and instructed him to sweep that area until the painted lines on the floor were gone. Another union supporter, who was left handed, was transferred to a side of the production line on which she had to work primarily with her right hand. When her production fell, the company found a pretext to discharge her. The employer also used a rather novel tactic. One weekend, shortly before the election, the entire supervisory staff came into the plant and completely removed two assembly lines, moving them to another plant several miles away. When the employees came in on Monday, they found only empty space in that part of the plant. This maneuver was apparently designed to demonstrate to the employees that the plant could and would shut down, and its operations would be moved if the union prevailed. After the election, which the union won, these assembly lines were returned.[8]

Implying that the Board Favors One Side Over the Other   The Board is very sensitive about the manner in which it is depicted to workers by employers and unions. Unions can tell workers about the safeguards the Board provides for workers engaged in union activities, but unions are not to tell workers that the Board favors unionization.

Employers and unions can distribute facsimiles of NLRB election ballots with an "X" in the box accompanying their choice. However, the facsimiles should not look too much like the real ballots, because the Board might set aside the election on the grounds that the culprit is trying to convey the impression that the Board favors it over the other side.

Silly as it may seem, the Board takes this matter very seriously as one organizer found to his surprise and disgust. When compared with the serious unfair labor practices committed by the employer which the union was able to overcome and win the election, a sample ballot that looked too close to the real thing seemed like too minor of a violation to have the election set aside.

Third-Party Conduct   Newspapers, employer groups like the Chamber of Commerce, "vote-no" committees, and the local police can create an atmosphere that prevents a fair election. Threats by "vote-no" committee members, undue police surveillance of union supporters, inflammatory articles in newspapers, and a cut-off of credit for union supporters by local merchants are examples of actions that union organizers should bring to the attention of the NLRB.

Events such as threatening phone calls and picket line violence can invalidate an election even though they cannot be attributed to either the union or the employer. One organizer had an election won by the union set aside because someone placed a union sticker inside an NLRB voting booth. The culprit could have been an anti-union worker as well as a union supporter. Yet, the Board ruled that the union sticker affected the laboratory condition necessary for the election by violating the Board's prohibition against campaigning in the election area.

WHAT TO DO ABOUT UNFAIR LABOR PRACTICES

If the organizer believes that an unfair labor practice has been committed, he or she should file a "charge" with the regional office of the National Labor Relations Board having jurisdiction over the geographic area where the violation occurred. The charge must be filed within six months of the alleged violation or else the Board will not act upon it. The Board has a simple one-page form upon which pertinent information related to the charge must be recorded. The new organizer should not hesitate to ask a Board representative for assistance with filling out the form.

The organizer's statements should be truthful during all phases of Board proceedings, although one union avoidance consultant is quoted as saying "Fortunately for all of us . . . there is no such thing as perjury in a Labor Board proceeding whether you go to trial or not. No such thing as perjury. The only thing that can be found is a lack of credibility."[9]

To a union avoidance consultant who travels extensively from employer to employer in many geographic areas of the country, the establishment of credibility with the agents of a particular regional office may not be important. But to union organizers who expect to be involved with a particular regional office for some time to come, the establishment of credibility with the Board is very important. Human nature and government bureaucracies being what they are, an organizer having credibility with the Board is more likely to get a "break" in situations that are not clear-cut.

Being truthful does not mean that the organizer fails to be assertive with the Board. As with any occupation, the Board has its share of incompetent agents. Many of the union avoidance consultants started out as agents for the NLRB, so the agents with whom you are dealing may not be predisposed toward "this union cause."

As with any government regulatory agency, the Board often has a heavy workload and a backlog of unsettled cases. Because cases differ as to complexity, it is difficult to specify what constitutes a reasonable length of time for the Board to complete various stages of the procedure for resolving unfair labor practice charges. It is reasonable, however, for the organizer to be kept informed of the progress the Board is making on pending cases and, if necessary, to prod the Board to speed up the process. Remember that the Board and its agents are there to serve you. Do not be shy about showing your inexperience or demanding your rights, but establish and maintain your credibility and do not hesitate to remind the Board of it when necessary.

The organizer should always file unfair labor practice charges on behalf of the union and not the workers who had the unfair labor practice perpetrated on them. By filing charges on behalf of the union, all correspondence on the charges will be sent by the Board to the union.

Unfair labor practice charges should be filed against employers. However, where an employer engages a union avoidance consultant, the consultant should also be named. If the NLRB upholds a charge against a consultant, the consultant risks contempt charges if he continues the practice with other employers. However, if only the employer is cited by the NLRB, the consultant is free to go on to another employer and do the same thing again.

Under the Landrum-Griffin Act of 1959, labor lawyers and consultants engaged in union avoidance activities are required to report their activities to the U.S. Department of Labor. A recent study published in the *Northwestern University Law Review* estimates that only a small fraction of attorneys engaged in union avoidance activities bother to file.[10] The law provides up to a $10,000 fine for willful violations, but that is not the primary reason to seek enforcement.

Unions must also file reports under the Landrum-Griffin Act which are part of the public record and which provide employers with information such as union officers' salaries that they in turn use as part of their message on why employees should not form unions. By having labor lawyers and consultants comply with the law, union organizers could supply workers with information on how much their employers are willing to spend to avoid unionization. Where this information has been obtained, it has proven to be a highly effective organizing message.

The AFL-CIO Department of Organization is coordinating the reporting of consultant and lawyer activities to the Department of Labor through the directors of organization for AFL-CIO affiliated unions. Report consultant and lawyer activities to your director of organization in addition to naming labor lawyers and consultants hired by employers to engage in union avoidance activities on unfair labor practice charges.

An excellent book on union organizing and the law advises organizers filing unfair labor practice charges to adopt "what some have called a 'shotgun' style. This technique helps to prevent you from tipping your complete hand to the employer too early. It is not necessary to spell out the intricate details of your case, the names of witnesses and all the rest, to the employer at that early stage." Also, "this type of charge does not lend itself to such an easy defense as one which spells out every fine point." An example of how to describe a violation of the law's prohibition on discriminating against workers for union activity would be to state: "On about March 15, the above-named employer fired John Smith to discourage union membership."[11]

While it is true that filing a general description of the unfair labor practice is sufficient to get the process started and that a representative of the Board will investigate the charge and attempt to ascertain all of the pertinent details, the organizer must not adopt the tenet "let the Board do it." It is extremely important for organizers to take a systematic approach to gathering evidence which supports unfair labor practice charges. "Letting the Board do it" will lead to disappointment. The organizer must be prepared to supply the Board with all pertinent details substantiating the charge.

A number of unions hire organizers with little or no experience in unions. They have zeal and endurance often unmatched by their older, more experienced peers, but they have never processed a grievance through to arbitration and, therefore, may be unfamiliar with supporting claims through evidence. Substantiating an unfair labor practice is much like substantiating a grievance.

If the organizer suspects that an unfair labor practice has been committed, he or she should IMMEDIATELY INVESTIGATE the incident, because memories fade as time passes and pertinent facts may be forgotten. Also, the employer's unfair labor practices are designed to instill fear in workers. Initially, the worker may be very angry and willing to divulge all the pertinent information about the incident. As time passes, tempers cool. Conversations with spouses and close friends may encourage the workers to not get "involved." Also, fear might set in, thereby making the workers reluctant to provide information. "Letting the Board do it" means delay and delay means that evidence literally disappears between the time the organizer files the unfair labor practice charge and the Board's investigation of the matter.

The format for gathering evidence supporting an unfair labor practice charge involves "The Seven W's": *Who, What, Where, When, Witnesses, in Writing,* and *Why.*

- Who did it? A foreman? A member of the "vote-no" committee? A consultant? A local merchant or clergyman?

- What happened? Threats? Promises? Discharge? Isolation?

- Where did it occur? The workplace? A local tavern? Over the telephone? A letter sent to the house?

- When? At work? After work?

- Who are the witnesses? Who else saw it happen?

- In writing? You bet! In order to systematize the evidence gathering process, the organizer should use a form upon which the pertinent information is recorded. An example of such a form is shown in Exhibit 2–1. Statements should be taken from all witnesses to the action. Supporting documents such as leaflets, letters, and other written materials distributed by the employer should be gathered. When the employer has made a speech, the organizer should attempt to obtain an accurate summary.

- Finally, why is employer action taken to discourage union organization? By gathering supporting evidence in a systematic

---

EXHIBIT 2–1. Union Record of an Unfair Labor Practice Committed by the Employer

1. Date the incident occurred:

2. Approximate time it happened:

3. Where did the incident occur?

4. What happened? (Attach leaflets, letters, or other evidence):

5. Who committed the unfair labor practice?

6. To whom did it happen?

7. Who else witnessed it?

   I believe that this statement is accurate.

_____   _____
Date   Signature

Signature Witnessed by _____   _____
                                                              Date

---

manner, the organizer has a better chance of proving WHY than by "letting the Board do it."

If the regional office of the NLRB determines on the basis of its investigation that the charge is true, it will attempt to reach an informal settlement with the employer. The Board will try to get the employer to agree to stop committing the unfair labor practice in the future and to remedy the situation. In cases of unlawful discharge, the employer is usually asked to reinstate employees with back pay. In cases where, for example, the employer has made threatening statements, the employer is usually asked to post a notice on bulletin boards admitting his wrongdoing and promising not to do it again. Big deal! The damage is done. If the employer disagrees with the settlement proposed by the Board's regional office, then the regional office will issue a complaint. The organizer need not have an attorney assist him or her.

A complaint results in a hearing before an Administrative Law Judge. The judges reside in New York, Washington, D.C., and San Francisco and travel to the regions for hearings. An attorney from the Board's regional office acts as the prosecutor in the case, because the regional office views the law as being violated and is seeking to uphold the law. While the union can have an attorney to assist the attorney from the regional office, it is not necessary. The Administrative Law Judge issues a "recommendation" to the NLRB's headquarters in Washington, D.C., which decides to either uphold or deny the recommendation. The Law Judge's recommendation can be appealed by either the union, the employer, or the regional office.

After the Board's decision is made on whether to uphold or deny the Administrative Law Judge's recommendation, the case can be appealed to the United States Court of Appeals. A new trial is not held. Instead, all evidence related to the case is reviewed by the court in determining whether or not to uphold the Board's decision. Overall, most of the Board's decisions are upheld by the Court, because the Court's power to overturn the Board's decisions is limited. This is in keeping with the intent of Congress at the time of the passage of the National Labor Relations Act to have the Board and not the courts govern labor-management relations. A Court of Appeals decision can be appealed to the Supreme Court.[12]

If an employer appeals a Board decision, the Board will supply the lawyers for the case and the union need not incur this expense. If a union appeals a Board decision to the courts, it will have to supply the lawyers.

By appealing NLRB regional office decisions, employers can delay union authorization elections for a year or more. As was discussed in Chapter 1, the longer an election is delayed, the greater the chance that the union will lose the election.

DISCHARGES FOR UNION ACTIVITY

The most serious and often the most difficult cases to prove to the Board are those involving discharge and other punishments for union activity. Employers attempt to justify the punishment on grounds other than union support. Therefore, the union must be systematic and thorough in its effort to demonstrate that a worker was in fact punished for union activity and not the reason given by the employer. A step-by-step approach follows:

1.   The organizer should investigate and determine whether the disciplined worker actually did what the employer has given as the reason for the punishment. Question witnesses. Get the

truth. If the worker did not commit the act, the Board should be convinced that some other reason accounts for the discipline.

2. Establish that the employer knew of the worker's union activity. If the worker wore a union button or other insignia, this may be cited as evidence. If supervisors or fellow employees observed the worker talking union or distributing union literature, their testimony may provide proof. Many organizers do not want to leave any doubt about the employer's knowledge of union supporters, so they send the employer a registered letter listing the names of all members of the in-plant organizing committee.

3. If the disciplined worker did what the employer gave as the reason for the punishment, the organizer should investigate whether the employer has applied the punishment consistently for similar infractions by employees who cannot be readily identified as union supporters. If the employer has given a union supporter a stiffer punishment, the Board is likely to view the punishment as motivated by the worker's union activity.

4. If there is a serious question of whether the punishment was motivated by the worker's union support, the Board may infer that it was, if the employer has committed other unfair labor practices. Therefore, it is important for the organizer to seek redress for punished workers in conjunction with other unfair labor practices committed by the employer.

5. Construct a record of all discharges and other punishments since the union campaign began. If a very high percentage of these actions has been against union supporters, the Board may view this as sufficient proof of anti-union discrimination by the employer.[13]

6. In order to prepare a comprehensive record of each instance of punishment for union activity, have the aggrieved party fill out the questionnaire provided as Exhibit 2–2. The form provides valuable information in those instances where the reason for punishment is not readily apparent.[14]

The organizer should advise workers fired for union activity to file with the state employment service, even though the discharged employee will be unable to immediately collect unemployment insurance benefits. When contacted by the state employment service

EXHIBIT 2–2. Employee Questionnaire for Determining Unfair Labor Practice Charges

Representative _____

International Union _____

Address _____ Phone _____

In the event of discharge in organizing campaigns the following information becomes tremendously important in order to complete investigation and the filing of charges with the National Labor Relations Board. Please complete and return to the above mentioned Union Representative.

UNFAIR LABOR PRACTICE CHARGES

I, _____, do solemnly state that my answers to the following questions are true and correct to the best of my knowledge and belief.

1. Print your name: _____
   Social Security Number _____ Phone No. _____

2. Street address _____

3. Name of Company involved _____

4. Address of Company _____

5. Name of Union involved in the case _____

6. How long did you work for Company? _____

7. Date of your discharge, or lay-off; or last day worked _____

8. (a) What reason did Company give you for discharge or lay-off and what Company official gave this reason?

   (b) Was it in writing? _____. If so, attach the paper.

9. Record of your employment with Company:
   (a) When did you start work for Company? _____
   (b) What job did you start at? _____
   (c) How much pay did you get? _____
   (d) What shift did you work on? _____
   (e) Who was your boss? _____
       Who was boss over him? _____
   (f) Did you receive any promotions and wage increases? _____
       If so, when and why? _____
   (g) Were you ever fired or laid off before by this Company? _____
       If so, when and why? _____

10. At the time you were fired, laid off, or demoted:
    (a) In what department did you work? _____
    (b) What was your job? _____

EXHIBIT 2–2 (Continued)

    (c) What was your pay rate? _____

    (d) What shift did you work? _____

    (e) Who was your boss? _____
        Who was boss over him? _____

11. Work record of person discriminated against:

    (a) Did you ever act as foreman or boss? _____

    (b) Were you ever chosen to do special jobs, new work, harder work than others, etc? _____. If so, describe the jobs or work _____
        _____

    (c) Did your boss ever criticize your work? _____. If so, when, and what did he say? _____
        _____

    (d) Give the names and, if possible, the address of fellow employees who can tell about your work: _____
        _____
        _____

12. How many employees did the same kind of work you did? _____
How many employees belonged to or were active in the Union? _____

13. How many employees were laid off or discharged at the same time you were? How many of those laid off or discharged with you either belonged to or were active in the Union? _____

14. (a) Is anyone now working on your job? _____

    (b) If so, what is his name? _____

    (c) Does he have more seniority than you? _____

15. Have any new workers been hired to do work similar to your work? _____
If so, about how many have been hired? _____

16. Is seniority followed by the Company in hiring and laying off? _____
If not, what plan is used in laying off and reinstating employees? _____
_____

17. Did you join the Union involved in this case? _____

18. If you joined the Union, when and how did you join? _____
_____
_____

19. Put a check mark opposite any Union work or activity which you did and give date. Check below—
    _____ Held Office   Title of Office _____ Date _____
    _____ Attended meetings   How many? _____ Date _____

EXHIBIT 2–2 (Continued)

_____ Solicited members   Whom, when and where? _____

_____

_____

_____ Distributed circulars	Dates_____
_____ Wore a union botton.	Date _____
_____ Member of Shop Committee.	Date _____
_____ Handled grievances.	Date _____
_____ Acted on picket duty.	Date _____
_____ Any other activities? _____	If so, describe them:

_____

_____

20. (a) How did the Company or your bosses know you belonged to or were active in the Union? (Give details with names and dates involved.)

    (b) Did you have any conversation with any of the bosses about the Union? _____. If so, give names and jobs of each boss, when and where it happened, and what was said. (Give names and, if possible, addresses of anyone else who heard the conversation.)

21. Did the company ever send you any leaflets and letters or make any speeches about the Union? _____. If so, attach copy of letter or leaflet, or give summary of what was said in speech describing when and where it was made and who heard it:

22. Did your boss ever criticize your Union? _____

_____

23. Did any boss ever threaten you about your Union activity? _____ If so, who was he and what did he say, when did he say it, and who heard it?

24. (a) Does the Union have an agreement with the Company? _____
    (b) If so, when does the agreement expire? _____

IMPORTANT

If you have a copy of the agreement, send it in with this questionnaire. If you don't have a copy on hand but can get a copy, get one and sent it to this office as soon as possible.

25. Did the company practice any forms of discrimination other than lay-off dis-

EXHIBIT 2–2 (Continued)

charge such as giving harder jobs to the Union workers or cutting their pay? (Give full details, names, etc.)

26. List the names (and addresses and phone numbers if you can) of any one else who can give information about the discrimination against you and the anti-Union acts of the Company:

27. Since you were fired, laid off, or demoted, did you talk to any company bosses about your discharge, about being reinstated, or about the Union? ___
    If so, who was it? _____
    What is his job? _____
    When and where did you talk to him? _____
    Who else was present? _____
    What did the boss say and what did you say? _____
    _____
    _____
    _____
    _____

28. Have you asked for your job back? _____
    (a) When? _____
    (b) Who did you talk with? _____
    (c) What did he say? _____

29. Employment since discharge or lay-off:
    (a) Where are you employed now? _____
    (b) When did you begin work there? _____
    (c) What kind of work do you do now? _____
    (d) What is your present rate of pay? _____
    (e) Do you wish to go back to work for the Company against whom this charge is filed? _____

30. Give any other information that you think will be helpful in your case and *attach* all pay envelopes, pay vouchers, letters, and any other papers connected with your job or discharge.

Date _____   Signed by _____

about the reason for termination, the employer will undoubtedly state that the worker was discharged for a reason that makes the worker ineligible for benefits. The organizer must assist discharged workers with appealing adverse decisions by the state employment service through the presentation of the evidence gathered by the method described above. Even if unemployment benefits are not granted, discharged workers must continue to report to the employment service regularly in order to be classified as "ready and willing" to work. Failure to attempt to find work can result in no back pay being granted through the NLRB procedure. If a worker is successful at obtaining other employment, the back-pay award will be reduced by the amount earned from the job, thereby making the NLRB procedure even more of a wrist slap for the law-breaking employer.

If the NLRB regional office upholds the unfair labor practice charge that the worker was fired for union activity, an informal settlement of reinstatement with back pay will be proposed, provided that the worker was actively seeking other employment.

The informal settlement procedure of the NLRB regional offices is similar to collective bargaining. The union, employer, and NLRB regional office negotiate a settlement. In discharge cases, the employer will often demand that the discharged workers not be allowed to return to work. If the workers have found other employment, they will often go along with this demand rather than face the possibility of further harrassment from the employer and a long delay before receiving back pay. Too often, the union's best in-plant organizing committee members are discharged and never return to participate in the organizing drive. Furthermore, the employer achieves its objective of instilling fear among the work force, if discharged workers do not return.

The organizer must attempt to persuade discharged workers to return so that the prospects for the union organizing drive are not diminished further. During periods of high unemployment, workers are more inclined to return than in a tight labor market. Long-term employees stand to benefit from a seniority system should the union be authorized and may retain credits under current or future pension plans. Short-term employees who are able to secure other jobs with similar wages and benefits to those from which they were discharged are the least likely to return.

Unions sometimes hire discharged employees to work as organizers until they are offered reinstatement, which helps to assure that they will return to the workplace. Ideally, unions could lend financial support to all workers discharged for union activity so that higher proportions would return to the workplaces from which they were discharged. The $33 million dollars awarded for back pay in 1980 is a very large amount of money; however, it represents less than $2 from every union member in the United States. Many unions maintain death and disability benefit funds and strike benefit funds. Why not a discharge for union activity fund? Low interest loans could be made to workers who demonstrate that there is a strong likelihood that they were discharged for union activity. Repayment of the loans would be made from back-pay awards. Additional meaning would be lent to the old refrain "You can't scare me, I'm sticking with the union!"

THE APPROPRIATE ELECTION UNIT

If there have been no unfair labor practices committed by the employer who is the target of the organizing drive, the first contact the organizer will have with the regional office of the NLRB regarding a particular organizing campaign is the filing of a "petition" for a union representation election. As with unfair labor practice charges, a simple one-page form must be filed with the regional office. The organizer must provide information on the collective bargaining unit whose organization is being sought, the nature of the employer's business, and the approximate number of workers in the unit. The new organizer should not hesitate to ask the Board for assistance in filling out the form.

Unions seldom represent all of the employees of a particular employer. In filing an election petition, a union carves out a unit of workers eligible to vote in the election and excludes other workers from participating in the election. The union has two goals when selecting the election unit. Naturally, it seeks an election unit that will support the union when the election occurs. Also, it seeks a unit that will be either large enough or strategic enough from the standpoint of the employer's operations to be able to exercise sufficient collective bargaining power after the election victory to be able to negotiate a contract, which represents an improvement of wages and working conditions over what they were before unionization. The employer, of course, seeks to carve out an election unit that will not support the union. If unionization seems certain, the employer may attempt to weaken the union's collective bargaining power by excluding or including certain employees.

The Labor Management Relations Act places constraints on the composition of election units:

No unit can be comprised of both professional and nonprofessional employees without the approval of a majority of the professionals. A professional is defined as a person working in an occupation that is nonrepetitive, varied, and intellectual in nature, and which requires the exercise of independent judgment. Professional employees usually need advanced education beyond high school. Doctors, lawyers, teachers, and certified public accountants are examples of professional employees.

A distinction is made between professional and technical employees. Technical occupations require advanced training, but technical employees do not exercise the degree of independent judgment that professionals do. Technicians are not allowed to choose whether or not they want to be included with other employees in the election unit. If the union and employer agree, technicians can be included or excluded. If the union and employer disagree on including or excluding them, the NLRB decides the issue.

No election unit may include supervisors or managers. They are specifically excluded from the protection of LMRA and can be fired for union activity. A supervisor is a person having the authority "to hire, transfer, suspend, lay off, recall, promote, discharge, assign, reward, or discipline other employees, or responsibility to direct them, or to adjust their grievances, or effectively to recommend such action" provided that this authority "is not of a merely routine or clerical nature, but requires the use of independent judgment." The law lists twelve different factors that make an employee a supervisor.

A person with the authority to carry out only one of these functions is classified as a supervisor even though the authority is never exercised. The title of an employee's job means nothing; it is the authority of an employee that counts. Job titles such as group leader, senior (whatever), and chief (whatever) cause the most confusion. Important considerations are whether the person can act independently and exercises judgment that goes beyond simple routine. Even though a worker's actions in regard to matters such as assigning work and transferring employees must be approved by someone of higher authority, this does not necessarily disqualify the person from being a supervisor. The approval may be routine. What is important is whether the person who must approve the action conducts his or her own investigation of the matter or merely follows the recommendation of the worker. Therefore, even though a person has no title suggesting a supervisory job, he or she will be classified as a supervisor if management calls upon her or him for advice and bases actions upon that advice without conducting an independent investigation.

Earlier in this chapter, a situation was described where an employer "promotes" union supporters into supervisory status in order to fire them. There are two other strategies. The employer may attempt to place "loyal" employees who really function as supervisors into the election unit in order to tip the vote against the union. Or, if the employer perceives a union election victory as inevitable, it may attempt to shift workers into supervisory positions. While the effort to reduce the number of workers in the election unit may not prevent union organization, the employer erodes the union's collective bargaining power by assuring itself of a built-in strikebreaking force.

No election unit may include guards hired to protect the employer's property or to enforce the company's rules. Guards can form their own union, but it cannot be affiliated with the same union as that representing other employees.

Children or spouses of the employer are automatically excluded from the election unit. While not required by law, the NLRB also as a matter of policy excludes employees whose interests are more closely allied with management than with the bargaining unit. Relatives of the employer other than spouses and children may be excluded if they are granted special privileges which make their interests more allied with the employer than with other employees in the election unit.

The Board also excludes certain other employees who do not meet the definition of supervisor, but whose interests are different than those of other employees in the election unit. Employees who receive special privileges or participate in the formulation of company policy by exercising independent judgment are classified as "managerial" and excluded from the election unit.

Confidential employees are excluded from the election unit and are defined as employees who regularly act in a confidential capacity to a person who develops or puts into action the employer's labor policy. Just because an employee deals with confidential information does not exclude him or her; the information must be related to the labor policies of the employer.

Part-time employees, seasonal employees, students, trainees, and probationary employees will be included in the election unit if they are in a "regular" status rather than a "temporary" status. The rationale is that if they can reasonably expect to be employed in the future, they will be affected by the outcome of the union authorization election.

There are a number of other factors taken into account by the NLRB in determining the election unit which complicate the matter even further and make it nearly impossible for the organizer to determine with certainty what the election unit will be in advance. Some of the issues which are very critical in determining the union's chances at winning the election and which are subject to different interpretations are the following: Must the election unit include more than one business location operated by the employer? Are production and maintenance workers to be included in one election unit? Should craft workers be included in the same election unit as production workers? Should office clericals and plant clericals be included in the same unit as production workers?

The NLRB examines each particular case and determines the appropriate election unit by taking into account a number of factors. No single factor governs its decisions; however, the most important factor in deciding these issues is the "community of interest principle." The more that employees have in common, the greater the chance that the NLRB will include them in one election unit.

Community of interest is determined by several factors. Do the employees perform similar types of work such as craft work, clerical work, or production and maintenance work? Do they work in the same location, or if they work in a different location, do they frequently transfer between locations? Do the employees have similar working conditions such as using the same locker room, cafeteria, and parking lot? Are the wages and benefits of different groups of employees related? Do the employees have common supervision? The Board also looks at the composition of bargaining units at other firms in the industry and the organizational structure of the employer in question.[15]

The Board will not accept the employer's argument that a particular unit would be the most efficient or convenient for collective bargaining; community of interest prevails. Likewise, the Board will not accept the union's argument that a particular group constitutes the election unit solely because they want the union to be their collective bargaining representative, while other groups of employees do not support the union. The Board will take these arguments into account, along with the other factors determining community of interest.

Even if the employer and union agree on the election unit, the NLRB is not bound by their agreement. This may seem incongruous, but the Board views its role as more than merely accommodating the interests of employers and workers. Many years ago, I attended a speech by the then-chairman of the NLRB. He had just returned from Europe and described how a Ford automobile assembly plant in Great Britain has something like fifteen different unions, while the same company's plant in the United States has one union. He went on to describe labor relations in Great Britain as turbulent. A number of skilled tradesmen from the auto industry were in attendance. They had recently been denied their request to break away from the United Auto Workers and form their own union comprised of skilled workers. What about the interests of workers?, they asked. After much verbal shadow boxing, the reply was that the Board, or at least this particular chairman, views its role as promoting stable labor relations. So, even if the union and employer agree on the election unit, the Board may view itself as seeking a "greater good."

If the employer and union do not agree on the unit, the organizer is at a disadvantage, because the employer has more detailed information on the operation of the business than the organizer. Therefore, the employer can present a more detailed argument before the NLRB than the organizer.

In order to protect the desired unit, the organizer should have a diagram of the workplace and a breakdown of the relationships between divisions and departments. Also, the relationship between supervisors and workers should be outlined. The organizer must try to anticipate who the employer will attempt to include and exclude, and must have evidence ready with which to combat the employer's arguments.

In a later chapter, there will be a discussion on researching the employer. By adopting those procedures, the organizer will have a systematized method for identifying potential union members, directing the activities of in-plant organizing committees, and gathering evidence to substantiate election unit requests with the Board.

SUPPORTING THE ELECTION PETITION WITH UNION AUTHORIZATION SIGNATURES

In addition to the one-page petition for election form, the union must supply the Board with documents demonstrating a "showing of interest" by at least 30 percent of the employees in the unit that the union is trying to organize. The supporting documents are usually in the form of "authorization cards," filled out by individual employees. Some organizers prefer using an authorization petition so that signers of the petition can see that they are not alone in desiring union representation and because they believe that it helps promote solidarity among the workers. The authorization card, however, is the most widely used document for proving a "showing of interest."

Organizers must follow a number of rules in obtaining a "showing of interest":

1. Authorization cards or petitions, circulated by the union, must indicate the desire of workers to be represented by the union in collective bargaining. Cards should *not* state that they are also authorization to petition for an NLRB election, because the NLRB has ruled that signers might want the cards to be used only for an election, not to show their desire to be represented by the union. This distinction can be very important if the employer commits unfair labor practices, which the NLRB rules to have destroyed the union's majority status. In a small fraction of these cases, the employer is ordered to recognize the union and bargain even if the union lost the election. If workers signed cards authorizing an election, the union may be unable to demand recognition and the right to bargain.

2. The organizer should not be ambivalent when asking union supporters to sign cards. The card should also be an application for union membership and an authorization for union dues checkoff. The organizer should make the prospective union member aware of these costs, because these are realities of union membership and attempting to hide them is not only dishonest but self-defeating in the long run. The organizer is not merely trying to win an election, he or she is also trying to build a union capable of success at collective bargaining. In "right-to-work" states, the distinction between voting for union authorization

and union membership is particularly important. The organizer does not want a union in name only, but an organization that has the commitment of the workers it represents.

3. Forging signatures on authorization cards is a felony punishable by fine and imprisonment. Forging signatures is also stupid, because while undetected forgeries will substantiate a petition for election, the union will lose the ultimate test.

4. The organizer should never tell workers that signing authorization cards is confidential and that the employer will never find out who supports the union. If the election is challenged, the authorization cards become part of a public hearing and the employer will have access to the names of union supporters.

5. The organizer should make sure that union supporters fill in the date on which they sign the authorization cards. The NLRB requires that signatures on authorization cards be "timely" in order to support a petition for election. Usually, this is interpreted as being within one year of the submission of the petition for election.

6. Signatures must be written legibly and not printed.

7. Organizers and organizing committee members should always initial cards signed in their presence. If a question arises later as to the authenticity of the signature, the organizer can testify that the card was signed in his or her presence. Also, when cards are mailed in, the envelope in which they were sent should be initialed by the organizer and stapled to the cards, because the envelopes may provide evidence substantiating the authenticity of the cards.

8. The organizer should not promise card signers lower union dues if they sign, or threaten higher dues if they do not sign, because the NLRB will invalidate signatures if these contingencies are attached to signing the cards.[16]

CERTIFICATION

Certification means that the NLRB orders an employer to recognize a union as the bargaining agent for a group of workers and that the employer must bargain in "good faith" with the union for a period of at least one year in an effort to reach a collective bargaining agreement.

A union is certified by the NLRB in one of three ways:

1. **Voluntary recognition by the employer based upon the union obtaining authorization signatures from a majority of workers in the unit.**

From 1935 until 1947 when the Taft-Hartley Act was passed, a union could be certified by presenting the NLRB with authorization cards or an authorization petition indicating that a majority (50 percent of the unit plus one) of workers desired the union to represent them. This procedure is called a "card check." As was discussed in chapter 1, the government of the Province of Ontario, Canada, will grant recognition on the basis of a majority of employees signing cards.

Since the passage of Taft-Hartley, unions are limited to demonstrating majority status through card signatures to employers. The employer is under no obligation to recognize the union on this basis, but if the employer chooses to grant recognition, the NLRB will certify the union as bargaining agent without an election.

The usual procedure followed by unions in demanding recognition is to send the employer a registered letter claiming that a majority of workers are represented by the union and offering to have a neutral third party check the authenticity of the authorization cards. Union avoidance consultants advise employers never to recognize unions on the basis of authorization cards, but to demand elections. Therefore, many organizers do not bother to demand recognition on the basis of an authorization card majority. If the employer agrees to have authorization cards checked by a third party, it is bound by the outcome of the card check.

2. **Based upon unfair labor practices committed by the employer, the Board rules that a fair election cannot be conducted and certifies the union.**

Where a union loses an election and files objections with the NLRB because of unfair labor practices committed by the employer, the Board examines the *totality* of conduct by the employer during the period of time between the union's filing of the petition for election and the actual election. Each case is examined on its own merits.

In some cases, the Board rules that the violations were so minor that the election results stand. In others, the Board finds that serious misconduct occurred and overturns the election. The employer is ordered to remedy the violations. Often, all this amounts to is a requirement that the employer post notices on bulletin boards admitting its guilt and promising not to engage in the prohibited activity. This is similar to a judge telling a jury to ignore a statement made in court. After the so-called remedy, a re-run election is held.

Occasionally, the Board certifies the union as bargaining agent even though it lost the election. The Board must view the employer's misconduct as being so "pervasive" as to forever impair the workers from participating in a fair election. Between 1962 and 1975, only about 2 percent of the certifications granted by the Board occurred for this reason.

3. The union wins an authorization election conducted by the NLRB.

An NLRB election can be conducted in a unit of workers provided that no NLRB election has been conducted among the unit within one year and provided that the petition for election is supported by authorization signatures representing at least 30 percent of the workers in the unit that the union is seeking to certify. If an election can be conducted, the NLRB regional office will either hold an informal conference or telephone the employer and union and attempt to have them reach a "consent election agreement." The agreement includes a description of the election unit, the time and place of the election, and payroll eligibility date by which a person must be employed in order to vote. If the employer and the union agree, a consent election will be held shortly after the filing of the election petition by the union. However, union avoidance consultants advise employers not to enter into consent election agreements.

A union avoidance consultant describes how employers should react to a request for a consent election:

> You tell the Board, "NO WAY!" We think the production and maintenance is an appropriate unit . . . this should include the warehouse. This should include the truck drivers. This should include our office clerical or whatever the hell else you can come up with your imagination.
>
> Or if you got several plants and several facilities in the area—this unit isn't appropriate. This is plant A. We also have

plant B. We are going to have twice as many employees in the foreseeable future.

. . . You create an issue, and actually go to a hearing. What do you do in a hearing? You have seventeen days. That is normal for the Board to process a new procedure. You hire some guy. You hire me. I tell the Board I have such an unbelievable schedule that there is no way in hell I can meet the seventeen days. The first time I had a free day is in three weeks. I got to have three weeks. We can't buy that, so we split it in two and I get away with ten days. I have twenty-seven days before we get to a hearing.

Now what happens? Go to a hearing. We litigate the various issues underlined in the bargaining unit.

. . . Suffice to say, you have at least 500 issues. So you litigate those issues. You don't give a damn whether you win or lose because you are not really interested in that. You are only interested in going over . . . the peak period . . . So, twenty-seven days out, you have your hearing . . . You come up with a few good issues. You could come up with them for almost a year, as we did in one case.[17]

If the parties do not agree to a consent election, then a hearing is held before an agent of the NLRB's regional office in an effort to resolve the disputed issues. The director of the NLRB's regional office resolves the issues and orders an election. "Board-directed elections" are usually held about seventy-five days after the union files the election petition. The decision of the regional director can be appealed to NLRB headquarters in Washington, D.C. However, NLRB headquarters retains the right to refuse to even hear the appeal. An appeal of the regional director's decision does not delay the election; instead, the election takes place and the ballots are impounded pending the outcome of the appeal.

The Board establishes a payroll eligibility date by which a worker must be employed in order to vote. Usually, this is the payroll period immediately preceding the date on which an election is directed by the Board or a consent agreement is signed. Employees who quit before the election is held are not eligible to vote and employees hired after the payroll eligibility date cannot vote.

Because of the long delays between the filing of an election petition and the time of the consent agreement or Board direction, employers have the opportunity to hire employees who are unlikely to support the union and, thereby, to stack the vote. A union avoidance consultant describes the process:

> Any employee you hire up until the regional director makes his decision . . . anybody you hire can vote.
> . . . Now those of you who have organizational activity with a small bargaining unit like fifteen employees . . . What do you do? You go out if you are a corporation and hire five of your relatives on a regularly scheduled part-time basis.
> You don't even have to go to that extreme. You can just go out and get five people who are not relatives and who you are very confident of and you work them on a regular schedule of four hours on Monday and four hours on Tuesday. And the second guy you regularly schedule to work the first four hours on Tuesday, or Wednesday, and the first four hours on Thursday, and you hire another to work the second four hours on Wednesday and Thursday, you hire another regularly scheduled guy to work eight hours a day on Friday.
> So you got one forty-hour employee. Right? But you got five employees who can vote. So the vote was 10 to 5. You picked up five votes. The election was held. Ten votes and ten votes—who wins?[18]

One organizer had the experience of attempting to organize a small clerical unit of a plant operated by a major manufacturing company whose production and maintenance employees had been organized in 1937. Immediately after filing the election petition, the company hired eight recent college graduates as "management trainees." The election unit increased by nearly 50 percent through the hiring of these future business moguls, and the outcome of the election was determined.

The employer must give the Board the names and home addresses of all employees eligible to vote within seven days after the consent agreement or the Board direction. This is called an "Excelsior List" after the Excelsior Underwear Company case in which the Board first enacted this regulation. The Board supplies the union with the Excelsior List. Failure of the employer to supply the list or supplying a substantially inaccurate list may be grounds for setting aside an election. Make sure to request a list with full names, not just first and middle initials.

The election is usually held at the workplace and on work time and is by secret paper ballot. The employer and the union are each entitled to an election observer. Unions may not insist upon using professional organizers as observers. The best union observer is one who is a respected leader of the workers and who knows the workers well enough to be able to identify ineligible voters.

The Board agent who conducts the election does not make decisions on voter eligibility. Challenged voters are allowed to vote. Their ballots are placed in sealed envelopes and impounded. The decision of whether or not to count their ballots is made by the regional director. After the polls close, a tally of the votes is made by the Board agent. Challenged ballots, of course, are not counted.

The number of votes cast, not the number of eligible voters, is the deciding factor in elections. In order to win an election, a union must receive a majority of the votes cast (50 percent plus one). If a tie occurs, the union loses the election. If there are two or more unions on the ballot and no single union has a majority of the votes cast but the combined votes for union representation are greater than the votes for no union, the Board will hold another election between the two choices receiving the most votes. One of the choices may be "no union."

Within five days of the election, any objections to the conduct of the election must be filed with the NLRB's regional office. The regional director resolves the disputed issues, and under certain circumstances the regional director's decision can be appealed to the NLRB's national office. The process of filing objections to the election and appealing the regional director's decision requires action on the part of the union. The novice organizer might need the assistance of a lawyer.

Employers do not have the right to appeal the Board's decision to the courts. If an employer disagrees with the Board's decision or is merely trying to stop union organization, it will refuse to bargain with the union. The union then must file an unfair labor practice charge. The Board then will provide the legal services as the case goes to the Court of Appeals and perhaps, ultimately, to the Supreme Court.

CONCLUSION

This chapter offers some suggestions for making the laws regulating the formation of unions work more effectively for unions. Organizers who establish their credibility, who gather evidence supporting unfair labor practice charges, and who research the operations of employers so that they can substantiate their election unit requests are more successful than organizers who "let the Board do it."

Adoption of these suggestions, however, is no substitute for fundamental changes in the law, because workers desiring union representation can be so easily frustrated by unscrupulous employers. Every organizer with whom I have spoken has cited deficiencies in the law as the major factor retarding the growth of union membership. I have yet to hear a union avoidance lawyer or consultant level much criticism against the law. Even the most diligent union organizer with superb legal training cannot help becoming cynical toward the law.

FOOTNOTES

[1] Report on Union Busters, Issue No. 15, April 1980, pp. 9–10.

[2] Bruce S. Feldacker. *Labor Guide to Labor Law* (Reston, Va.: Reston Publishing Company, 1980), pp. 81–82.

[3] U.S. House of Representatives, Subcommittee on Labor-Management Relations. *Pressures in Today's Workplace* (Washington DC: Government Printing Office, 1979), Vol. I, pp. 205–214.

[4] "NLRB Revokes Its Ban on Campaign Deceptions," AFL-CIO News, August 14, 1982, pp. 1–2.

[5] "How They Fight Unions," UAW *Washington Report*, June 20, 1980.

[6] "Probe To Hear Guns for Hire," *Memo from COPE*, December 24, 1979.

[7] "Union Busters' Dirty Tricks," *r w d s u RECORD*, May 1981, p. 9.

[8] U.S. House of Representatives, Subcommittee on Labor Management Relations. *Pressures in Today's Workplace.*

[9] Report on Union Busters, Issue No. 9, October 1979.

[10] Report on Union Busters, Issue No. 6, July 1979, pp. 3–6.

[11] Stephen S. Schlossberg and Frederick E. Sherman. *Organizing and the Law—A Handbook for Union Organizers* (Washington DC: The Bureau of National Affairs, 1971), pp. 26–28.

[12] Feldacker, *Labor Guide*, pp. 13–24.

[13] Industrial Union Department, AFL-CIO, *A Layman's View of the National Labor Relations Act for Organizers* (Washington DC: IUD, AFL-CIO, n.d.), p. 20.

[14] Form distributed at an "Organizing Conference" conducted in 1978 by Roosevelt University, Labor Education Division, 430 South Michigan Avenue, Chicago, Illinois 60605.

[15] Feldacker, *Labor Guide*, pp. 41–42.

[16] Schlossberg and Sherman, *Organizing and the Law.*
[17] U.S. House of Representatives, Subcommittee on Labor-Management Relations. *Pressures in Today's Workplace.*
[18] U.S. House of Representatives, Subcommittee on Labor-Management Relations. *Pressures in Today's Workplace.*

ADDITIONAL RESOURCES

A Layman's Guide to Basic Law Under the National Labor Relations Act. Washington, D.C.: U.S. Government Printing Office, 1980.

Busman, Gloria. *Union Representatives' Guide to NLRB RC and CA Cases.* Los Angeles: Center for Labor Research and Education of the Institute of Industrial Relations, University of California, 1977.

Getman, Julius; Goldberg, Stephen; and Herman, Jeanne. *Union Representation Elections: Law and Reality.* New York: Russell Sage Foundation, 1976.

Morris, Charles J., et al. *The Developing Law.* Washington, D.C.: The Bureau of National Affairs, 1971.

National Labor Relations Board Caseholding Manual, Parts One and Two. Washington, D.C.: U.S. Government Printing Office, 1979.

Taylor, Benjamin J., and Witney, Fred. *Labor Relations Law—3rd Edition.* Englewood Cliffs, N.J.: Prentice-Hall, Inc., 1979.

3

Keeping Unions Out

About twenty years ago, I was an office worker at an automobile assembly plant. The United Auto Workers represented production and maintenance workers at the plant and one day distributed authorization cards at the gates of the unorganized, salaried employees' parking lot. Within a week, plant management announced plans for a dinner party at a fancy hotel, and circulated a memorandum advising salaried employees that they would soon be receiving a cost of living adjustment just as the union contract for hourly employees stipulated. Also, we were reminded that salaried employees received all other improvements stipulated in the union contract and that merit increases were received every eighteen months by most salaried employees, which hourly employees in the bargaining unit did not receive.

The top shelf liquors, oysters and shrimp in every conceivable configuration, prime rib, baked Alaska, and gift certificates from a department store helped convince recently hired employees that the employer had their best interests at heart. Besides, the money was better than in the union contract for those salaried employees who were "meritorious." Be "meritorious" enough and one could be in the position of doling out the gifts.

For older employees who had experienced a nearly 50 percent

reduction in the salaried employee work force when mechanical data processing equipment was introduced a few years earlier, the response to the union organizing effort was one of fear. A twenty-four-year employee who was on tranquilizers advised me: "They got rid of the people they thought were troublemakers when we changed over. Don't sign a card. They have ways of finding out." A fifty-three-year-old employee with high blood pressure and ulcers and eighteen years of continuous service told me that he had only two years to go, because it was his understanding that firing a twenty-year employee required a vice president's signature. His brother had been a congressman and he described how his career skyrocketed while his brother was in office. After his brother's retirement, he was bounced from a management job at corporate headquarters down to a clerk's job at the assembly plant. The union could give him job security, but why take a chance? Only two more years to go and the last performance review was "meritorious."

The union's organizing effort was limited to the one day of distributing authorization cards and an election petition was not filed. As a union committeeman at the plant told me: "We knew you guys wouldn't sign up. We just wanted to get a rise out of management." They sure did. The carrot and the stick were amply displayed and that is what "keeping unions out" is all about.

Union avoidance activities that do not violate the law are examined in this chapter. The purpose of the chapter is to set the stage for other sections of the book. When selecting organizing targets, for example, it is necessary to evaluate employer programs for union avoidance so that the chances of winning campaigns can be evaluated. Likewise, the development of organizing tactics requires an understanding of union avoidance techniques. Also, some of the same techniques used by employers can be adapted by unions for organizing and preventing decertifications.

Union avoidance activities can be divided into two categories. Short-run activities are triggered by the initiation of union organizing campaigns and are likened by management to emergency repairs of broken machinery. Long-run activities occur without any indication of an organizing effort and are likened to preventive maintenance of capital equipment such as the physical plant and machinery. We will first examine the easier of the two categories for unions to combat—short-run union avoidance strategies.

SHORT-RUN STRATEGY: THE MEDIA

The instant an employer is aware of a union organizing effort, keeping the union out becomes the overriding concern of the organization. Employers with foresight will have already developed a short-run strategy for meeting this "emergency." Now is the time to put the plan into action, the time to fix this organizational "breakdown."

The authority for conducting the union avoidance campaign for the duration of the "battle" is given to a manager or "task force" of managers who operate out of a "war room" where information relevant to the campaign is received, tactics are planned, and orders emanate.[1,2] Large organizations may have a department or section whose sole responsibility is union avoidance. Small employers or employers who have not planned a strategy and are caught off guard by the organizing drive may hire an outside law firm or union avoidance consulting firm to direct the campaign.

The person or persons responsible for directing the campaign establish a plan for the entire union avoidance effort from the first day of the campaign through the day of the union authorization election. Letters to employees' homes, leaflets distributed to employees, speeches by management, and the contents of day-to-day conversations between supervisors and workers are prepared in advance, ready for their respective slots on the timetable. If necessary, the plan is altered to meet changing circumstances as the campaign progresses.[3] Exhibit 3–1 is the calendar for the last two weeks of an actual campaign.

Regardless of whether the campaign is directed by a member of the organization or outside lawyers or consultants, a key to successful union avoidance is the granting of nearly absolute power to the person or persons placed in charge. Beating the union is the primary objective of the organization for the life of the campaign. Production of goods or services may become secondary. Employees can be called from their work stations at any time for meetings intended to convince them to reject union representation. Even at hospitals and nursing homes, patient care may take a back seat to beating the union.[4]

The short-run union avoidance campaign can be expensive. The major costs are lawyers' fees and production time lost by employees because of required attendance at meetings held during work hours.

EXHIBIT 3–1. Calendar of Events in an Organizing Campaign

COMPANY NAME

Month _____ Year _____

MONDAY	TUESDAY	WEDNESDAY	THURSDAY	FRIDAY
15	**16**	**17**	**18**	**19**
Meeting with supervisors Distribute election calendar	Distribute union constitution in morning	"What's the Score" flyer	Pre-election conference	Staff meeting Q&A's Mail "Everyone Loses in a Strike"
20	**21**	**22**	**23**	**24**
Meeting with supervisors Election day checklist Distribute baggies	Show film to employees Mail "Did You Know" letter	Contest drawing	Final meeting with employees "Details of Election"	ELECTION DAY 10:00 a.m. to 11:30 a.m. Lunchroom Warehouse I

A study conducted in 1975 estimated that the cost to a company with 100 employees was about $123 per employee. Companies with 1,000 employees encountered a cost of approximately $101 per worker. These are conservative estimates based upon an average hourly wage of $3.50 per hour and $1 for fringe benefits.[5] The costs in 1982 are, of course, much greater, particularly when union avoidance consultants are hired. A fee of $500 or more per day plus expenses is not uncommon for their services.

Between 1975 and August 1981, the Consumer Price Index increased by 72 percent. Assuming that the change in CPI reflects the approximate change in the cost of union avoidance, the cost to a company with 100 employees in August 1981 was about $212 per employee. The cost to an employer with 1,000 employees was approximately $174 per employee.

It must be emphasized that these are only the costs incurred during the campaigns immediately preceding union authorization elections. The true costs of union avoidance are much greater when account is taken of the costs incurred by employers who adopt a long-run union avoidance strategy of paying wages and benefits equal to or greater than those in union contracts.

The Troops   For the duration of the short-range union avoidance campaign, the major concern of foremen and other first-line supervisors—the "troops" in the campaign—is union avoidance. Supervisors are told that they have no protection under the laws prohibiting disciplinary action for union activity and that they will relinquish their authority to shop stewards should the union win the campaign. Otherwise, effective supervisors who do not demonstrate sufficient skill or commitment to beating the union are subject to transfer or discharge. Likewise, supervisors who are unpopular with workers may be transferred or discharged, because they are poor spokespersons for the employer's point of view.

The "troops" perform two major functions. They feed information to the "war room" on developments in the union's organizing campaign and the positions for or against the union of individual employees under their direction. A tally of employee positions is kept by the "task force" so that it can measure the effectiveness of the campaign and, ultimately, determine the necessity of "pulling out all of the stops," including illegal activities.

The second function of the "troops" is to implement the tactics developed by the "task force." This includes distributing leaflets, answering questions, and engaging employees in conversations revolving around anti-union themes developed by the "task force." Exhibit 3–2 is an example of such a directive to supervisors.

The "troops" are trained to perform these functions. To be most effective, the training occurs prior to any hint of an organizing drive and continues throughout the campaign. The training consists of persuading supervisors that they will be better off without a union, instructing them of their roles in the campaign, and apprising them of their rights under the law.[6]

The reason why the "troops" are so important to the campaign is that their daily face-to-face conversations with workers are the most persuasive media available to management for the campaign— more effective than letters, posters, leaflets, films, and large group meetings. This conclusion is supported by studies of union organizing campaigns.[7]

Simply put, many people do not bother to read letters, leaflets, and posters. The "troops" can rather easily conduct face-to-face communications on a daily basis. Also, foremen and supervisors may have more credibility with workers than top management or outside lawyers or consultants because they have communicated regularly with employees prior to the "emergency." Despite the heavy reliance upon the "troops," all means of written and oral communications are used in the campaign.

Bulletin Boards   Anti-union messages are posted on bulletin boards. The messages are short and to the point, and through the use of headlines and illustrations, are designed to capture the attention of employees. Bulletin board postings are changed frequently in order to keep the campaign fresh and are designed to reinforce the messages conveyed orally by first-line supervisors.

Employers are advised to have bulletin boards in locked glass cases to prevent tampering and to adopt a long-run strategy of prohibiting employees from posting messages. If employees have always been allowed to post messages on bulletin boards, the employer will not be allowed by the NLRB to prohibit employee access once a union organizing campaign begins.[8]

Displays   Employers sometimes construct displays in lobbies, cafeterias, and other areas of the workplace frequented by employees.

EXHIBIT 3–2. Supervisors' Fact Sheet

Efforts are being made to misinform your employees on certain points regarding the union situation. Your counter-effort to see that the truth is told will be appreciated and will be a service to those who look to you for accurate information. Please try to get the following points across over the next week or two.

I

The union is losing. This is clear (1) from the number of employees who are asking for letters to send to the union to revoke their union cards, and (2) from the dwindling number of patches and buttons seen in the plant.

The union *knows* it is losing. When someone knows he or she is losing a fight, he/she may show it by resorting to unfair tactics. The union is doing that now, circulating rumors that are untrue, in a desperate effort to stop their downward slide.

For instance:

II

People are being told that the union could close down this plant in a strike by cutting off deliveries. The union's supporters are saying the union truckers would not cross a picket line. Your employees should know the following:

1. We have a rail siding. We could use that to bring in what we need.

2. There are plenty of non-union truck lines who would be more than glad to cross a picket line.

3. All common carriers and motor carriers are *required by law* to render service, and can lose their operating licenses if they don't. If their drivers refuse to cross a picket line, they will send supervisors to do so.

4. There are also many owner-operators who will gladly drive their trucks across picket lines. Most owner-operators have payments to make every month, and cannot afford to turn away business.

There would be no problem getting deliveries at this plant in the event of a strike. Those who tell you otherwise are not telling you the truth.

III

Union supporters are saying the union could get rid of certain foremen and supervisors.

This is totally false.

Under the law, a company is not required to negotiate, or even to discuss, with a union the hiring or discharge of supervisory personnel. Nor does a company have to discuss with a union the matter of who gets promoted to supervisory positions.

The Company publicly states: No union will ever have *anything to say,* or *any voice at all,* as to the hiring, firing, or work assignment of any supervisor in this plant.

The intent of the displays is usually to convey the cost of union membership. A basket full of groceries or barrel of money equal to the cost of union dues for one year or a "BA's new Cadillac" are examples. Employees may be invited to participate in a raffle for the items on display after the union authorization election is held.

Vivid Depictions of Union Dues   Simply telling employees about the cost of union initiation fees and dues is not nearly as effective as a vivid portrayal of their effects upon employee paychecks. Employees are sometimes issued two checks on paydays. One check is for the regular amount less union initiation fees, dues, and potential special assessments. The other is for the cost of union membership. Sometimes, play money representative of the cost of union membership is distributed to employees. The NLRB views these tactics as proper.

Anti-Union Insignia   Bumper stickers, T-shirts, "Vote NO!" buttons, and other items bearing anti-union slogans are sometimes made available to employees during campaigns. Employees cannot be asked to display anti-union insignia by management, but the materials can be left at places throughout the workplace where employees can obtain them.

Letters Home   Letters sent to the homes of employees have two purposes. They are intended to arouse the opposition of spouses or other household members against union organization. Therefore, frequent themes of the letters are the costs of union membership and strikes.

The other purpose is to convey to employees that management takes a personal interest in them. Therefore, employers are advised to make the letters as personal as possible by referring to employees by their first names and reproducing the letters in a manner that makes them appear as if they are individually typewritten.[9] Exhibit 3–3 is an example of such a letter.

Leaflets   A more impersonal and inexpensive form of written communication is the leaflet. They may be distributed on the job by first-line supervisors, in pay envelopes, or as workers enter or leave the workplace, making them a convenient way of communicating all of the themes of the anti-union campaign. While leaflets are usually

EXHIBIT 3–3. Letter to Employees Against Unionization

COMPANY LETTERHEAD

Date

Dear John and Sue,

On Thursday and Friday, you will vote in an election that is most important to you and to your future.

During these final hours before the election, I ask that you seriously think about the following questions and to honestly evaluate your answers in your own mind:

1. Last year the two of you together received a gross income of $22,677. Are you making more money now than you have or could make by working someplace else?

2. Will you never have to go out on strike if the Union gets in the plant? If the Union calls you out on strike, both of you will lose your income from this company.

3. Do you want to pay a part of your paycheck every week to go to the Union? *Both* of you will have to pay dues to the Union. On your current combined income, these dues would total approximately $288.00 a year.

4. Can the Union really make good on their promises?

5. What has the Union ever done for either or both of you?

I don't know how you will answer these questions. But, I ask that you think about this—it did not take the Union to get what you have received, and it did not cost you any money in dues, fines, fees, and strikes.

For fourteen years we have seen this plant grow and expand, the products we make have been broadly diversified, wages have been increased many times, there have been no strikes, and, working together, each one of us has shared in the progress of this plant. We have attained this record of progress and peace without a union and without strikes. This is not a perfect plant, but it is a very good plant. Our record is one for each of us to be proud. I hope you will agree with me that to bring a union into the plant would work to your serious disadvantage, and to keep it out would be in your very best interest.

By all means vote in this election next week!

Sincerely,

Signature
Name
Title

designed to gain and hold the reader's attention, their major short-coming is that many employees may not bother to read them.

Captive Audience Speeches   During the campaign, management usually brings employees together in a cafeteria or other central meeting place on company time for speeches discouraging union organization. A captive audience speech is often made just prior to twenty-four hours before the NLRB-conducted election. A popular member of management usually makes the speeches, although an outside person is sometimes used, particularly when the speech is coercive so that management is less likely to be associated with the threats.

In order to reduce opportunities for union supporters to prepare to challenge management during the speeches, captive audience speeches are seldom announced in advance. Union avoidance consultants advise employers to deny requests from the union to debate management or equal time to rebut management's presentations.

Voluntary Meetings   Employers sometimes hold parties and dinner meetings in order to provide additional forums for presenting anti-union messages. As long as attendance is voluntary, the meetings can even be held within twenty-four hours of NLRB-conducted elections. Spouses are often invited to these meetings in an attempt to bring additional pressure on employees to reject union representation.

Films and Slide Shows   Employers sometimes present films and slide shows to captive audiences. Films like *And Women Must Weep, A Question of Law and Order,* and *Springfield Gun* depict unions as violent and un-American. These emotionally charged films are quite old and outdated, so that they are shown less frequently today. In their place, union avoidance consultants have developed slide shows, which are cheaper to produce and easier to keep current.

Outside Influence   Employers sometimes enlist the aid of outsiders to convey anti-union messages. Editorials in newspapers, and captive audience speeches by local radio and TV personalities, professional athletes, and clergy have all been used in attempts to persuade employees to reject union organization. Exhibit 3–4 is a follow-up letter from a local radio personality.

EXHIBIT 3—4. Anti-union Letter from Radio Personality.

Dear Family:

How much I enjoyed coming over and visiting with you at the plant. Because our relationship through my radio ministry goes back a long time, I do think of you as one large family.

Last week I was in Ohio visiting a boyhood friend and his family. My friend is a union member and I was expecting a defense of unions from him. Was I shocked! He told me to do everything I could to keep people from joining. Thousands of people in Ohio are out of work because factories have closed and moved overseas. My friend has been lucky so far but he is afraid of the future, because he has seen other good workers and family men like himself, 30% of the people at his plant, out of work with no hope of employment in sight. He blames unions for this sad situation. "Unrealistic demands and long strikes have killed the goose that lays the golden eggs. And when I tried to speak up at a union meeting about burying the hatchet with management and working with them to keep our jobs, I was hooted down by the union bosses and their cronies." His advice was "Tell them to stay the hell away from unions!"

Let me remind you of one of my points when I visited you. You are too good a people to join the union. You have always stood for honesty and hard work. The opposite of the union! Like me, you've taught your children to be honest and I wonder how I would answer if my child asked: "Dad, you've taught me to be honest, but if you're honest, Dad, how can you carry a union card in your wallet, with all that I learn in school about them?"

Again, I'm so proud to be associated with you and who you are, and what the company does in our community. You're honest, hard-working people. You're too fine to join the union.

My thoughts, affection, and prayers are with you.

Yours devotedly,

Vote-No Committees

Employers encourage the active support of employees opposing union organization. The line between permissible and nonpermissible behavior under NLRB guidelines is narrow. Employees cannot be told to campaign against the union, but they may be told that they have a right to campaign. Employers can tell employees what to say and how best to say it, if they should choose to campaign. Employers can receive information from employees regarding union campaign activities, but they cannot ask employees to report union activities.[10] Given this legal hairsplitting, it is no wonder that vote-no committees often emerge during organizing campaigns.

SHORT-RUN STRATEGY: THE MESSAGE

The messages conveyed by employers during union organizing drives fall into two categories. The initial messages appeal to loyalties that employees may have toward the employer as a result of the long-run strategy of "making unions unnecessary." Hence, the employer may cite its record on wages and fringe benefits and the provision of job security, the personal relationships that exist between supervisors and workers, the "open door policy," and the participation of workers in the management of the enterprise.

To a greater or lesser extent, depending upon how effective the long-run strategy has been, the other messages are designed to arouse fear among employees. The possibilities of plant closings, fines and assessments imposed by the union, strikes, permanent replacement of economic strikers, and corruption of union officials are communicated to unorganized workers in a vivid manner.[11] In short, messages are orchestrated to "sweet talk" workers, and if those do not work, to "scare the hell out of them."

Within these two categories, some messages are used more frequently than others, and some messages are more effective than others. A study of thirty-three election campaigns discloses that the most frequently used messages are as follows:

1. Improvements in wages and working conditions are not dependent upon unionization.
2. Wages are good and equal to or better than under union contracts.
3. The financial costs of union dues outweigh the benefits to be gained.
4. The union is an outsider.
5. Employees should get the facts before deciding. The employer will provide facts and accept the employees' decision.
6. If the union wins the election, strikes may follow.
7. A loss of current benefits may follow a union win.
8. Strikers will lose wages during a strike and ultimately lose more than they gain.

9. Unions are not concerned with employee welfare.

10. Strikes may lead to a loss of jobs.

11. The employer has treated employees fairly and treated them well.

12. Employees should be certain to vote in the election.[12]

Strikes   Of the twelve messages most frequently conveyed to employees, three of the messages involve the strike theme. An eminent union avoidance consultant states: "Because information about strikes may be the single most important theme that an employer may communicate, . . . [there are] essential facts that must be articulated with clarity and force. . . ."[13] In other words, the prospect of strikes is one of the messages most likely to instill fear among employees.

Employers may stress a number of the aspects of strikes. The union will fine members who cross picket lines and will provide meager strike benefits. Wages and employer payments of medical and life insurance premiums will stop. Strikers are eligible for state unemployment insurance benefits in only three states. Also, recent changes in federal government guidelines make strikers ineligible for food stamps. The employer may summarize the financial disadvantages of striking with a statement that employees are unlikely to ever regain the money lost due to strikes. In addition to these short-term financial losses, workers are told that strikers face the possibility of losing their jobs to permanent replacements. Picket-line violence vividly completes the message on strikes.

Here are some examples of the strike theme as expressed in letters and leaflets from employers:

> I do not need to stress to you the dangers of strikes, and the trouble and dissension—the strain, the strife, the violence—which comes with them. You have heard and read about all of this—many times. Some of you have seen it in your own experience, and you know that it is the truth.
>
> You should remember that if a union calls people out on strike in order to force a company to agree to what the union wants, it is definitely the right of the company to fill the jobs of those who see fit to go out on strike, if necessary to operate. And remember this: THOSE WHOSE JOBS ARE FILLED WHILE THEY ARE OUT ON SUCH A STRIKE HAVE NO RIGHT TO RETURN TO THEIR JOBS OR GET THEIR JOBS BACK—

EVEN WHEN THE STRIKE HAS ENDED, SO LONG AS SUCH JOBS REMAIN FILLED BY SUCH REPLACEMENTS.

Incidentally, you should not overlook the fact that when employees follow a union and go out on strike, their company does not have to continue paying for their insurance. I am not saying what this Company would do under such circumstances, but I do think you should realize that in such a situation a company is legally at liberty to cease paying and carrying insurance for employees who are out because of a union strike.

Employees and The Union drew up a contract asking for higher wages and benefits which the company could not and would not agree to.

The Union went on STRIKE. After sixteen months of walking the picket line, members went back to work *without reaching an agreement.*

This was not "Some Union" or "Some Company in Another State!" This was the SAME Union trying to organize US. The Union only gives you "THEIR SIDE." We think you should know "BOTH SIDES."

No Guarantees   The three messages of improvements not being dependent upon unionization, wages being comparable to those in union contracts, and losses of current benefits possibly following unionization are often embodied in the theme "unions cannot guarantee anything." The employer may stress that union organizing campaigns are based upon promises of higher wages, better fringe benefits, and more job security—promises unions cannot guarantee. Workers will be told that the employer has the right under the law to refuse to grant the union its demands. Present benefits may even be lost. All that is required of the employer is "bargaining in good faith." The absence of a union guarantee and an explanation of the legal guidelines for collective bargaining are used to substantiate three of the messages communicated most often during organizing campaigns.

An example from a leaflet distributed by a vote-no committee follows:

What Would Happen if The Union Should Be Voted In?

Nothing—for a long, long time (maybe never). We have seen and read about other employees who have voted to go union, then the company would contest the election—prolong—put off—resist—using every legal means available to the company. Isn't this what the company has already said they will do? Think just a little bit ahead. In less than three months it will be time to fill up the fuel tanks, time for the added expense of putting the kids back in school, higher electric bills and not to mention Christmas. If we cannot reach a contract by then (and you can be certain we will not), how will this affect you and your family? Then think how this might affect our plant. Production would go on as usual. At the other plant the employees will get their annual raise in wages and benefits (we will not get ours because the Federal Courts prohibit a wage increase during negociations (sic)) And employees at the other plant will probably be told "Look what happened at our plant."

Do you want this to happen to you?

Here is an employer's version of the same message:

If the Union were voted in here, all that the law would require of us would be to "bargain in good faith" with the Union. This definitely does not mean, as many people mistakenly believe, that we would have to consider the wages and benefits you now have as irreducible minimum. There is no law which requires us to pay more than the Federal minimum wage. We have every right to bargain for a reduction in any phase of wages and fringe benefits if economic factors indicate that we should do so, and would not hesitate to bargain in that fashion. We want you to realize that many companies have in fact ended up paying less after bargaining with a union than they did before they started bargaining.

Plant Closing   The ultimate guarantee which the union is unable to provide is complete job security. Strikes and higher labor costs due to inefficiencies imposed by the union contract may result in higher prices, a loss of customers, and ultimately, the most terrifying consequence of all, a plant closing. Under the law, employers cannot "guarantee" this scenario, but they can and do allude to it.

Here are examples of the plant closing theme:

MEMBERS of the Union went on strike two years ago. About *one year later* the Company went into bankruptcy. They CLOSED DOWN—Hundreds of people no longer had a job!!!

These are just a few. There are many more. We can show you where huge companies, larger than ours, with employees belonging to the Union, have gone into bankruptcy—CLOSED DOWN! When this happens, thousands of people lose their jobs.

"The Union is an Outsider"   message has a number of congruent themes. The employer may charge that "friendly relationships" between management and employees in the election unit will be lost, because the union will promote strife and divisiveness through the establishment of an "us versus them atmosphere."

The employer may also infer that employees will no longer be able to approach management directly; instead, employees must pursue solutions to workplace problems through union channels. Pay increases and promotions will no longer be based on individual merit; instead, standardized rates will be imposed. In short, "workers lose their individuality through the interference of this outsider."

The following is an example of the frequently used message that the employee relinquishes his or her right to bring workplace problems to the attention of management without the participation of a union representative:

In our shop we know each other much better than people do in big shops. We see each other during the entire work day. You can stop me anytime I'm in the shop and talk to me about a work problem. If you prefer, we can go to my office. Now, if a Union was in our relationship, that would not be possible. You would have to go through another employee or a Union representative. I'd rather talk directly to you and do the best I can to help you with your problem. The Union has no way to force me to do something more than I am willing to do for you when we talk direct with each other. You have to make up your mind what it is you want—union or *no union*. It will not be the best of both worlds, it will be one or the other.

The statement is not true and may be particularly unsettling to workers who enjoy good relations with their immediate supervisors. Under the Taft-Hartley Act, workers have the right to handle their grievances individually without union representation.

Need To Vote   Employers usually stress the need for workers in the election unit to vote. The reasoning is that avid union and company supporters will surely vote. Workers who are apathetic about the outcome of the election or who are unsure of whether unionization will benefit them are less likely to vote. However, these workers are likely to be more fearful about changing the status quo through unionization than keeping the employment situation as it is, because change entails risk and uncertainty. Furthermore, the outcome of authorization elections is determined on the basis of the number of votes cast rather than the number of eligible voters in the election unit. Employers generally reason that a vote not cast in the election is a de facto vote for union representation.

Three issues were remembered most by employees in the thirty-three election units surveyed:

1. Improvements in wages and working conditions are not dependent upon unionization.

2. The financial costs of union dues outweigh the benefits to be gained.

3. The plant may close if the union wins the election.[14] Even though the threat of closing the plant was not one of the twelve messages most frequently communicated in the thirty-three campaigns, it was the third most freqeuntly remembered message.

There are other messages conveyed by employers during union organizing campaigns. These messages are designed either to appeal to loyalties employees may have toward the employer or to instill fear in them.

Union Authorization Card Signing Should Be Halted

This is usually the first subject addressed by the employer and is intended to stop the union in its tracks. If effective, the union will be unable to gather a sufficient number of signatures to support an election petition before the NLRB.

Critical to the employer's success at stopping authorization card signing is an effective "early warning system" for detecting union activity. While the employer may periodically tell employees not to sign cards, a media blitz usually occurs once union activity is detected. Handbills, letters to employees' homes, posters, captive audience speeches, and conversations with supervisors on this topic may all occur.

The truth may be twisted in an effort to intimidate employees.

They may be told that by signing cards, the union may be certified as the bargaining agent without an election being held. This may come as a surprise to employees who are somewhat unsure of their support of unionization, but who want an election campaign to occur so that they have the opportunity to weigh the arguments presented by the employer and the union.[15] What the employer may not tell them, however, is that the only ways the union can be certified are if the employer agrees to a card check or commits substantial unfair labor practices so as to make a fair election impossible in the view of the NLRB. There is virtually no chance that either of these scenarios will occur.

The major thrust of the employer's communication may be that card signing is not confidential. This is true. But the employer may dwell on the point to such a degree that workers feel intimidated even though no overt threat is made.[16] If the employer stresses repeatedly the lack of confidentiality of the cards, an unfair labor practice charge should be filed with the NLRB, which may view the employer's statments as threats.

Employees may be told that if they have second thoughts about signing the cards, they should request the cards back from the union. The employer may supply the address of the union and a sample letter to be sent. However, the union is under no obligation to return the cards. If the union succeeds at filing an election petition, employees will be told that they are under no obligation to support the union if they have signed authorization cards.

No Local Union Autonomy   Employers may stress that union locals are subject to the rules of the international union with which they are affiliated and will go so far as to say that there is no such thing as "local control." The per capita dues earmarked for the international union and, if applicable, the AFL-CIO are cited as evidence to substantiate the claim along with the international union's constitutional provisions on trusteeships and, where applicable, international union approval of contract settlements and strikes.[17] If the international union has imposed sanctions on local unions or dissident groups among the membership, these incidents will be publicized.

Unions Mean Trouble   Employers will usually level a broad attack upon the labor movement in general and the particular unions attempting to organize their employees. The information for these attacks is gathered systematically by the "task force" directing the anti-union campaign.

In election units with a high proportion of women and minorities, the relatively low representation of women and ethnic minorities within the leadership ranks of organized labor may be emphasized. The downward trend in the proportion of the labor force represented by unions, and the increase in the number of union decertifications may be cited as evidence that workers in the United States are finding unions to be "more trouble than they are worth."

An examination of a union's constitution and bylaws discloses the grounds for which union members can be disciplined and the procedures for determining guilt or innocence. The union's authority to level fines and special assessments is also contained in the constitution and bylaws, and this information is conveyed to employees.

Employers often interpret provisions from the union's constitution and bylaws in ways that make the union look bad. Exhibits 3–5 and 3–6 are examples of actual employer communications. In Exhibit 3–5, the provision allowing only union members in good standing to vote on strikes is reasonable. Why should workers who do not belong to the union have a voice in union affairs?

Realistically, there is little likelihood of a strike if only a small percentage of the bargaining unit belongs to the union. Employees not belonging to the union probably would not honor the union's picket lines, thereby making a successful strike difficult to conduct.

The rationale behind the union's executive board determining the membership eligible to vote on a strike is to give the union increased bargaining power in situations where, for example, two contracts with the same employer expire simultaneously. If one bargaining unit chose to strike and the other did not, the employer could shift production to the unstruck location, thereby weakening the strike. By having both bargaining units vote together on the strike and abide by the decision, a strike would be more effective. If the local has a history of not allowing members with no direct interest in the contract negotiations under review to vote, this fact should be communicated.

Less than one percent of union contracts in the United States allow strikes to be conducted during the life of the contract for the purpose of general enforcement of the agreement. The usual contract provision is a grievance procedure culminating with final and binding arbitration. More than likely, the local has no contracts allowing strikes during the life of the agreement. If so, this fact should be conveyed.

This anti-union communication is rather easy to debunk. However, it would be best not to be required to clarify the overly legalistic language in the union's constitution and bylaws. More on this in the next chapter.

In Exhibit 3–6, the organizer is again placed in the position of explaining the rationale behind provisions in the union's constitution. Words like "discipline," "charges," "fine," "expulsion," and "trial" are very powerful and apt to intimidate potential union supporters. Couldn't this problem be minimized if the constitution and bylaws were written in a less legalistic manner and with the inclusion of examples clarifying the provisions? Couldn't the reasons for the provisions be provided in plain language within the constitutions and bylaws? Of all the topics contained in anti-union messages, the constitution and bylaws and their clarification are the areas where the union exercises its greatest control. Why not reduce the opportunities for employers to interpret these documents at will?

From the reports filed by unions under the Labor Management Reporting and Disclosure Act, the salaries and expenses of international union officers and even the union staff directly involved in the organizing campaign are available. The employer may level the charge of "high-paid union bosses" based upon this information. An example:

> By the way, where does the money come from to pay for these organizational meetings the pro-union people have been attending? Who pays for the flowers, the badges, the paper, and the copier at the Local? Just who pays for all these Union organizing efforts, including the organizer's $53,709.39 in salary and expenses? Each and every member of the Union, that's who!

Clipping services like that of the Bureau of National Affairs provide information on strikes, permanent replacement of economic strikers, picket-line violence, criminal accusations, alleged Communist Party affiliations, plant closings, and negotiated wage freezes and reductions. This information is then conveyed to employees in an effort to portray unions as the source of "trouble," with a particular emphasis, as noted above, on strikes.[18] Exhibit 3–7 is an example.

EXHIBIT 3–5. Anti-union Letter to Employees Regarding Strike Vote

COMPANY LETTERHEAD

Date

TO: All Employees

NO STRIKES WITHOUT
A 2/3 VOTE!
TRUE OR FALSE?

The union has been saying you couldn't be called out on strike unless two-thirds of *you* voted to strike. True or false? We say FALSE!
The official *bylaws* of the local union (as filed with the federal government) say
1. Only members of the union can vote on strikes:

"Members at each separate division, craft, or place of employment authorized to hold separate meetings . . . may vote . . . on approval of . . . contracts . . . and strikes . . ."

In other words, if only a FRACTION of our employees actually joined the union, a fraction of THAT GROUP could call a strike affecting all of you.
2. If you are not a member, with all dues, fees, fines, and assessments paid up, you cannot even go to a union meeting or vote on ANYTHING:

"The Warden shall have charge of the inner door and shall not admit any member who is in arrears . . "

3. The unions' executive board (president, vice president, secy-treasurer, recording secretary, and three trustees) decides WHICH members can vote on strikes, and could allow the ENTIRE local membership of several thousand to vote on a strike at our company:

"The executive board is authorized and empowered to conduct and manage the affairs of this organization . . . . Determine the membership which shall vote on agreements and strikes . . ."

4. Strikes can be called WITHOUT any vote being taken:

"Strike votes shall not be required where a collective bargaining agreement does not prohibit strikes for the purpose of enforcing the terms of such agreement. In such cases, the President may call a strike, or in his discretion refer the matter to the membership directly affected as *he* shall determine."

These union bylaws are on file in the personnel department. You are welcome to read them at any time.

LET'S SUM IT UP!

A. You cannot vote on a strike unless you are a MEMBER. Since this is a right-to-work state, you will never have to become a member, and a great many of our employees undoubtedly NEVER WILL. This means that some of our employees could vote a strike affecting ALL!

B. The union could permit thousands OUTSIDE THIS COMPANY to vote and decide whether YOU have a strike!

C. The local president CAN call strikes without any vote!

WHAT DOES THIS MEAN?

It means the union has given you a FALSE story.

If you can't believe them about one thing—can you believe them about anything else? Think it over!

Signature
Name
Title

We've Made Mistakes, But . . .   If management perceives that its long-run strategy has not made unionization "unnecessary" and that the union is winning the organizing campaign, it may admit that it has made mistakes. Underlying this admission is a veiled promise that if given another chance, wages and working conditions will improve. Employees may be led to believe that if the union loses the election and the employment situation does not improve, they retain the option of unionization at a later date. The organizer must dispel this notion. The following is an example of an employer's "mea culpa:"

> Problems do exist. For some of them I accept responsibility. Perhaps you were not kept as well informed as was possible or were not listened to so that your problems could be better understood or your questions answered promptly. That there was not a full comprehension of some issues of the past few years, I hold myself responsible. But, whatever the mistakes and problems may be, I am convinced that we can solve them by working

EXHIBIT 3—6. Anti-union Letter to Employees Regarding Discipline

COMPANY LETTERHEAD

Date

To All Employees:

The National Labor Relations Board has set the date for the secret ballot election for Friday. As a result, questions have been raised by employees which I would like to answer.

Question: Does the union have rules and regulations controlling our activities as members of the union?

Answer: Yes, these rules and regulations and obligations of membership may be found in the union's Constitution, which serves as the legal document binding *all* members to the union.

Question: What are the requirements and obligations of membership as spelled out in the union Constitution?

Answer: You may care to review the following Articles.

"Any member . . . shall be subject to discipline after charges and a hearing thereon in accordance with the provisions hereof for any of the following offenses:

1. Engaging in any conduct or committing any acts forbidden by or in conflict with any of the union or AFL-CIO Codes of Ethical Practices.

2. Violating any provision of the Constitution of the International Union or the constitution or bylaws of any subordinate body or the oath of office or membership.

3. Refusing to carry out the decision of any Executive Board or membership of a subordinate body . . .

4. Engaging in any activity or course of conduct contrary or detrimental to the welfare or best interests of the International Union or of a subordinate body."

"The term "discipline" when used in this Article shall include but not be limited to a fine, removal from office, . . . expulsion from membership or suspension . . ."

"Unless otherwise provided herein, trials shall be conducted in accordance with the constitution . . ."

Between now and the day of the election, I urge each of you to study and consider the union rules and regulations. Your supervisor has copies of the union constitution. Read it for yourself.

> Signature
> Name
> Title

---

together. Many of you, I feel, share with me the belief that a union is a poor substitute for the individual freedom we all cherish and do not want to lose.

Employers will sometimes charge that workers have been coerced into signing authorization cards and wearing union insignia without ever substantiating these serious charges. Here are some examples:

> It has come to my attention that a few people have been coercing employees into signing cards for the union. *Let there be no mistake—this type of behavior will not be tolerated!* Any employee or person from the union found engaging in such tactics will be dealt with firmly. Employees have a right to come to work each day without fear of coercion. We will protect that right.
>
> We will continue to keep you fully informed concerning this matter. In the meantime, should you have any questions, please do not hesitate to contact your supervisor or me.

Employees are falling away from the Union. We can see it in many ways. More and more employees are asking for copies of our letter on cancellation of Union cards. Others are saying that they wear Union buttons only to avoid harassment, and really don't want the Union. This is understandable, but those who wear Union buttons just to avoid harassment may be giving a false impression. *You* are an important person! Many others who think well of you may vote as they *think* you will. We wouldn't try to tell anyone what to do about this, but remember—you may be creating an image of yourself that will be hard to shake.

Where a vote-no committee is formed, the organizer can usually anticipate the most ludicrous charges. Examples of the charges in-

EXHIBIT 3–7. Anti-union Flyer with Newspaper Clippings.

VOTE NO FOR YOUR KIDS

GOONS KEEP CIO STRIKE BOOMING WITH 7 BLASTS

Bomb Rips Roof Over 5 Children

Danville, Va., April 26 (Special)— The seven state strike of 45,000 CIO Textile Workers unionists was booming today— with seven new dynamitings here and at Wake Forest, N.C.

Five children of Wesley Cook, a nonstriker at the Royal Cotton Mills, narrowly escaped death at Wake Forest last night when a bomb thrown at their home blasted a hole in the roof over the children's bedroom. The children were asleep in the room at the time.

Teamster President Charged With Murder in Dillard Death

Teamster Local 515 president David L. Halpenny was charged with Murder Friday after a non-union man, Mark

Howard Dillard, 37, of 260 E. 45th St. was shot and killed at the Teamster Hall on East Oaks Drive.

Woman Killed In Georgia Mill Strike Violence

Summerville, Ga., June 1—A woman was killed Monday when a car of non-striking employees tried to enter a struck textile mill at nearby Berryton. Solicitor General John Davis said the woman, Mrs. Nellie Turner, was crushed to death when strikers overturned the car in which she was riding. Mrs. Turner attempted to jump from the vehicle and it turned over on her, he said. Two other women in the car escaped serious injury.

Worker's Car Blasted At Cedartown, Ga.

Atlanta, Ga.—Violence in the strike at Cedartown Textiles, Inc., at nearby Cedartown has flared up once more with the dynamiting of a mill employee's automobile.

The automobile, reported to have been owned by Harold Edge, worker in the Cedartown mill—which has been strike-bound since February—was parked in the yard.

Dynamitings and Rifle Fire Mark Textile Strike Scene

cluded in vote-no committee leaflets are that workers will need the
permission of union stewards to use the restrooms and will need to
pay for entering company parking lots.

In addition, the vote-no committee can make coercive statements which would be considered illegal if made by the employer:

> IS YOUR NAME ON THE IN-PLANT ORGANIZING COM-
> MITTEE? Many people who were told that if they signed cards
> the front office would never know have found their names on
> that list. You don't have to sign anything to be on that committee.
> If you signed a card or attended a meeting your name may be
> on that list. You can see the list in the Personnel Office or discuss
> it with your foreman.

The release of "doomsday reports" just prior to the election
can be a very effective management tactic. "The Story of the Plant
at Other City" (Exhibit 3–8) is an example.

Another forum for a "bomb-shell" is the captive audience speech.
The following is an excerpt from a speech delivered just prior to
twenty-four hours before an NLRB-conducted election:

> Many of you know that before coming here, I worked at another
> plant in this organization. I worked at that plant for six years,
> bought a house, and settled down. My family and I were happy.
> We were close to our relatives and our childhood friends.
>
> At one time that plant was the largest one in our organi-
> zation, but over the years jobs were lost and that plant no longer
> plays a prominent role in our company. That plant has a union.
> Strikes have occurred and relations between employees and su-
> pervisors are strained. You might say that my family and I were
> transferred here because of a union.
>
> We are happy here. We have made new friends and actively
> participate in church, school, and civic affairs. We do not want
> to be transferred again.
>
> The decision is yours. I respect you enough to go along
> with your decision. All that I can do is ask you to please consider
> seriously all of the consequences of bringing a union in here. I
> urge you all to vote tomorrow and when you mark your ballot,
> ask yourself: "What is best for me and my family?"

The employer's melancholy description of how he and his family
were uprooted from another company location presumably because

---

EXHIBIT 3–8. Anti-union "Doomsday Report"

THE STORY OF THE PLANT AT OTHER CITY

At one time, the plant at Other City was one of the largest plants in this company. It employed almost 5,000 *unionized* employees.

In the early 1960s, we got the new process for making our product. We told the union at the Other City plant we would install the new process there if the union would agree to necessary changes. The union refused, thinking we would go ahead whether we got the changes or not. Instead, we built a new plant elsewhere for the new process.

After that happened, the union came and *asked* for a new process operation, but it was too late. In the years that followed, the number of jobs at Other City dropped down to 300 or so. This is what the union did for the Other City employees. Thousands of jobs lost.

We now have plants throughout the country where our employees refuse to have any union.

At one time, this company was 95 percent unionized. A few weeks ago, you saw a Union handout saying we are now only one-third to one-half unionized. The Other City story is one of the reasons, and there are many similar stories in this company. We will be talking about some of them in the days to come.

Let's not turn our town into another Other City. We all have a good thing here, and we have made a lot of progress in these first fifteen years. We know that we now have the best wages and benefits in our area and industry. Why turn it all over to a union with whatever risks that may involve?

Protect what you have!

Vote NO!

YOUR MANAGEMENT

---

of union activity at that location is a tough act to follow, particularly just prior to the election. Now let us turn our attention to the long-run union avoidance strategy.

LONG-RUN STRATEGY

The major thrust of the long-run strategy is to "provide employees with those things promised to them by a union."[19] Wages and benefits comparable to those in union contracts reduce the advantages of unionization for the worker. Where an employer has both organized and unorganized employees, changes in the wages and benefits of the unorganized follow in lock-step fashion those of the organized. For employers with no unionized employees, wages and fringes may be equal to or greater than those of other area and industry employers. Unorganized employees are made aware that their wages and benefits are tied to those in union contracts, industry averages, the Consumer Price Index, or whatever factor is used in order to reduce their anxiety about the future and to convey the impression that union representation will not cause the employer to deviate from the plan. Where employees are held directly responsible for productivity, wage increases may be based upon merit with the system for determining merit agreed to by employees.[20]

Many unorganized employers make it a practice of keeping employees in the dark as to what their fellow employees are earning. A recent survey of 248 manufacturing companies disclosed that more than half of the companies do not discuss salary ranges with employees.[21] The primary reason is that employers attempt to pay individuals who perform satisfactorily what they believe it will take to keep them from quitting, thereby reducing the cost of hiring and training new employees. The likelihood of a fifty-year-old, twenty-year employee quitting, for example, is much less than that for a twenty-five-year-old, two-year employee with comparable educational qualifications and job performance. At raise time, the employer is likely to grant a higher increase to the younger employee. Sealed pay envelopes, a payroll register available only to top management, telling each employee "confidentially" that he or she is drawing the top salary, and the natural secrecy of employees are usually sufficient to keep employees from knowing salary ranges. This strategy encourages "individualism" and yields the employer a healthy profit.

Bonuses, raffles, vacation trips, and other rewards paid to employees are also a way of discouraging unions. Employees are made aware that the employer can withhold these forms of compensation and will attempt to do so if a union should be successful at organizing. The cost of these glittering prizes is often less than the wage structure that would exist under a union contract, but they make more of an impression on employees than extra dollars in every paycheck.[22]

The grievance procedure is an important benefit of union representation, particularly in cases where the employer takes disciplinary action against workers. Increasingly, unorganized workers are enjoying the benefits of grievance procedures resembling those in union contracts. It may be called an "open-door policy" or "employee judicial system," but the procedures are basically the same regardless of the name. Employees are encouraged to bring problems to the attention of management which, in turn, promises to listen. The program is most effective when management gives its answers to employee complaints within a day or so, because employees perceive that their complaints are important to management and that management is not giving them a runaround. Appeals of decisions by first-line supervision to higher levels of management are common. However, unlike the grievance procedures in union contracts, binding impartial arbitration is seldom stipulated.

The seniority system in union contracts is designed to reduce favoritism by management, which forces workers to engage in demeaning behavior unrelated to work performance in order to attain promotions and job security. Employers interested in avoiding unionization install job posting systems and "promotion-from-within" policies. Education and training opportunities enabling employees to take advantage of the organization's promotion policies are also instituted. While seldom the sole consideration, seniority is taken into account when layoffs occur. However, seniority is often the sole consideration in matters such as vacation selection and parking lot assignments.

In addition to matching or surpassing the provisions of union contracts, the long-run strategy has other aspects that can be used by themselves in an attempt to thwart organization. Employers choosing to provide employees with less than union representation would provide must rely heavily upon these other aspects of the long-term strategy.

Physical Environment   The physical environment of the workplace can be manipulated to reduce the likelihood of unionization. A retired executive at a major U.S. corporation told me that his company's policy is to limit the size of new manufacturing facilities to 200 employees and to locate new plants in rural areas, particularly in the South. This policy is expressly designed to make new plants an unattractive target for union organization, while large organized plants in the urban North are being phased out.

The police and other local authorities can harass union organizers and assist in strikebreaking. Civic and religious leaders and the media can influence workers about union organizing. For these reasons, employers curry their favor, often through financial contributions, in order to affect the community environment in which union organizing might occur.

Plant layout can be altered to reduce the access outside union organizers and members of in-plant organizing committees have to workers. Locating plants and parking lots down long private driveways makes the distribution of leaflets difficult. Having enough entrances and exits so that employees do not wait in line to punch in and out reduces the access of organizers. Likewise, the workplace might contain a sufficient number of drinking fountains, vending machine areas, and rest rooms to prevent employees from congregating in large groups. Isolation reduces the likelihood of collective action.[23]

The Communication Network   Another key element of the long-term strategy is the communication between management and employees. Although both are used, face-to-face communication is much more effective than written communication. As a part of their job responsibilities, managers and supervisors are expected to speak to workers on a personal level. Furthermore, personal contacts between management and workers in the potential bargaining unit are fostered. A single parking lot without reserved spaces for top management, workplace entrances used by both labor and management, and a common cafeteria reduce the distinctions between managers and workers and provide opportunities for personal contacts. Employer-sponsored golf, bowling, and softball leagues, recreation facilities, and trips to concerts and sporting events are additional examples of ways to promote communications between managers and workers.[24]

These informal contacts are meant to convey management's concern for employees and to serve as the early detection network for alerting management to union organizing activities. The longer the time management has to implement its "emergency" short-term union avoidance activities, the more effective they are. Also, during the time before an actual organizing drive surfaces, management can commit what would later be ruled as unfair labor practices without sanctions imposed by the NLRB. Actions such as the dismissal of workers perceived as union supporters and unscheduled improvements of wages, benefits, and working conditions will not be considered to be unfair labor practices if the union cannot demonstrate to the satisfaction of the Board that the employer was aware of union organizing activity.

In addition to providing rather informal opportunities for communication, a more structured approach is used. Workplace-wide meetings and departmental, divisional, or other small group meetings are held on company time along with "voluntary" dinner meetings held off the clock. The management approach is often very subtle. The intention is to convey to workers that they are part of the "team." So-called inside information on the company's sales, productivity, and profitability is conveyed to employees.

Also on a systematic basis, first-line supervisors are responsible for conducting individual face-to-face discussions with the workers under their direction on a selected topic, whether it be the need for increased productivity to meet foreign competition or a reminder that the company prefers to operate non-union and will become part of the foreign competition in order to remain non-union.

Consultants encourage employers to continually remind their employees that they prefer to operate non-union. The non-union policy is conveyed at the initial employment interview, the orientation sessions for new employees, in the employer's handbook and newspaper for employees, and through periodic letters to workers' homes.[25]

This broadly based communications policy, coupled with efforts to reduce the status differentials between labor and management, along with the elimination of time clocks and the placement of all workers on a salary basis promote allegiance to the employer. An additional benefit of the continuous long-term communication and status equalization policies of employers is immunity from criticism for insincerity during union organizing campaigns because of sudden interest in the welfare of employees.

Attitude Surveys   A rather sophisticated tool used for union avoidance is the attitude survey. Questionnaires are distributed to employees on company time in a cafeteria or other central meeting place. Usually, surveys are short—about twenty questions—and take only a few minutes for employees to complete. Individual employees retain their anonymity. Employers administer the questionnaires at intervals as frequently as once each year. Results of the surveys are summarized and released to employees, even when the employer does not receive good ratings. However, employers only ask questions about matters they are willing to change. Results of the surveys and any resulting changes are publicized through letters to employees' homes, the employer's newspaper, and meetings with employees.[26]

Questions are asked about favoritism by supervisors and how consistently management applies its policies and procedures. Answers to the questions provide a good indication of a union's chances at organizing workers. Some questions are rather subtle:

> My idea of a good department is one in which:
>
> - Employees are allowed to get ahead and achieve their career goals without anyone holding them back.
> - Employees stick together and help each other when the going gets tough.
> - The needs of the employees are a little more important than the needs of the department.[27]

Employees are asked to assign a numerical value to each statement. Similar questions are asked about supervision, wages and fringe benefits, promotions, and job security.

Employee reactions to statements more specific to union organization are sometimes requested:

> It may be that the only way employees at my level can get a fair shake is if they join a union.
>
> The longer I worked for _____, the more I see a need for a union.
>
> A union would help employees like me get what I need from __.
>
> A union would get us the kinds of benefits we want.
>
> A union would improve job security.[28]

Attitude surveys accomplish several objectives. Management assesses the degree to which its personnel policies meet the needs of employees and gauges the likelihood of a successful union organizing drive. Also, the impression is conveyed to employees that management is concerned about their welfare and willing to adopt their suggestions. The message is "Why organize a union? Management listens!"

Employee Organizations   The National Labor Relations Act specifically prohibits employer-sponsored labor organizations and for good reason. During the 1920s and early 1930s company unions outnumbered legitimate labor unions. Some non-union employers, however, still support employee organizations. Often, these organizations restrict their activities to planning and conducting sporting and social events. Sometimes they serve as advisory groups on matters such as "work enrichment." While some employers grant these groups permanent status, others relegate them to temporary ad hoc status whereby specific tasks are assigned and after the tasks are completed, the groups are disbanded.

The reason for granting the employee groups temporary status is that the groups can become forerunners of unions. If employees are able to bring about changes through collective action, they may believe that the employer is responsive to their needs. However, if the employer rejects some of their suggestions, employees having previously experienced success through collective action may believe that the greater strength provided by unions and collective bargaining is desirable.

Union avoidance consultant Charles Hughes uses a "jelly bean theory" to explain why employee advisory groups should be temporary and limited to studying specific issues such as employee performance appraisal procedures and promotion policies. A tourist at a national park who feeds jelly beans to a bear will satisfy the bear as long as it is fed the jelly beans. When the tourist runs out of jelly beans, the bear will continue to expect them and may take off the tourist's arm, because no more jelly beans are forthcoming.[29]

Let us examine how the long-run union avoidance strategy is implemented by one employer.

LONG-RUN AVOIDANCE STRATEGY AT HYATT HOTELS[30]

Before the Hyatt Regency Hotel opened in downtown Minneapolis, Hotel, Motel, Restaurant Employees Local 17 attempted to reach an agreement with the employer to recognize the union as bargaining agent on the basis of authorization card signatures by a majority of employees. Hyatt rejected the proposal, asserting in a full-page ad in *The Minneapolis Star* that it preferred giving its employees the opportunity to express their views on unionization in an NLRB-conducted election. This was a portent of things to come. In September 1981, six months after the Hyatt Regency opened, union representation was rejected by two thirds of the hotel's employees who voted. What happened in those six months?

Hyatt instituted a wage scale that exceeds the wage rates in union contracts at Minneapolis hotels by several cents an hour. The benefits package is comparable or better than the package in union contracts. The grievance procedure at Hyatt is patterned after that in Local 17's contracts and seniority governs scheduling and layoffs. During its first nine months of operation, nearly half of Hyatt's 400 employees received promotions. In addition, there are monthly gripe sessions with the hotel's manager, tuition reimbursement for qualifying school work, employee sports teams, drug and alcohol counseling, and frequent social events.

One twenty-four-year-old employee is quoted as saying: "Things could change, but right now, the company is so fair—what's the need for a union?" Not surprisingly, major support for the union came from older employees, who had seen elsewhere that what the employer gives, it can also take away.

CONCLUSION

It is convenient to blame the organizing difficulties confronting unions on the weaknesses of the law and the lawlessness of employers and union avoidance consultants. But as discussed in chapter 1, there is much more involved. Particularly disturbing is the reality that some workplaces are unorganizable because employers match or surpass the provisions in union contracts by the union avoidance technique of "making unions unnecessary." Through collective bargaining, unions establish local labor market and industry standards of wages, benefits, and working conditions. Unorganized employers can then use these union-negotiated standards as bench marks for developing personnel policies designed to convince their employees that these standards are not dependent upon unionization.

On the union's loss at the Hyatt Regency Hotel in Minneapolis, Local 17's president at the time, Cal Wright, is quoted as saying: "Do all these benefits outweigh the social consciousness we should have in the younger generation? In this case, yes they do."[31]

Wright is addressing a fundamental issue determining the organizing potential of labor unions in the United States. If employers remove the incentive for gaining union contracts, what other incentives can unions provide for workers to organize? If that additional incentive is "social consciousness," do workers lack it or do labor unions fail to appeal to it?

For nine years, I lived in upstate New York close to the major facilities of IBM and Eastman Kodak, the country's two largest non-union employers. Wages, benefits, and working conditions at the two companies surpass or equal those in their respective local labor markets and in union contracts in their respective industries. Their employees are unorganizable unless IBM and Kodak change their personnel policies. However, IBM and Kodak workers are not necessarily anti-union. The workers with whom I spoke attributed the companies' personnel policies to unions and the employers' desire to remain unorganized. This connection is obvious to unorganized workers who enjoy the benefits of unionization without the costs of membership. Yet it does not provide them with a motivation to organize. Why organize when the benefits are free?[32]

The answer is that unions in the United States in the 1980s do not provide workers with a reason for organizing other than pure self-interest. In the terminology of Eric Hoffer, American unions are "enterprises" and not a "mass movement"[33] whose members are motivated by self-sacrifice for a higher good beyond the provisions in union contracts which benefit them directly.

This is not to say that the sole concern of organized labor is collective bargaining or that a mass movement is not envisioned by some labor leaders. Organized labor has been an important lobbying force assisting in the passage of progressive social legislation benefitting union members and non-members alike. However, one need not be a union member or even support the concepts of labor unions and collective bargaining to actively support the same social legislation as organized labor. Political parties and other interest groups also provide the opportunity to express a person's "social consciousness." Organized labor is not unique.

The late Jerry Wurf, organizer and president of the American Federation of State, County, and Municipal Employees once said: "The labor movement can be a force for not just the economic well-being of workers, but for peace, tranquility, and a better tomorrow for all mankind."[34] A similar vision is shared by some other labor leaders and by some observers outside organized labor.

Ultimately, those who are concerned about the formation of a

"movement" are led to a political solution.[35] Of necessity, this solution goes far beyond Samuel Gompers' prescription of organized
labor's role in politics as "rewarding friends and punishing enemies."
While an independent political course for organized labor, perhaps
even the formation of a labor party, is appealing, it does not provide
a solution to the issue under examination—reasons for workers who
enjoy the benefits of union contracts without union membership to
join unions. Even if a labor party could gain the support of the vast
majority of American workers, both organized and unorganized, every
November, there is no assurance that the unorganized would choose
union representation and collective bargaining at the workplace in
those instances where its benefits are free. Ultimately, government
could mandate compulsory union membership, but unions would not
be a "movement" but rather an "enterprise" of government itself.

The union avoidance consultants are right; matching and surpassing the provisions in union contracts removes the incentive for
workers in the United States in the 1980s to organize. This is hard
to accept, but it is not an admission of defeat or, more important, a
lack of resolve, but only a realistic assessment of organizing potential.
Of necessity, the selection of organizing targets must be limited to
those workplaces where unions can identify distinct advantages to
be obtained from union contracts.

All is not lost. Every employer does not follow the formula,
because it is costly, not in back-pay awards to workers fired for union
activity, but instead in wages, benefits, and working conditions comparable or better than those provided in union contracts. Employers
who institute or promise to institute the formula are tempted to
cheat on it. This temptation to cheat helps to explain why the union
"win" record in 1980 for NLRB second elections was 61 percent
and 82 percent for third elections.[36]

Unions can hold their own when confronting employers who
have not developed a comprehensive long-run union avoidance strategy. Persuasive arguments for unionization can be mounted during
organizing campaigns which surpass or equal those of employers
against union representation.

The examination of the short-run union avoidance strategy of
employers in this chapter was rather long, but its purpose will be
clearer in a succeeding chapter. It is my conviction that the short-
run strategies of employers are limited, although it is too presump-

tuous to claim that all of the possible strategies are included in this chapter. If employer strategies are limited, then they are predictable. If they are predictable, unions can enhance their organizing strength by anticipating the employer's campaign and neutralizing its impact by forthrightly addressing the objections to unionization that will ultimately be raised by the employer.

The stage is set for the next two chapters.

FOOTNOTES

[1] James L. Dougherty. *Union-Free Management—And How to Keep It Free* (Chicago: The Dartnell Corporation, 1972), p. 87.

[2] A. T. De Maria. *How Management Wins Union Organizing Campaigns* (New York: Executive Enterprises Publications Co., Inc., 1980), p. 5.

[3] Dougherty, *Union-Free Management,* p. 87.

[4] Presentation by Robert Muehlenkamp, Organizing Director, National Union of Hospital and Health Care Employees, Local 1199, at the 1979 AFL-CIO Education Conference.

[5] Woodruff Imberman. "How Expensive Is an NLRB Election?" *MSU Business Topics,* Summer 1976, p. 15.

[6] De Maria, *How Management Wins,* p. 97.

[7] De Maria, *How Management Wins,* p. 115.

[8] De Maria, *How Management Wins,* pp. 115–116.

[9] De Maria, *How Management Wins,* p. 117.

[10] De Maria, *How Management Wins,* p. 100.

[11] De Maria, *How Management Wins,* p. 345.

[12] Julius Getman, Stephen Goldberg, and Jeanne B. Herman. *Union Representation Elections: Law and Reality* (New York: Russell Sage Foundation, 1976), pp. 78–81.

[13] De Maria, *How Management Wins,* p. 345.

[14] Getman, et al., *Union Representation Elections,* pp. 78–81.

[15] J. W. Lawson. *How to Meet the Challenge of the Union Organizer* (Chicago: the Dartnell Corporation, 1977), pp. 265–271.

[16] Lawson, *How to Meet the Challenge,* pp. 265–271.

[17] Lawson, *How to Meet the Challenge,* p. 63.

[18] Lawson, *How to Meet the Challenge,* p. 249.

[19] Lawson, *How to Meet the Challenge,* p. 8.

[20] Charles Hughes. *Making Unions Unnecessary* (New York: Executive Enterprises Publications Co., Inc., n.d.), p. 110.

[21] "The Workplace," *Minneapolis Star,* July 15, 1981, p. 2C.

[22] Tony DeZiel. "Inside the Union Busters' Conference," *Union Advocate,* May 18, 1981, p. 5.

[23] Eric Hoffer. *The True Believer* (New York: Harper and Row, 1951).

[24] Dougherty, *Union-Free Management,* p. 56.

[25] Hughes, *Making Unions Unnecessary,* pp. 8–9.

[26] Hughes, *Making Unions Unnecessary,* pp. 28–29.

[27] AFL-CIO, *Report on Union Busters,* Issue #16, May 1980, p. 4.

[28] AFL-CIO, *Report on Union Busters,* Issue #8, September 1979, pp. 10–11.

[29] Hughes, *Making Unions Unnecessary,* Chapter 6.

[30] Dave Hage. "Hyatt's Technique Keeps Union Out," *The Minneapolis Star,* December 24, 1981, pp. 1C–2C.

[31] Hage, "Hyatt's Technique," pp. 1C–2C.

[32] The same arguments supporting taxation imposed by government in order to provide public goods such as national defense, a criminal justice system, and universal education can be applied to labor unions. Where the personnel policies of employers are motivated by union avoidance, an agency shop fee should be paid by unorganized workers to unions for services rendered. The prospects for such legislation, however, are laughable.

[33] Hoffer, *The True Believer.*

[34] *John Herling's Labor Letter,* December 19, 1981.

[35] For examples, see the articles by Sidney Lens.

[36] "If You Don't Win the First Time, Don't Give Up," AFL-CIO Department of Organization Statistical and Tactical Information Report, August 1981, Issue No. 4, p. 1.

Preparing to Organize

4

"Organizers are a special breed." "Not everybody can organize." These statements seem too obvious to even mention, yet some unions cling to the view that anyone can organize. The first step in preparing to organize is to recognize that organizing is not for everyone.

Organizing is the most difficult job in unions. Rejection is nearly a daily occurrence and some prospects are belligerent and insulting. There is a strong likelihood that the organizer will be arrested and convicted for, at least, trespassing, and as a consequence, find it difficult to obtain personal credit. While not as prevalent as in the 1930s, there is still the danger of violence, enough so that some organizers feel compelled to carry a handgun. Frequent overnight travel is common. Organizing is very uncertain; there is no formula guaranteeing success. The organizer must become immune or, at least, accustomed to rejection and, more important, proceed to the next prospect with the same enthusiasm as he or she had the first day on the job.

A few years ago, I was in the midst of teaching a class on organizing techniques to the full-time staff of a union, when the union president, who had not been in attendance but who had arranged for the class, walked into the classroom and interrupted my presentation with words to the effect that what I was doing was fine but it would not solve the organizing problem of the union. The problem was how to motivate the staff to organize new members; they already knew enough techniques. What did I suggest?

Because the staff was organized into its own union and in the midst of negotiations over a new contract with the president, I was on the spot. I went into an academic soft-shoe offering various hypotheses that did not answer the question. The president then gave an impassioned lecture on the need for housecalls when organizing and left the room. My head spinning, I continued the presentation at the point of interruption, not knowing what to make of the situation.

After the class, I went out for a drink with a few members of the staff. The conversation naturally centered around the union president's outburst. Admittedly, the president was right. Staff members did not like to make housecalls, which the union president, formerly an organizer, believed were the best method for organizing. Those who had made housecalls encountered hostility from prospects who viewed the visits as an intrusion. After having doors slammed in their faces and obscenities directed at them, staff members had an aversion to making housecalls.

Eventually, the staff and the president did reach an accord. The union president stuck to his position on the importance of housecalls and hired an experienced organizer from another union who was willing and able to make them. Other full-time union staff assist the organizer in target selection, leafleting, and other aspects of organizing.

It would be encouraging to report that the union is growing by leaps and bounds. While this has not happened, tension between the staff and the president has been reduced appreciably.

The problem in this situation was the union president's initial view that anyone on the union's staff who handled grievances and negotiated contracts should be able to organize, probably because he had done both. It is similar to the old adage about members of the Baseball Hall of Fame making poor managers, because they cannot accept the mediocre baseball talents of others. Organized labor draws upon people with different talents: grievance handlers, actuaries, lawyers, negotiators, and organizers. Without the training and mathematical aptitude, one would not expect an organizer to function as a pension actuary. Likewise, a proficient grievance handler will not necessarily be an effective organizer.

Unions that place the responsibility for organizing on the shoulders of union officials, whose major responsibilities are negotiating and administering contracts, often find that little organizing activity is conducted. "Overworked," and "lazy" are usual explanations. Overlooked is the explanation that good negotiators and contract administrators do not necessarily have the aptitude for organizing.

It must also be recognized that some aspects of organizing require other aptitudes. Some time ago, I attended a presentation on organizing by two staff members of a union. The first speaker was an organizer, energetic and demonstrative, definitely an extrovert. The second speaker was a research department staff member, quiet and reserved, almost shy, a marked contrast from the organizer. These two individuals comprised an effective organizing team. From the union's headquarters, the researcher provided the organizer in the field with information on organizing targets that the organizer did not have the time and resources to gather. The researcher's activity was not limited to passively answering requests for information from the organizer. Instead, the researcher suggested information to the organizer that demonstrated the advantages of union representation. This was particularly true of data on wages, pensions, health care plans, and other fringe benefits.

CLARIFYING THE UNION'S CONSTITUTION

A favorite employer tactic is to quote extensively from the union's constitution and bylaws, and to use the quotes in an attempt to substantiate charges that the union is undemocratic and self-serving. As part of its preparation for organizing, the union should have a lawyer with expertise in the area of union internal governance review its constitution and bylaws. Provisions that are unlikely to be upheld by the courts in light of similar cases involving other unions should be recommended for removal by the convention, executive board, or other body having the authority to amend the constitution and bylaws.

In addition, the documents should be rewritten to eliminate overly legalistic language which lends the constitution and bylaws to wide interpretation. Stating the intent of the provisions, and under what circumstances they have been invoked in the past, if at all, would be of valuable assistance to organizers. Presently, organizers are placed on the defensive and must provide explanations preceded by statements like "this is what it really means" and "the union has never used this provision." A member of the union's newspaper staff or public relations department is a likely person to conduct this project in consultation with a lawyer.

A COMMITMENT TO DEVELOPING LOCAL UNION LEADERSHIP

Most of the jobs created in the last decade are in small units of less than fifty employees. Where unions succeed at organizing workers in these small units, the bulk of the collective bargaining and contract administration activities tends to be conducted by full-time union officers. These full-time officers are often overworked and unable to provide adequate service to small units. As will be discussed in a succeeding chapter, this failure to provide adequate service is a major reason for union decertifications. Because of their inability to provide adequate service, some unions shy away from organizing small units.

Labor unions in the United States have more full-time officials than unions in most other Western industrialized countries. In 1962, unions in the United States were estimated to have one full-time official for every 300 members. In sharp contrast, Great Britain had one full-time official for every 2,000 members; Sweden one for every 1,700; and Australia one for 900.[1] While this data is quite old, it is reflective of an important difference—unions in other countries rely heavily upon local activists to handle the day-to-day affairs of the union at the workplace.

Reducing dependence upon full-time officers and, as a consequence, removing an important internal barrier to organizing workers in small units requires two changes—increased and improved education and training of local union activists and, more important, a willingness to share power through the development of an effective steward system at each workplace.

Workplaces with small numbers of workers constitute the organizing territory of the present and future and reflect the long-term union avoidance strategy of diffusing employees among many isolated workplaces. "Unserviceable" need not be synonymous with "unorganizable."

MAINTAINING ORGANIZING RECORDS

Unions vary as to the adequacy of the records they maintain on organizing campaigns, particularly those that failed. Some unions maintain files that amount to no more than a few bits and pieces of information about campaigns. Couple the lack of information about previous campaigns with a turnover in the organizing staff and the result is sometimes the launching of campaigns that should not have even been contemplated, the repetition of previous mistakes, and the loss of valuable time.

Attempts to rectify the inadequacy of data by requiring voluminous reports may result in a great deal of useless information and resentment among organizers. All that is really necessary are the issues in the campaign, the tactics used, why the campaign was won or lost, and particularly if lost, a list of union supporters. Some organizers accomplish this recordkeeping task by tape recording a post-election session of organizers and in-the-workplace organizing committee members where the issues, tactics, and reasons for the outcome are discussed. Reporting the results of a campaign orally is often much easier for organizers than written reports, because the nature of their job requires strong oral communication skills.

COORDINATION OF ORGANIZING WITH CONTRACT NEGOTIATIONS

Regardless of how committed the union is to developing local union leadership among the rank and file of newly organized workplaces, the initial contract will undoubtedly have to be negotiated by experienced, full-time union staff. The organizing and contract negotiation functions are performed by different people in many international unions. This is fine, except that some organizers win representation rights for workplaces that have little or no likelihood of ever securing a contract or make unrealistic promises of what the union can attain, leaving contract negotiators to pick up the pieces.

Largely for this reason, ultimate authority over organizing within some international unions rests with local union officials who negotiate and service contracts. Where organizing is controlled by the international, the quickest way to undermine the union's organizing commitment is to present local union officials with units that they find to be unserviceable. Selecting organizing targets that are winnable in terms of both union representation and collective bargaining requires coordination between organizers and the staff who negotiate and service contracts. The target selection process outlined in this chapter attempts to merge these two considerations.

IDENTIFYING POTENTIAL TARGETS

Potential organizing targets are identified in many ways. Because of their wide jurisdiction, some Teamster organizers, for example, make it a practice of responding to only unsolicited telephone calls. The calls are indicative of interest in union representation by at least one employee who is willing to enumerate the issues in a potential campaign. The caller is also a potential leader of the workplace organizing committee.

The AFL-CIO Food and Beverage Trades Council in the Washington, D.C., area has used television advertisements. The ads dramatize some of the benefits of union representation and close with information on how unorganized workers can contact the Council.

Various departments of the AFL-CIO provide information on potential organizing targets. The Industrial Union Department, for example, provides computer print-outs listing all of the organized and unorganized plant locations of large companies. The lists also provide information on which unions represent workers at the organized locations and NLRB election results for plants that remain unorganized.

Organized employers will also alert unions of potential organizing targets. Competition with non-union firms in the product market may hamper the sales of organized employers' products and diminish the union's strength in collective bargaining, thereby making organizing the unorganized a mutual concern of both employers and the union.

Other unions and city and state AFL-CIO central bodies are also sources of information on potential targets.

Some organizers run classified advertisements in newspapers for "dissatisfied employees" in the particular occupation or industry they desire to organize. Generally construed by respondents to mean "an excellent opportunity" for a new job, the organizer can explore with them the means for improving conditions at their present job.

With the majority of the U.S. labor force unorganized, the identification of potential union organizing targets is not difficult. However, determining whether to make a potential target one of the union's organizing targets requires careful consideration.

TARGET SELECTION

I moonlight on weekends delivering newspapers to over 200 customers on the tundra. Periodically, the district sales manager asks me to solicit new customers. The pay is determined strictly on commission, according to how many people agree to a two-week free-trial subscription to either the morning or afternoon papers.[2] Not having much time available for telephone soliciting, it is important for me to identify or target the people who will be most responsive to my sales pitch.

The *Minneapolis Star and Tribune* provides me with computer print-outs for entire residential areas listing names, addresses, phone numbers, and current subscriptions to the company's newspapers. It did not take long to devise a targeting strategy. People who do not subscribe to a newspaper either do not know how to read or, otherwise, are not interested in newspapers. People with Mildred, Clarence, and other "old-fashioned" names tend to be old and set in their ways. An additional newspaper subscription tends to intrude on their routine. People who already subscribe to either the morning or afternoon papers are unlikely to subscribe to another daily newspaper, because they "can barely read one paper." Suggesting that the extra paper would be useful if they have a fireplace or a puppy has not been a successful approach.

The people most likely to agree to an additional subscription have "modern" names and already subscribe to a paper, but not a daily newspaper. My targets are the Cheryls and Kevins who subscribe to only the Sunday *Tribune.* This is not to say that all people who do not subscribe to newspapers or have "old-fashioned" names or already take a daily paper will not agree to a two-week free-trial. Some do, but my time is limited and I want the biggest return for my expenditure of time.

The development of this targeting strategy represents my preparation for selling newspaper subscriptions. Selecting the targets is certainly as important a determinant of success as the actual contact with potential customers. The same is true of organizing. Selecting the target is at least as important as conducting the actual organizing drive.

All unorganized workplaces are potential union organizing targets. However, because union financial resources are limited and the salary and expense for maintaining one full-time organizer in the field for a year range from about $25,000 to $80,000, choices must be made. Regardless of whether organizers are on their own when selecting targets or must gain approval of targets from higher echelons within the union, the considerations involved in choosing targets are the same.

The approach to target selection described in this book is slightly different from the approach taken by many organizers. Except in those cases where the union must launch campaigns in order to protect its collective bargaining power from non-union competition, organizers often make their own decisions to launch campaigns on the basis of a demonstration of interest in unionization by workers at unorganized workplaces. Sometimes the level of interest is so high that workers virtually demand to sign authorization cards. If a vast majority of workers sign authorization cards, the best strategy, of course, is to push for an early election. But, this is usually not the case. More often, some workers, a minority of the unit, are rather enthusiastic union supporters. From this base of support, an in-the-workplace organizing committee is formed. At about this time, the organizer and the committee identify the issues in the campaign. The problem is that often considerable effort in recruiting and training the committee has been expended on the campaign before the organizer determines whether union representation is likely to win the support of a majority of the workers in the unit and whether the union, if authorized, is likely to obtain a contract.

The approach in this book alters the sequence of events. Prior to forming a committee of union supporters and in effect launching the campaign, the organizer assesses the likelihood of unionization and obtaining a contract. Where the organizer has a number of potential targets, information is gathered on all of them and they are ranked from "best" to "worst."

WHO IS MOST LIKELY TO ORGANIZE?

In 1977, the University of Michigan's Survey Research Center asked unorganized workers whether they would unionize if given the opportunity. Thirty-nine percent of unorganized blue-collar workers and 28 percent of unorganized white-collar workers said that they would organize. The survey shatters stereotypes that Southern workers and women workers are hostile to unions; 35 percent of unorganized workers in the South and 40 percent of unorganized women workers said that they would organize. Black workers are the most favorable toward joining unions; 67 percent said that they would organize.[3]

While only a minority of the unorganized U.S. labor force indicates that it would organize, if unions could in fact organize these workers, total union membership would more than double. The objective of organizing target selection is to identify those workplaces where workers desiring to join unions are most likely to be concentrated, and whether the union is likely to negotiate a contract. The process is similar to the one I use to identify potential newspaper subscribers—pick the targets where the odds for success are greatest.

We have a pretty good idea why workers organize into unions. Workers organize because they are dissatisfied with the terms and conditions of employment. Within this apparent general explanation, however, two specific "bread and butter" issues are most important:

1.   Wages and fringe benefits.
2.   Favoritism and unfairness resulting in an absence of job security.[4,5,6,7]

The academic studies cited in the footnotes merely confirm what organizers will tell you. Workers organize over issues that affect them daily on the job—wages, benefits, favoritism, unfairness, and job security are the usual categories. Organizers generally agree that it is a mistake to launch organizing campaigns at newly established workplaces immediately after they open their doors unless wages and fringe benefits are significantly out of sync with those at organized workplaces. Instead, it is advisable to wait until management has an opportunity to create organizing issues.

In addition to job dissatisfaction, workers will only form unions if they are convinced that unionization will improve wages and work-ing conditions.[8] Hence, two elements must be present for workers to organize—job dissatisfaction and the belief that unionization will lead to improvements. A broad overview of the U.S. labor force indicates that these two factors are sufficiently present to result in a substantial increase in the proportion of the labor force represented by unions.

A majority of the American public appears to believe that unions have a positive effect upon the two issues over which workers are most likely to organize. A recent poll conducted by the *Washington Post* and ABC News discloses that more than two out of three people approve of unions in general and a strong majority say that workers are "better off belonging to a union than not." The often heard nostrum that unions might have been needed at one time, but are not needed today, is rejected by 60 percent of the public. Two thirds agree with the statement that "labor unions ensure fair treatment for workers." Eighty percent agree that unions improve wages, working conditions, and job security and 70 percent agree that wages and working conditions would not have reached today's level if there were no unions. The public's view of labor leaders, however, is decidedly negative.[9]

There is strong factual evidence, particularly in regard to wages, to substantiate the public's beliefs on the benefits of unionization. According to the U.S. Department of Labor's Bureau of Labor Sta-tistics, unionized workers earn more than non-union workers. In 1977, organized workers earned an average of $262 per week in comparison with $221 by unorganized workers, a $41 per week differential. The differential between organized and unorganized blue-collar workers was $72. For service workers, the union–non-union differential was $77.

While there was a differential between unionized and unorga-nized white-collar workers, it was only $15 per week, an indication that employers of white-collar workers are the most likely to adopt the long-run strategy of "making unions unnecessary." This may be an important explanation of the lack of success unions have among white-collar workers, because they appear to form unions for essen-tially the same reasons as blue-collar workers.[10] Apparently, white-collar workers on the average can expect to gain less by forming unions than blue-collar workers.

The union–non-union differential varied significantly between industries. The biggest differential was in the construction industry where organized workers earned 49 percent more than their non-union counterparts. The differential for local government workers was 32 percent, for retail trade workers 31 percent, for teachers 27 percent, for transportation workers 22 percent, and for workers in the printing industry 21 percent.

Likewise, the wages of unionized workers increased by more than those of unorganized workers during a period of high inflation. From 1970 through 1978, the wages of organized workers increased by 71 percent, while those for unorganized workers increased by only 56 percent.

Unionized workers also receive better fringe benefits than unorganized workers. In 1977, the Bureau of Labor Statistics estimated that the average organized worker received $2.75 per hour in fringe benefits, while non-union workers received only $1.13 per hour in fringes.[11]

Pensions will become an even more important fringe benefit as the average age of the labor force increases in the future. According to the U.S. Department of Labor, 90 percent of organized employers had pension plans for their employees in 1981, while only 40 percent of unorganized employers provided pension benefits upon retirement.[12]

Statistics for the economy as a whole and for particular industries are of interest, because they indicate the overall potential for demonstrating to unorganized workers the benefits to be gained through unionization. However, comparisons between organized and unorganized workers on so large a scale fail to provide the union with information on its opportunities for improving wages, benefits, and working conditions at specific potential organizing targets. Therefore, it is necessary to develop criteria which can be applied to specific unorganized workplaces. This investigation consists of three interrelated sections:

1. The Economic Prospectus
2. Working Conditions
3. Getting a Contract

Gathering this information is very time consuming, particularly where the organizer seeks to rank a number of potential targets, but it is not nearly as time consuming as the long delays between filing a petition and the actual election under NLRB procedures nor the length of time in negotiating an initial contract. In addition, if a campaign is launched, the organizer will have already compiled much of the information to be communicated to workers during the campaign.

THE ECONOMIC PROSPECTUS

Wages and benefits are one of the two major reasons why workers organize into unions. It is best to conclude before launching a campaign whether wages and benefits are an issue and whether unionization can in fact improve economic conditions for workers at the potential organizing target. If wages and benefits are not an issue, or if they are an issue, and unionization is not likely to improve economic conditions, the union should weigh carefully the importance of non-economic issues before launching a campaign.

Preparing an economic prospectus for a potential organizing target is different than costing a wage-fringe benefit package during collective bargaining, because some of the information necessary for costing a package is unavailable. Therefore, an economic prospectus is not as precise as the cost of a package. However, it goes without saying that the economic prospectus should provide an honest appraisal of the union's potential for improving the wages and benefits of workers at the organizing target. Misrepresentation can lead to unfair labor practice charges being filed by the employer and ultimately to union election victories being overturned should inaccurate information be released to the election unit. Furthermore, misrepresentation inflates the expectations of newly organized workers, making realistic contract negotiations and satisfaction with union representation difficult to achieve.

The first step in preparing the economic prospectus is to determine the wage and benefit levels at the organizing target. The following items should be identified:

1. Hourly straight time wage rates or straight time salaries per pay period.
2. Shift premium
3. Overtime premium
4. Call-in pay

5. Rest periods

6. Vacations

7. Holidays

8. Bereavement pay

9. Jury duty pay

10. Military reserve pay

11. Pensions

12. Life insurance

13. Medical-hospital insurance

14. Dental insurance

15. Prescription plan

16. Bonuses, gifts, prizes, etc.

The best way of organizing the information is to maintain a $4'' \times 6''$ file card on each one of the sixteen categories.

Obtaining information on the wages and fringe benefits at a potential organizing target usually requires some detective work. While employers frequently exchange information on wage and benefit levels among themselves through a local employer's association, this data is not available to the organizer unless he or she has a friend working in an employer's personnel office. Because this is not usually the case, the organizer must piece together the information through a variety of sources.

A union activist can apply for employment at a potential organizing target and during the course of the interview process acquire information on the wage structure and fringe benefits. Conversations with workers at local taverns and restaurants can also uncover this information prior to any discussion of the prospects for unionization.

Even where a large number of employees are seriously interested in exploring the prospects for unionization, obtaining precise wage information may be difficult. As discussed in the previous chapter, employers have an incentive to treat wages as a confidential matter in order to keep labor costs down. More importantly from the standpoint of preparing an economic prospectus, workers are often reluctant to disclose information on this "personal matter." An organizer has developed a successful method for obtaining wage information in these circumstances. At a meeting of workers interested in unionization, they are asked to write their wage rate or salary on slips of paper and to drop the slips into a hat so as to maintain their anonymity. The organizer can then provide the group with information on wage ranges and average wage rates.

Employers are required by law to furnish their employees with information on the benefits provided by pension, life insurance, and health benefit plans. This information is often contained in an "employees' handbook." If contact has been made with employees regarding unionization, they should be able to readily provide fringe benefit information. Employer pension and health benefit plans must file reports with the U.S. Department of Labor. These reports are classified as public information and, therefore, are available to labor unions even though they have no collective bargaining relationship with the employer. These detailed annual reports can be the source of valuable information for the economic prospectus.

After obtaining information on wages and benefits at the potential organizing target, the organizer must then provide a basis for comparison with the potential wage and benefit levels likely to occur through unionization. This information comes primarily from union contracts. However, most union contracts do not contain detailed information on life insurance, medical and dental plans, and pensions. This information is usually provided by insurance and pension trustees in the form of booklets addressed to workers covered by the plans.

The comparison of wages and benefits at the potential target with those in union contracts serves two purposes. The organizer can determine whether wages and benefits are in fact an issue. That workers receive the legal minimum wage and have no fringe benefits is not an issue unless the union can demonstrate its ability to improve the situation. Widespread publicity of "take aways" in the automobile, airline, construction, meat packing, and rubber industries makes union wage influence less of an article of faith than it may have once been.

It is not enough that issues exist. Workers must be convinced that collective action—unionization—will improve wages, benefits, and working conditions. Comparisons with union contracts emphasize the path to improvement.

There are approximately 195,000 collective bargaining agreements in the United States. Out of those 195,000 union contracts, the organizer should be able to find at least two or three for units having many of the same characteristics as the potential organizing target. Size, geographic location, and industry are the most important similarities. If these characteristics are not met, the employer is likely to retort that comparisons are inaccurate—"Larger, produce a different product, and located in a region with a higher cost of living." In addition, comparisons should only be made with units experiencing steady or increasing employment, lest the employer level the charge that high wages and benefits at organized firms are the cause of unemployment.

When organizing targets are located in a geographic region with little union representation, finding comparable union contracts may be difficult. In those cases, contracts for units in other geographic areas must be used, but the organizer should "deflate" wages and fringes if there is an appreciable difference in the cost of living between regions. The method for making this adjustment will be discussed later in this chapter.

In those rare instances where a union is organizing workplaces in an industry with no comparable union contracts, it should examine closely the work being performed and identify job characteristics similar to those in industries where unionization exists. Likewise, the education and training required by the unorganized industry may be comparable to that in industries where unionization exists. While these analogies may be criticized as being inapplicable by unorganized employers, the economic prospectus also includes an assessment of the employer's ability to pay, which can make the comparisons more applicable.

Information on contracts can usually be obtained from the union's national headquarters. In addition, the U.S. Department of Labor maintains a collection of union contracts in Washington, D.C., and will send copies of entire contracts or portions for a nominal charge.[13] The AFL-CIO also provides information on contracts. The Industrial Union Department and Food and Beverage Trades Department, as examples, will provide computer print-outs listing major provisions of contracts including units represented by the Teamsters. Provided are the lowest and highest regular hourly job rates, negotiated wage increases including the details of cost-of-living adjustments where applicable, overtime pay provisions, report pay, recall pay, shift premiums, number of paid holidays, vacation pay, military reserve pay, paid rest periods, jury duty pay, bereavement pay, and sick leave pay.

Straight Time Wage Rates   Making comparisons between wages at the potential target and wages in union contracts is not always a simple matter. While union contracts in industries like construction, retailing, and transportation may specify only a journeyman or top rate and the steps for reaching that wage level, union contracts in the utility and manufacturing industries and in the state and local government sectors tend to have dozens of job classifications, each with its own wage rate. An additional difficulty in making comparisons is that job classifications and job titles in union contracts may bear little resemblance to those at the organizing target.

Let us examine the wage provisions in three contracts:

Millwrights Journeyman, May 1, 1980

Base Wage	$11.91
Health & Welfare	.60
Pension	.60
Vacation	.60
Dental	.20
Training Fund	.02
Total	$13.93

The minimum scale for foremen is .85 per hour above the journeyman rate. The minimum scale for general foremen is .85 above the foreman's scale. Apprentice wage rates are governed by the provisions of the Millwrights Joint Apprenticeship Standards.

Presenting this information in an economic prospectus is relatively easy. Wage rates and even employer contributions for fringe benefits are clearly spelled out. The joint union and employer apprenticeship committee's agreement provides information on the step progression for apprentices to the journeyman's rate.

Another straightforward type of wage structure, easily comparable with those at potential organizing targets, has wage rates increase as workers acquire experience on the job. An example is the wage structure in a United Food and Commercial Workers' grocery store contract:

Position:	
Assistant Manager	$11.00
Produce Manager	11.00
Head Checker/Bookkeeper	10.90
Frozen/Dairy Manager	10.80

Full Time:

1st. 6 months	$ 8.10
2nd. 6 months	8.30
After 1 year	8.50
After 2 years	9.00
After 3 years	9.30
After 4 years	9.70
After 5 years	10.00

Part Time:

0–500 hours	$ 4.62
501–1040	4.80
1041–1560	5.05
1561–2080	5.55
2081–2600	6.30
2601–3120	6.80
3121–3640	7.60
3641 and over	8.10

Utility:

0–1040 hours	$ 3.75
1041–1560	4.10
1561 and over	4.40

A United Auto Workers contract with a defense contractor provides an example of a more complicated wage structure.

BASE RATES*

LABOR GRADE	STEP 1	STEP 2	STEP 3	STEP 4
I				$ 8.65
II				8.88
III				9.04
IV			$ 9.04	9.22
V			9.22	9.40
VI		$ 9.29	9.47	9.70
VII		9.47	9.70	9.94
VIII	$ 9.47	9.70	9.94	10.09
IX	9.88	10.09	10.30	10.52
X	10.11	10.33	10.59	10.78
XI	10.34	10.60	10.82	11.02
XII	10.66	10.88	11.10	11.28

* All rates are to be increased by the Cost-of-living Allowance in effect.

Each labor grade includes a number of specific jobs. In all, there are 125 job classifications. Progression to higher "steps" on the wage schedule come every six months, provided that the employee has worked satisfactorily during that time. The union reserves the right to file grievances where the employer judges an employee's performance to be unsatisfactory.

Every three months, wage rates are to be increased by a Cost-of-living Allowance. For every one percent increase in the Consumer Price Index, wages are increased by six cents per hour. Therefore, a 10 percent increase in the CPI for a given year would mean approximately a sixty-cent per hour wage increase or $24 per week.

Presenting this rather complicated wage structure with its myriad of job titles in the economic prospectus requires some thought, because simply reproducing the wage structure provides little insight into the potential benefits of unionization, if the job titles at the potential target differ significantly from those in the union contract. Because unorganized employers seek to maximize their flexibility at transferring workers from job to job, they tend to assign fewer and broader job titles than occur at organized workplaces.

Presenting the highest rate and the lowest rate is informative but only one job classification (Janitor) is in Labor Grade I. The wage range may be presented more accurately in the following manner: "Janitors earn $8.65 per hour while the lowest wage rate received by any other workers is $9.04 per hour to start. The top hourly wage rate is $11.28."

Because employers sometimes pay all workers on a salary basis as part of their long-term union avoidance strategy and because some workers are more familiar with their weekly or bi-monthly wage than their hourly rate, it is advisable to present wages for a normal pay period: "In a forty-hour workweek, most workers earn between $361 and $451."

This $90 dollar per week range between the high and low rates is appreciable and workers will be interested in where they place within the range. The best way of conveying wage rates within the wage range is to select job titles that are clearly descriptive of the actual work performed and are capable of being performed by many workers at the potential organizing target:

> Lift truck operators start at $369 per week and after six months receive $376 per week. Power shear and heat treat operators

start at $379 per week and after one year receive $398 per week. Foundry workers and material handlers start at $379 and progress in three steps over two years to $404 per week. Welders and building maintenance workers start at $404 per week and progress over two years to $431 per week. Molders, platers, and sheet metal workers start at $414 and after two years receive $441. Machine repair workers and maintenance electricians start at $426 and progress to $451.

Local Labor Market Wages   In addition to examining wages in union contracts, a comparison should be made with the wages paid for the types of work performed at the potential organizing target by other employers located in the geographic area where the potential target is situated. The U.S. Department of Labor's Bureau of Labor Statistics keeps track of what is being paid to various occupations in the major geographic regions of the country. These "Area Wage Surveys" are available free of charge from the regional office of the Bureau of Labor Statistics listed under "United States Government" in the telephone directory.[14]

Here are some examples of available data. "Secretaries" in the Minneapolis-St. Paul area had an average weekly salary of $231 in January 1980. "Class A Computer Systems Analysts" in the Twin Cities had an average weekly salary of $458. Hourly pay rates for maintenance, toolroom, and powerplant jobs varied from highs of $10.39 for "Maintenance Pipefitters" and $10.31 for "Maintenance Electricians" to lows of $8.59 for "Boiler Tenders" and $8.63 for "Maintenance Trades Helpers." "Tractor-Trailer Truck Drivers" had an average rate of $10.13. "Janitors," "Order Fillers," and "Material Handling Laborers" in Minneapolis-St. Paul had average hourly rates of $4.82, $7.42, and $8.68 respectively in January 1980.

Pay levels in the Twin Cities area were 6 percent below the U.S. average for "Office Clerical Workers" and 4 percent below for "Computer-Related Jobs." "Unskilled Plant Workers" were 13 percent above the national average and "Skilled Maintenance Workers" 4 percent above.

Between January 1979 and January 1980, average hourly wages for "Unskilled Plant Workers" in the Twin cities increased by 10.8 percent. "Office Clerical Workers" received a 9.1 percent increase over the same period of time.

In addition to these average wage rates for broad occupational classifications, BLS compiles average wage rates for occupations in a number of specific industries in the geographic areas surveyed. For the Twin Cities information is available on the building and printing trades, local transit, local trucking, retail groceries, hospitals, auto dealer repair shops, electrical appliance repair shops, banks, life insurance companies, and savings and loan associations. These studies of specific industries are not always kept up to date by the BLS, and studies of other industries are added from time to time. When you request from BLS the "Area Wage Survey" for the geographic area in which the potential target is located, be sure to ask them if there are studies available on the target industry.

The average wages for various occupations included in the "Area Wage Survey" include both union and non-union wage rates. In geographic areas with little union organization, the rates will, of course, reflect what non-union employers are paying. Regardless of whether the geographic area has a high or low degree of union representation, the organizer should be prepared for the employer's argument that it is paying rates prevailing in the local labor market. Where wage and salary rates at the potential organizing target are below the rates in the "Area Wage Survey," an organizing issue is readily apparent. However, this is often not the case, because employers adopt a long-term union avoidance strategy of paying the average wage in the local labor market. The organizer must investigate whether average wages in the local labor market are a proper means for determining wages at the potential target. Three potential deficiencies in the "Area Wage Survey" should receive attention:

Job titles and actual job responsibilities vary significantly among employers. Just because workers at two companies have the title of "Secretary," for example, does not mean that they have the same job responsibilities. The primary duty of some "Secretaries" is typing, while others perform duties that amount to managing an office. This divergence between job title and actual job responsibilities is true for all occupations listed in the "Area Wage Survey." If significant differences exist, the organizer should illustrate this point in the economic prospectus.

Working conditions vary significantly among employers. Other things being equal, we would expect workers in hazardous, dirty, and noisy places of employment to receive higher wages than workers employed in safer, more pleasant surroundings. Differences in the quality of the work environment are not reflected in the "Area Wage Survey."

Even where job titles and actual responsibilities are the same and work environments are comparable, another factor—the most important—is missing. The "Area Wage Survey" shows what workers receive from their employers, but it does not indicate what employers receive in return. Some workers produce more than others. They are more productive because they try harder or because they have more training or education or because they are physically stronger or more agile or mentally more alert than others. If the employer didn't believe that workers are different, it would not have an employee selection process administered by the personnel office. Instead, it would hire workers on a first-come, first-hired basis. Point out that the employer gets what it pays for.

Cost-of-Living Differences   When investigating a potential organizing target in a geographic region with little union representation, it is necessary to consider cost-of-living differences between the region in which the potential target is located and the geographic region from which union contracts used for comparative purposes emanate. Without adjustments for cost-of-living differences, the employer may claim that comparisons are inappropriate.

The Bureau of Labor Statistics compiles "Urban Family Budgets"[15] which demonstrate how much it costs a family to live at three different living standards—a lower budget level, an intermediate budget level, and a higher budget level. The budgets are not standards recommended by BLS. Instead, they are intended simply to show how much it would cost to live at those standards which are comprised of precise amounts and qualities of food, clothing, transportation, housing, etc. Unions frequently use the intermediate budget as a benchmark against which to measure their members' earnings.

The BLS computes the budgets for the urban United States as a whole and for various large metropolitan areas. In addition, family budget data are compiled regionally for nonmetropolitan areas, which are defined as areas in which the population ranges from 2,500 to 50,000 people.

Suppose that the potential union organizing target is located in North Dakota and that the closest organized workplaces of comparable size and industry are in Minneapolis-St. Paul, Minnesota, and Cedar Rapids, Iowa. There are no metropolitan areas in North Dakota for which the BLS compiles "Urban Family Budget" data. North Dakota is, however, included in the data for "North Central Region: Nonmetropolitan areas." The following data are applicable:

URBAN FAMILY BUDGETS

Area	Intermediate Budget
Cedar Rapids, Iowa	$18,224
Minneapolis-St. Paul, MN.	19,389
North Central Region:	
Nonmetropolitan Areas	17,363

As expected, the cost of living is substantially lower in nonmetropolitan areas of the region than in Cedar Rapids and Minneapolis-St. Paul. One can estimate that the cost of living in North Dakota is about 89.6 percent of that in Minneapolis-St. Paul ($17,363 divided by $19,389) and 95.3 percent of that in Cedar Rapids ($17,363 divided by $18,224). It is appropriate, therefore, to deflate wages in the union contracts by the differences in the cost of living between geographic areas.

Suppose that hourly wage rates for the organized workplaces in Minneapolis-St. Paul are $11 and in Cedar Rapids, $10.50. Applying the cost-of-living ratios of .896 and .953 respectively to the hourly wage rates results in an hourly rate for Minneapolis-St. Paul of $9.86 and $10.00 for Cedar Rapids adjusted for the lower cost of living in North Dakota. A brief explanation of the cost-of-living adjustment and how it was calculated should be included in the economic prospectus.

Hours: Overtime, Call-in Pay, Shift Premium, and Rest Periods   Under the Fair Labor Standards Act, workers in the private sector are to receive time and a half pay for any hours worked over forty hours in one week. Unorganized employers usually comply with the law, but they often do not compensate their employees for overtime in a manner stipulated in many union contracts which require time and a half for work over eight hours in any given day. In addition, many union contracts require double time for any hours over twelve in one day and for Sunday and holiday work and time and a half for Saturday work. The difference between the legal requirement and many union contracts can be significant if work schedules are irregular. Conceivably, a worker could be required to work two twenty-hour days in a week and not receive any overtime pay under the law.

Where work schedules are irregular, workers often experience the disruption of reporting for work and being told that work is unavailable that day. Unorganized employers often do not compensate their employees in these situations, while many union contracts stipulate that workers receive call-in-pay, usually ranging from two to four hours at the straight time wage rate.

The eight-hour day, five days per week is not customary in industries such as retailing, food service, health care, and public safety so that overtime and call-in-pay may not be issues. But unions in these industries often negotiate provisions that reduce the employer's discretion in assigning undesirable work hours and, therefore, opportunities to reward and punish individual workers.

Shift premium is a common element in union contracts and generally rather easy to present in an economic prospectus: "Employees on the second shift receive a 50 cents per hour shift premium and those on the third shift receive a 65 cents per hour shift premium."

Unorganized workers often believe that the law requires rest periods and lunch breaks. Without a union contract, rest periods and lunch breaks are at the discretion of the employer. During heavy work schedules or "emergencies," the employer is tempted to require employees to forgo breaks. Rest periods and lunch breaks are provisions in virtually all union contracts. Furthermore, many contracts recognize that there may be occasions when rest periods and lunch breaks are not feasible. In those instances, provision is often made to compensate workers at time and a half, thereby giving the employer an incentive to require employees to forgo breaks only in situations that are genuine emergencies.

While workers covered by union contracts tend to be paid for rest periods, paid lunch breaks are not common. Check whether workers at the potential organizing target are paid during breaks.

Vacations and Holidays   The vacation schedule in contracts is easy to present in an economic prospectus:

Years of Service	Weeks of Vacation
1	1
2	2
7–14	3
15+	4

Some contracts provide that employees who work overtime will receive vacation pay that includes both straight-time pay and average weekly overtime pay for the year.

Holidays are also easy to present: "Nine paid holidays per year."

Bereavement, Jury Duty, and Military Reserve Pay   These three items are commonly found in collective bargaining agreements. Jury duty pay is usually at the straight-time hourly rate less any compensation received by the juror. Bereavement pay provisions vary in regard to two factors—the number of relatives whose death qualifies the employee for bereavement leave and the number of days for which the leave is granted. Employers are required by law to grant leaves for military reserve duty. The major difference in contract provisions is whether the reservist is compensated for the difference between regular wages and reserve pay. These provisions are quite straightforward and easy to express in an economic prospectus.

Life Insurance   Many contracts provide life insurance coverage. Often, all workers in the bargaining unit receive the same amount of coverage: "A group life insurance policy of $17,000 is provided to all employees." In other contracts the amount of life insurance varies with income and/or seniority: "With three or more months of service but with less than five years of service, the life insurance benefit is $9,000. With five years but less than ten years, $9,500. With ten or more years of service, $10,000."

An important aspect of the life insurance provision is whether the employer pays the entire premium or only a portion with the remainder paid by the employee. Most negotiated life insurance provisions provide a base amount of life insurance paid by the employer free of charge to the employee. Additional coverage is usually optional with the employee required to pay all or part of the additional premium.

Medical, Hospital, and Dental Insurance   Non-union employers desiring to avoid unionization but desiring at the same time to cut financial corners are quick to institute all of the fringe benefits commonly found in union contracts but to make the actual benefits for each category of fringes very meager. Many workers, particularly young, healthy workers, do not discover that health plans are not full coverage health plans until they are confronted with a large bill, after the insurance company's payment has been deducted. Imagine my consternation when I had to "Mastercharge" a $750 bill that was not covered by the New York State Employees Blue Cross-Blue Shield plan in order to secure the release of my wife and newborn child from the hospital, when my first son's delivery two years earlier cost only $25 under the United Auto Workers negotiated Blue Cross-Blue Shield plan in Michigan.

Health insurance plans are rather complicated, because they contain a number of exceptions, deductibles, and maximums. The best way to organize the information is by completing the check list in Exhibit 4–1 for the potential target and the union contracts being used for comparative purposes.

After completion of the "Health Plan Coverage Checklist," analysis might disclose significant discrepancies between health provisions at the potential target and the union contracts used for comparative purposes. These items should be highlighted in the economic prospectus.

An inequity that some employers perpetrate is to have good health insurance coverage for individual employees but to charge an exorbitant fee for family coverage. Sometimes the contribution out of employee paychecks for family coverage is greater than the actual cost of the coverage. Each year the insurance carrier returns to the employer the difference between the money received for family coverage and the actual disbursement for the coverage. Some employers return this money to employees by reducing family coverage premiums, others simply pocket this rebate from the insurance carrier. Whether the employer is receiving a rebate from the insurance carrier is a matter of public information.[16] The organizer must be certain that the employer has not returned the rebate to employees. The best way of determining this fact is to examine the paystubs of workers interested in gaining union representation. Organizers for the Western Conference of Teamsters and the Food and Commercial Workers have found the disclosure of pocketed family coverage rebates to be an effective organizing message.

Pension Benefits   Pension plans, like health insurance plans, differ significantly between employers with some constituting a fringe benefit in little more than name only. While generally not as com-

---

EXHIBIT 4–1. Health Plan Coverage Checklist

1. How many days of HOSPITALIZATION are provided for general hospital admissions? _____
   Semi-private room? _____   Other? _____
   Is the full cost of a room in the hospital covered? _____
   If not full cost, how much? _____
   Usual charge in the area for a semi-private room: _____

2. Is the full cost of SURGERY covered? _____
   If not, is there a SURGERY SCHEDULE? _____
   Does the SURGERY SCHEDULE cover the usual surgeon's charge? _____

   Is any provision made to cover charges by surgeons exceeding the schedule? _____

3. Is ANESTHESIOLOGY fully covered? _____
   If not, how much of the ANESTHESIOLOGIST'S fee is covered? _____

4. Are X-RAYS and laboratory TESTS fully covered? _____
   If not fully covered, how much is covered? _____

5. Are VISITS TO DOCTOR'S offices fully covered? _____
   If not fully covered, how much of the cost of OFFICE CALLS is covered? _____

6. Are MATERNITIES treated differently than other medical procedures? _____

   If treated differently, estimate the cost of a normal pregnancy and delivery: _____.

7. What is the cost for PREVENTIVE MEDICINE such as regular physical examinations, well-baby care, immunizations, injections, and allergy shots? _____

8. Is MENTAL HEALTH coverage provided on an inpatient basis? _____
   an outpatient basis? _____
   If MENTAL HEALTH coverage is provided, what is the maximum outpatient coverage and cost? _____
   and the maximum inpatient coverage and cost? _____

9. Is CHEMICAL DEPENDENCY coverage provided on an inpatient basis? _____
   an outpatient basis? _____

10. How much, if any, of the cost of EYEGLASSES is covered? _____

11. Do participants pay the full cost of PRESCRIPTIONS? _____ If not the full cost, what is the charge per PRESCRIPTION? _____

12. Is there an amount of medical expense or DEDUCTIBLE that an individual must incur before the health insurance begins to pay? _____ If "yes," what is that amount? _____
What PERCENTAGE of medical expenses above the deductible does the health insurance cover? _____

13. In the case of CATASTROPHIC ILLNESS what is the MAXIMUM coverage of the health insurance? _____

14. What is the cost to the employee for the coverage of the employee's DEPENDENTS under the health insurance plan? _____

15. Is DENTAL expense coverage provided? _____

16. If a dental plan is provided, what is the coverage for regular DIAGNOSTIC and PREVENTIVE services (e.g., six month check-up, fluoride for children)?
_____

17. What is the coverage for RESTORATIVE services (e.g., fillings)? _____
_____

18. What is the coverage for PROSTHETICS (e.g., bridges, crowns)? _____
_____

19. What is the coverage for ORTHODONTICS, i.e., braces? _____
_____

20. Is there an annual DEDUCTIBLE before the dental plan begins to cover the expense?
_____

21. Is there a MAXIMUM amount covered by the dental plan each year? _____
_____

22. What, if anything, is charged employees for DEPENDENT or FAMILY COVERAGE?
_____

---

plicated as health insurance, a number of aspects of pension plans should be examined when preparing an economic prospectus:

1. **Contributory or noncontributory?** Most pension plans do not require financial contributions from employees for participation. However, some do, and these contributions represent a deduction from net take-home pay.

2. **Normal retirement age?** The normal retirement age under most plans is 65.

3. **Early retirement?** Some plans provide a full pension after an

employee has accumulated a number of years of service regardless of age or on the basis of a formula accounting for both age and years of service. Other plans provide early retirement but at a reduced level of benefits.

4. **Disability retirement?** Disabled workers ineligible for normal or early retirement may be entitled to a pension in addition to any workers compensation and disability insurance benefits they may receive.

5. **Benefit increases for retirees?** Pension plans seldom increase the benefits of retirees despite high rates of inflation which erode purchasing power. While not a mandatory collective bargaining issue, some unions have negotiated benefit increases for retirees. A small number have cost-of-living adjustments built into the plans.

6. **Social Security offset?** Most pension plans provide benefits as an addition to Social Security benefits. Some pension plans, however, have what is termed a "Social Security offset," meaning that the employer agrees that retirees, usually in relation to their years of employment, will receive certain levels of retirement income consisting of both Social Security benefits and pension benefits. Two effects are possible. As Social Security benefits increase, total retirement income may not necessarily increase, meaning that benefits from the pension plan as a portion of retirement income decline. The other effect is that if Social Security benefits exceed the total retirement income specified by the pension plan, the retiree receives in effect no pension benefit, even though he or she is fully vested under the plan and the law.

The Social Security offset is found in both union-negotiated plans and pension plans established solely by employers. Because it is somewhat complicated, often workers do not understand the effect of the provision until the time that they apply for retirement. Then it comes as a shock. Exposing the Social Security offset in the pension plan of a potential organizing target can be an effective organizing message, because the Social Security offset can result in a pension plan that provides little or no benefit to a substantial number of workers regardless of whether or not they are fully vested. (Entitlement to a pension or "vesting" normally occurs after ten years of continuous service with an employer.)

7. **Monthly retiree benefits?** Most pension plans are of the "de-fined benefit" category, meaning that the monthly pension ben-efit is established at the time of retirement and, in the case of organized workers, negotiated by the union. The employer's obligation is to make contributions to the plan sufficient to insure the benefit. Usually, the monthly retirement benefit is based upon a formula dependent upon years of service. For example: Monthly benefit per year of service times years of credited service equals monthly benefit at age 65.

A defined benefit based solely on years of service is easy to present in the economic prospectus. In other plans, the monthly benefit per year of service depends upon earnings in the last year of service or average earnings in a number of years of service with the result that benefits may vary between workers with the same years of seniority. In these cases, the economic prospectus should present pension benefit information reflec-tive of what an average employee would receive.

In addition to defined benefit plans, there are "defined contribution" plans, notably in the unionized sector of the con-struction industry where workers tend to be employed by many employers over the span of their careers. These multi-employer plans provide a valuable service to their participants because of the relatively short tenure of employment with any one em-ployer, which would make vesting difficult or even impossible. Each worker has in effect an account kept in his or her name for the accumulation of employer contributions under the plan. For each hour of work, the employer is usually required to make a pension contribution. The trustees of union-negotiated defined contribution plans can provide information on typical pension benefits.

Bonuses, Gifts, Prizes, etc.   The grab bag category of "bonuses, prizes, gifts, etc." may strike one as being relatively unimportant because of its miscellaneous character. But it can be the most decisive economic factor in an organizing campaign.

Organizing campaigns have been lost because employers pro-vided unusual fringe benefits to unorganized workers and implied that these benefits would be lost if the workers chose union repre-sentation. An organizer believes that the union lost an authorization election at a food processing plant because the workers were con-vinced that they would lose their unlimited access to free soft drinks throughout each workday. A union loss at an automobile rental company's maintenance facility is attributed to the employer's policy of allowing mechanics to take home used tires and batteries and, subsequently, to sell them on the side (tax-free, of course). A relatively large printing plant located in a rural area virtually shuts down in the spring and fall to enable its employees who also farm to plant and harvest their crops. Even though the wages and benefits in union contracts far exceed those at these unorganized plants, the free soft drinks, used tires and batteries, and guaranteed time-off during planting and harvesting seasons are very important to employees at these unorganized workplaces.

Convincing unorganized workers that the employer cannot remove these benefits unilaterally after a union is authorized as bargaining agent but instead must bargain with the union over retention of the benefits is often difficult. Two strategies are available to the organizer confronted with a potential organizing target providing unusual fringe benefits.

The dollar value of unusual fringe benefits should be determined. In the case of cash bonuses and prizes, this calculation is relatively easy to make. Determining the cash value of merchandise is only a bit more difficult. In order to emphasize the actual value of the unusual benefits, a comparison should be made between the yearly income of union members and workers at the potential organizing target receiving the unusual benefits.

In addition to monetizing the unusual benefits and comparing yearly incomes, the organizer should determine whether organized workers in the bargaining units that are being used for comparative purposes receive any unusual benefits. Employer subsidization of sports and social clubs is common at organized workplaces. Some organized employers also conduct contests and present bonuses and gifts to their employees. These benefits often are not specified in the union contract so the best source of information on them is the officers of the local union.

Some contracts, however, specify all benefits to be received. The following is an excerpt from a United Auto Workers contract:

The employer agrees that it will:
a. Provide parking facilities.
b. Provide parking lot snow plowing.
c. Provide parking lot car starting.

d. Give Christmas gift at the plant to current employees and employees having retired subsequent to January 1 of the current year.

e. Provide vending machine service and cafeteria facilities.

f. Give assistance to authorized recreational programs on all shifts subject to the continued availability of the facilities currently used.

g. Send flowers to employee when hospitalized and in case of death.

h. Provide hunting and fishing leave as work schedules permit.[17]

The last item is nearly the same as leave for the planting and harvesting of crops. Certainly, a union could negotiate a right to used tires and batteries and unlimited access to free soft drinks. The challenge is to demonstrate this fact to unorganized workers.

Union Dues   The employer will make an issue of the cost of union membership. Therefore, initiation fees, if any, for employees at a newly organized workplace, and dues should be depicted in the economic prospectus as a cost item and compared with the benefits of unionization. Typically, union dues are about equal to two hours of wages per month or about one percent of gross straight time hourly wages. What is the rate of return on this investment? Will the employer "pay" the union dues with a nickel per hour raise? Make sure to stress that union dues are tax deductible.

EMPLOYER'S ABILITY TO PAY

If it is determined that the potential organizing target provides wages and benefits below those for union organized workplaces of approximately the same size, producing essentially the same product, located in the same geographic region, and providing relatively stable employment, it is then necessary to establish whether the unorganized employer has the ability to pay the union scale. Simply relying on "pattern bargaining" to justify an employer's likelihood of matching the provisions in union contracts may have been acceptable at one time, but the breaking of pattern negotiations in the automobile, construction, meat packing, and rubber industries demonstrates that "ability to pay" is a much more realistic criterion in union-management negotiations of the 1980s.

However, evaluating the employer's ability to pay is often very difficult. There are many books and courses on financial analysis which will serve you very well if you have some money saved and want to invest it in the stocks of corporations or if you are deciding whether to loan money. These courses and books rely heavily on analyzing the financial statements of corporations. However, unions too often find themselves in the position of not having financial statements to analyze or of having financial statements that are rather meaningless.

Companies with at least 500 stockholders and $1 million in assets must file a great deal of information with the U.S. Securities and Exchange Commission (SEC). These completed forms are available to anyone at many large urban and university libraries or directly from the SEC.[18] Information from these reports is used to compile *Moody's Manuals* which contain information on the finances of most companies filing with the SEC. *Moody's Manuals* are an easy way to get financial information and are often found at local branch libraries. Form 10K is the most important form filed with the SEC. It includes information on the history and structure of the company and its subsidiaries, the company's products, operations in other countries, number of employees, income and expenses, and plant locations.

If all of this information is available, why then are unions too often unable to employ the same financial analysis techniques as investors and creditors? Some very large companies have less than 500 stockholders, are not required to file with the SEC, and are considered to be "privately held." For most of its history, the Ford family owned all of the stock of the giant Ford Motor Co. Only a handful of people know the assets, sales, and profits of Cargill, believed to be the world's largest grain dealer. Mars Candies, Hughes Aircraft, Dubuque Packing, Hallmark Cards, Lennox Air Conditioning, and Strohs Brewery are other privately held corporations.

Because most firms in the construction industry are quite small, they do not file with the SEC. While the Freedom of Information Act gives the public access to most of the files of government agencies, the public does not have the right to investigate the income tax returns of companies filed with the Internal Revenue Service.

The second reason why unions too often cannot use customary financial analysis techniques is that they usually do not seek to represent all of the employees of a corporation, and the SEC requires corporations to file financial information for only the entire company, not information broken down on a division, subsidiary, or plant basis. In the era when Mobil Oil Company was only in the oil business and didn't own Montgomery Ward and before the establishment of companies like SCM Corporation which produces Smith Corona typewriters, Durkee spices, and Proctor-Silex coffee makers, conventional financial analysis could be used by unions to a greater degree than today. Since World War II, diversification and concentration have characterized American business. Companies have merged with other companies in their own industries to form larger companies and with companies in other industries to form "conglomerates"—companies producing a wide variety of products. In 1977 alone, 100 corporations worth over $20 billion were taken over by other conglomerates. SEC financial reporting requirements have not kept pace with the growth of conglomerates. Business opposes the disclosure of information on divisions, subsidiaries, and plants on the questionable premise that such disclosure would aid competitors. Consequently, unions are too often in the position of seeking to represent workers at a plant, division, or subsidiary of a giant conglomerate and not having applicable financial information.

Where financial statements applicable to potential organizing targets are available, the union must determine the employer's ability to pay. There is only one true measure of ability to pay—*return on owner's equity*. To illustrate the point, if a business—a small grocery store, for example—can be sold for $100,000 and the owner has a mortgage and other debts of $60,000, one cannot say that the business is worth $100,000 to the owner, or that he has an "owner's equity" of $100,000. The mortgage and other debts must be deducted from the market value of the business to determine the owner's equity, which in this example is $40,000 ($100,000 market value less $60,000 mortgage and other debts). The seller of the business is now free to purchase another business, using the $40,000 as a down payment, or he might decide to invest the money in stocks, bonds, gold, a money market account, or any other asset.

The economic principle involved in assessing ability to pay is called "opportunity cost." If a business is earning a profit on its owner's equity that is less than what it could earn in another type of investment, it would be to its advantage to sell its current business, take the cash, and invest in some other endeavor. This principle is utilized by business in making its investment decisions. Certainly, businesses that are not making profits and that look as if they cannot be made profitable will stop producing. But even businesses that do make profits will languish if there are investment opportunities available that yield higher profit rates. Mobil Oil, for example, felt that its rate of profit from purchasing Montgomery Ward would be greater than if it expanded its oil produciton capabilities. A reason why American steel companies did not modernize their plant and equipment is not that producing steel was unprofitable, but rather that higher profits could be earned in other industries. An example of this reasoning is the acquisition of Marathon Oil by U.S. Steel in 1982.

The percent of profit on net worth or owner's equity is easy to compute (Profit/Owner's Equity) by yourself or you can find it in *Moody's Manuals*. Having the ratio for the company is not enough; the ratio must be given a frame of reference by examining how the potential target compares with that of other companies in the same industry. *Standard and Poor's Industry Surveys*, often available at local branch libraries, provides information on the ratios of profits to net worth for the top 25 percent, top 50 percent, and bottom 25 percent of companies in various industries. If you are doing research on a tool and die company, for example, you would compute its ratio of profits to owner's equity and compare it with other companies in the "Metal Working Machinery and Equipment" industry. *Standard and Poor's Industry Surveys* shows that in 1977, the top 25 percent of companies in the industry had profits on net worth of 13.99 percent. Over half the companies earned over 9.31 percent and 25 percent earned 2.74 percent or less. If the potential organizing target is as profitable as union organized firms in its industry, it should be expected to meet union wage and benefit scales.

What does the future hold for the potential organizing target? Does available information indicate that profits will increase or decrease? There is no central source for obtaining information on the future outlook for potential organizing targets. Instead, predictions of future profitability must be pieced together from a variety of sources.

Union organizers should read the same industry publications as management. If you are unaware of these, check with your local library. It will have lists of all available trade publications. Another way of finding out what the employer reads is to walk into the employer's reception area and examine the reading material laid out for visitors. Most magazines have a tear-out subscription card. Special publications such as *Iron Age, Women's Wear Daily,* and *Automotive News* provide valuable information on their respective industries.

The Wall Street Journal and *Fortune* and *Business Week* magazines are more general than trade publications, but they can provide valuable information on projected profits. Another way of obtaining information on the industry and company is to examine the periodical indexes at the main branch library. The indexes list articles pertaining to the industry and company. If you have the money, there are organizations that will locate the available information for you and give you a brief synopsis of each published article. One of these organizations is The Information Bank, a subsidiary of The New York Times Company.[19] Librarians are very helpful, so do not avoid conducting this research if you have not done it before. In addition to information on the employer's future outlook, you may obtain other valuable information about the potential target.

If the potential target issues stock that can be purchased by the public, consult a stockbroker at one of the major firms. They employ research specialists who study various industries and issue reports on current and future profitablity. A good way of making contact with stockbrokers is through a union pension trustee, because brokers know that they exercise control over large investment funds.

In addition to published sources of information, much can be learned about ability to pay by observing the day-to-day operations of the workplace. Analysis of this information at work is particularly important when the potential organizing target is privately held or a plant, division, or subsidiary of a giant conglomerate. This information can be gathered by talking to workers at the potential organizing target. While dollars and cents forecasts are not possible, the organizer can gain insights as to ability to pay by asking the right questions:

1. Are any workers laid off?

If unemployment exists, sales of the employer's products are down, unless some new labor-saving production process has been introduced. Because the cost per unit of production tends to be lower when the workplace operates at full capacity due to fixed costs such as mortgage payments on plant and equipment and property taxes, management generally attempts to operate at full employment. Unemployment indicates that profitability or ability to pay is hampered.

2. Has the amount of overtime work increased substantially?

Using overtime as an indication of ability to pay is tricky. While overtime work necessitates premium pay and managers generally agree that workers become less productive after periods of steady overtime, these additional costs must be balanced against the savings from not hiring additional workers. The cost of fringe benefits like health insurance, vacations, holidays, and pensions are generally constant whether a worker is employed forty or sixty hours per week. As a consequence, some employers make it a practice of maintaining heavy overtime schedules as a normal operating procedure. However, if the total work force has remained relatively constant over a period of years and heavy overtime work schedules are not the usual practice, a marked increase in overtime indicates that sales are brisk and profitability is improved.

3. How much competition does the employer face in selling the product?

If the employer is the sole producer of a product or one of only a few firms producing a product, this may be interpreted as an indication of profitability. Monopolies or near monopolies can usually charge higher prices and earn larger profits than firms in industries with a large number of producers. Patents, exclusive control over raw material sources, and brand names well established with customers can result in monopolistic or near monopolistic positions. Research in the library can provide information on the extent of foreign and domestic competition.

4. Is the plant and equipment being adequately maintained?

Management can exercise a great deal of discretion in spending on the maintenance of plant and equipment. Paint jobs can be put off, machines can run without being overhauled, and floors need not be cleaned every day. The employer can save money and thereby increase profits by neglecting maintenance. But a dirty, unpleasant workplace can affect employee morale and productivity and be the cause of industrial accidents. Machinery that is not properly maintained can end up in the scrap heap. An employer who finds a workplace to be a profitable endeavor is likely to provide proper maintenance, lest it break down and cease to produce. An employer who finds a workplace to be unprofitable is likely to cut back on maintenance and milk it for every dollar that can be extracted without any thought toward long-term profitability.

As with overtime, one must be cautious in interpreting maintenance policies. Managers are too often rewarded on the basis of the short-term profitability of the workplaces they direct. Hence, maintenance may be neglected at workplaces that are very profitable. It is perhaps best to interpret maintenance policies as indicating profitability in conjunction with investment policies, the two factors discussed next.

5. Is worn-out capital equipment being replaced?

When machines and other equipment at the workplace break down and cannot be repaired, management must decide whether to invest in replacements. The return on owner's equity criterion confronts management head on. Replacement investment indicates that the employer plans on remaining in operation because of the profitability of the workplace. Failure to replace worn-out productive capital indicates that the return on this investment is projected to be less than what the employer could earn elsewhere.

6. Is the employer expanding the productive capacity of the workplace?

More than the decision to replace worn-out capital, the ultimate test of a workplace's profitability is the decision to expand productive capacity through the introduction of new plant and equipment. Employers project the profits from the investments they make. An addition to plant and equipment represents a decision that investing in the operation will yield one of the best returns for the money. The prediction may turn out to be faulty, but nevertheless, this is how the employer views the investment. If the employer believed that a better return of profits on investment could be earned elsewhere, the addition to existing plant and equipment would not be made.

7. What are the sales prospects for the employer's product?

Industry trade publications can provide information on future sales for the product of an industry or firm. However, these projections are general and usually do not pertain directly to the operation comprising the bargaining unit. It is useful to establish how much of a sales backlog the employer has and whether the backlog is increasing or decreasing. While overtime schedules are a good indicator, direct information on sales backlogs is useful. Shipping clerks often have an idea of sales backlogs as do truck drivers. By establishing the employer's sales outlook for the near future, the organizer can assess the likelihood of full employment at the potential target from the time an organizing campaign might be started to the time of an authorization election. The likelihood of high unemployment in the near future might be a reason to disregard the potential target.

8.   What is the composition of production between new and replacement parts?

Some manufacturers produce both new products and replacement parts for products sold in previous years. Production of new products usually takes precedence over replacement parts. If the operation is producing new products to almost the total exclusion of replacement parts, this can be an indication that sales and profits are strong. If replacement part manufacturing comprises a growing proportion of production, this may indicate that sales and profitability are weak.

Caution: A danger with economic analysis in general and with the economic prospectus in particular as a means for identifying organizing targets is that an unwarranted sense of certainty is conveyed. The fact that an economic prospectus provides overwhelming evidence that unorganized workers would clearly benefit from union representation does not mean that they will organize. The union may conduct a poor organizing campaign or the employer, within or outside the letter of the law, may be able to instill enough loyalty and/or fear in the workers to beat the union.

All of the people with "modern" names who subscribe to only the Sunday newspaper do not purchase subscriptions from me. But the odds of them buying are much better than for people with "old-fashioned" names who do not subscribe to a newspaper or already take a daily paper. The same is true of the economic prospectus. Economic issues are one of the two most important reasons why workers join unions. The economic prospectus identifies targets where wages and benefits are an issue and, therefore, where the odds for success are good.

WORKING CONDITIONS

In addition to identifying economic issues at potential organizing targets, it is necessary to identify working conditions which are sources of problems to unorganized workers and which are capable of being alleviated through provisions typically found in union contracts. Conversations with a few workers at a potential target or examination of an employees' handbook distributed by the employer should disclose most of the necessary information on the employer's formal personnel policies such as disciplinary procedures, job posting, and grievance procedures. Less certain from a discussion with workers is whether the employer is arbitrary and unfair in administering personnel policies, because the workers with whom the organizer has contact may not be representative of the potential target's work force. Therefore, in assembling information on working conditions and assessing the likelihood of organizing issues, a distinction should be made between formal personnel policies and the views of workers on how the policies are in fact administered. The survey in Exhibit 4–2 illustrates this distinction and should facilitate the assessment of working conditions.

As with the economic prospectus, the organizer determines through this survey whether working conditions are organizing issues and whether the union is likely to resolve the issues. By identifying the formal personnel policies of the employer, the organizer can gauge the employer's degree of sophistication at implementing a long-run union avoidance strategy and how formidable an opponent the potential target would be to organize. A grievance procedure, particularly one culminating in impartial third-party neutral arbitration, is an example of a formal personnel policy which indicates that the employer has adopted a long-run union avoidance strategy, because this is a provision found in most union contracts. Likewise, if formal policies are counter to those typically found in union contracts, there is prima-facie evidence of organizing issues whose existence can be substantiated by employees at the potential target.

If employees indicate that working conditions are poor and the working conditions identified by employees are likely to be improved through union-negotiated seniority systems, health and safety provisions, promotion policies, grievance procedures, etc., the organizer has good evidence that organizing issues exist and a good case for

EXHIBIT 4–2. Survey of Working Conditions

FORMAL PERSONNEL POLICIES

1. Are personnel policies in writing and readily available to employees?

2. Does the employer have specific rules and regulations governing the conduct of employees at the workplace?
    If so, what are they?

3. Does the employer have a grievance procedure?

4. If there is a grievance procedure, does it culminate in final and binding arbitration by a third-party neutral?

5. What is the employer's policy in the event of layoffs?

6. Is seniority a factor in layoffs?

7. Are employees entitled to leaves of absence? If so, for what reasons?

8. Are job openings posted?

9. Does the employer have a policy of promoting from within the workplace?

10. Is seniority a factor in promotions?

11. What is the employer's policy in regard to overtime?

12. Do workers performing the same job receive the same wage rate or are wages based upon "performance?"

13. Does the employer have "quality circles" or some other worker participation program?

14. Does the employer have a program promoting health and safety on the job? If so, do employees participate in directing the program?

15. Has the employer communicated to employees its intent to remain non-union?

EMPLOYEE VIEWS ON WORKING CONDITIONS

1. Is the employer arbitrary in its discipline of employees? If so, give some examples:

2. Is there a "progressive" discipline procedure (e.g., oral warning, warning letter, suspension, discharge)?

3. If there is a grievance procedure, are employees afraid to use it? If yes, why are employees fearful?

4. If there is a grievance procedure, do employees view it as being fair? If viewed as not fair, give some examples.

5. If layoffs have occurred, is the employer viewed as being arbitrary in selecting employees for termination? If viewed as arbitrary, give some examples.

6. Have there been layoffs as a result of subcontracting? If so, give examples.

7. Is the employer viewed as disregarding ability and playing personal favorites when making promotions? If yes, give some examples.

8. Is overtime work allocated fairly? If no, give examples.

9. If workers performing the same job are not paid the same wage, is the employer viewed as being unfair in evaluating performance? If viewed as unfair, give examples.

10. Do employees believe that the work pace is reasonable? If viewed as unreasonable, give examples.

11. Are leaves of absence readily granted? If no, give examples.

12. Are there unhealthy and unsafe working conditions? If unhealthy and unsafe, give examples.

---

union representation can be made. Judgment must be exercised, however, in assuring that employees with whom the organizer has contact are representative of the potential target's work force. If a campaign is launched, the survey of "Employee Views on Working Conditions" will be expanded to include a larger number of workers and will provide the basis for important messages to be conveyed to the election unit during the campaign.

GETTING A CONTRACT

The employer's profitability is an indication that it can improve wages, benefits, and working conditions, but it is no guarantee that it will in fact do so. Ultimately, ability to pay is a prediction of what is possible, but not necessarily of what is probable.

One might think that highly profitable employers are more likely than unprofitable employers to agree to union demands, because they can afford to make improvements. But the matter is not quite so simple. Profitable employers may resist unionization even more than unprofitable ones. To profitable employers, unionization may be viewed as the path to reduced profits. Because of their profitability, they may be able to withstand strikes more easily than marginally profitable employers who may view unionization as just another obstacle to their day-to-day survival. Reaching collective bargaining agreements may be more acceptable than encountering the losses due to strikes. Clearly, ability to pay is not the same as willingness or, perhaps more accurately, resignation to pay, although ability to pay remains an important factor in selecting organizing targets.

With workers at an estimated one out of five newly organized workplaces unable to secure their first contract,[20] organizers must attempt to select organizing targets that are likely to be successful at not only gaining representation rights but negotiating collective bargaining agreements. There is no formula for successfully predicting the likelihood of securing a contract, but there are a number of questions the organizer should answer prior to launching a campaign, which provide a framework for analyzing the issue:

1. **Are most other firms in the industry—the employer's competition—union organized?**

Unorganized employers fear that unionization will raise labor costs and "force" them to raise prices. If the bulk of the competition in the industry is organized, the employer may view a union contract as less of a threat to profitability than if it is the only firm or one of a small proportion of firms in the industry to be organized.

2. **In the event of a strike, could the employer suffer a permanent loss of customers to its competitors?**

If the employer is in an industry with many competing firms, the employer may fear a permanent loss of customers to the competition, because customers may view the struck firm as an undependable source of supply and take their business elsewhere. If there is little competition in the industry or a high degree of brand loyalty among customers, the loss of business due to a strike is likely to be temporary in nature. The stronger the threat of a permanent loss of customers to the competition, the more likely an employer will attempt to avert a strike.

3. **If the employer has union organized workplaces, have their labor-management relations been relatively cooperative or highly combative?**

The employer is likely to adopt the same posture toward a newly organized workplace as it has toward its workplaces that have been organized for some time. Often, it is a matter of corporate policy.

If, for example, the employer has withstood long strikes or had decertifications occur at other workplaces, resistance to negotiating a contract can be anticipated. While a poor labor relations history should not necessarily persuade a union against attempting to organize an employer, the historical record cannot be entirely ignored either. International unions and the AFL-CIO can assist the organizer at compiling a profile of the employer's policy toward unionization.

4. **If the union has contracts at other plants of the employer, could it successfully apply pressure on the employer to agree to contract terms at a newly organized workplace?**

While the law restricts secondary boycott activities, unions can influence the policies of employers toward unorganized workplaces and newly organized workplaces without contracts. An example is the United Auto Workers' agreement with General Motors that the corporation adopt a neutral position toward the unionization of unorganized plants. Through the collective bargaining process at organized workplaces, the union succeeded at combating the corporation's alleged "Southern strategy."

5. **If a union represents other workers at the workplace, would they honor a picket line by the union of newly organized workers?**

While the union may be prohibited from authorizing a sympathy strike, individual union members may within the letter of the law choose to honor picket lines. This factor is especially important when unions attempt to secure contracts for white-collar workers at workplaces where production and/or maintenance employees are already organized.

6. **What is the likelihood of conducting a successful consumer boycott of the employer's product in the event of a collective bargaining impasse?**

The success of a consumer boycott depends upon the degree to which consumers can identify the employer's product, the union's "case" for engendering the support of consumers, and the union's resources for publicizing the boycott. While boycotts can be a successful tool for resolving bargaining impasses, they should be assessed realistically. Boycotts can be costly, very long in duration, and above all, unsuccessful, as many unions can attest.

7.   Could the employer easily shut down its operation and move to another location?

A "runaway shop" is more likely in industries where the employer's investment in plant and equipment is low, or the equipment is relatively portable, and the location where the work is performed is relatively unimportant. Using these criteria, a chemical plant is unlikely to run away because of the large capital investment and relative immobility of capital even though the location where the work is performed may be unimportant. Likewise, a fast-food restaurant is unlikely to run away, because the location where the work is performed is important despite the high mobility of capital equipment. In contrast, a light manufacturing plant with a national or large regional market, low capital investment, and portable capital equipment is a likely runaway candidate.

8.   In the event of a strike, would the employer be able to shift production to another workplace?

Multi-plant employers can play one bargaining unit off against others by shifting production during strikes. If the employer has a number of workplaces producing essentially the same product and the productive capacity to pick up the production lost due to a strike at the potential target, the possibility of diminished bargaining power must be faced.

If the union already represents employees at some of an employer's workplaces, it might strive for a contract expiration date at the potential target conciding with that at the other plants. Following this strategy, the union should time its organizing campaign to coincide with the bargaining schedule of plants where it already has contracts. For example, it may be unadvisable to launch a serious organizing campaign when organized workplaces have just signed a three-year contract; better to wait until the middle of the contract period.

Where the union does not represent employees at any of the employer's workplaces or at only a small number of the workplaces, the union might attempt to organize all of the workplaces simultaneously. This strategy was used by the United Steelworkers in its recent unsuccessful campaign at Du Pont, because the employer could play the fourteen plants off against one another during collective bargaining, if the union had succeeded in organizing only a portion of the plants.[21] Conducting a simultaneous campaign at a number of workplaces is difficult, but it is often the only alternative available to unions.

9. **In the event of a strike, could the employer continue to operate by using supervisors, other nonbargaining unit personnel, or strikebreakers?**

In general, the more capital intensive (more "automated") the production process, the more difficult it is to shut down production. A good example of an industry that is virtually impossible to shut down is oil refining. The organizer should always assume that the employer will attempt to operate during a strike and will utilize nonbargaining unit personnel to do so. The issue is whether the attempt would be successful. In order to resolve the issue, the organizer must be thoroughly familiar with the production process, which in the case of industries with low union representation may require a thorough analysis of the workplace, including a diagram of the plant.

Historically, union organizing efforts have often been thwarted by strikebreakers brought in by employers from the outside. The meat packing industry, while it was based in Chicago, is a stunning example of waves of foreign immigrants and migrants from rural areas of America gaining entrance into the industry by scabbing on workers who formed unions and who had gained their entrance by scabbing on other workers who had formed unions.[22] The prerequisites for the successful use of strikebreakers are timeless: relatively unskilled jobs that take little time to learn, unemployment and poverty among a substantial number of workers, and a lack of class consciousness or empathy toward the strikers among strikebreakers.

10. **Could the employer stockpile an inventory of the product so as to withstand a strike for a long period of time?**

The longer a strike the more difficult it is to maintain solidarity among strikers in the event of a "back-to-work movement." If the employer is capable of stockpiling a large inventory of its product, it may be able to withstand the pressures of a strike more than the bargaining unit.

11. **If the employer engages a law or consulting firm, what is its reputation?**

The AFL-CIO Department of Organization and state and city AFL-CIO central bodies can provide information on the activities of law firms and union avoidance consulting firms. One must anticipate the outside firm engaging in activities at the potential target which are similar to those it has used elsewhere.

12. **If strikes have occurred in the community where the potential target is located, what was the role of the media, police, courts, community leaders, and the public?**

Often, strikes are not confined to the employer and the union. The community becomes involved and can help shape the outcome of the confrontation. Local unions can provide the details.

CONCLUSION

Preparing to organize involves reducing potential barriers to organizing, such as a union constitution subject to inaccurate interpretation, and instituting procedures to improve organizing, such as a thorough target selection process. Adequate preparation will not guarantee success, but it will improve the odds and can be as important as the actual conduct of organizing campaigns. The preparations recommended in this chapter require changes, but none so drastic as to prevent unions from adopting them.

Engaging personnel with the aptitude for organizing sounds too obvious to mention. Yet some unions do not recognize that not everyone can organize.

Clarifying and cleaning up union constitutions and bylaws would make the job of organizers a bit easier and need not change the basic governance of unions. All that is needed in most cases is a clarification of the often uncertain and misleading language used by the legal profession. With one out of every five adult Americans estimated to be functionally illiterate, union constitutions and bylaws need to be written in a more comprehensible style. Certainly, the unorganized workplace is not the proper location for unions to attempt to improve literacy with documents originally drafted by lawyers two or more generations ago.

Improving the skills and increasing the power of local union activists is a challenging proposal because of the uncertainty it generates. Can local activists adequately direct more of the day-to-day affairs of their bargaining units? Will they usurp the power and ultimately the positions of full-time officials? These are legitimate fears, but as will be discussed in chapter 8, "Staying Organized," the development of an effective steward system at each workplace is the most effective way to prevent decertifications. Likewise, a commitment to develop effective steward systems at workplaces with fifty or fewer employees is necessary if unions are to attain the resources to both organize and service the preponderance of new unorganized workplaces of the 1980s.

The importance of maintaining organizing records is clear. Some organizers accomplish the task by tape recording post-campaign sessions among organizers and in-the-workplace organizing committee members. By knowing the successes and failures of the past, the union is better prepared to organize in the future.

Failure to coordinate the efforts of union staff who organize and those who negotiate contracts can undermine a union's organizing efforts because of the inevitable conflicts that arise. Short of placing the responsibility for organizing on those who negotiate and administer contracts, the union can institute a target selection process whose objective is campaigns that are likely to result in both certification as the bargaining representative and a negotiated agreement.

The target selection process described in the chapter emphasizes the ranking of potential targets according to the prevalence of organizing issues and the likelihood that the union will secure a contract representing an improvement in wages, benefits, and working conditions. The process recognizes that workers organize over issues, that workers must believe that collective action—unionization—will result in improvements, and that unions face obstacles in securing contracts.

The process of gathering information on potential targets is time consuming. Rather than being the sole responsibility of organizers in the field, it is best to share the responsibility with the union research departments. Likewise, state AFL-CIO and city central bodies can pool their resources to provide research. Some AFL-CIO Food and Beverage Trades Councils, for example, have hired full-time staff to conduct this type of research. In the 1980s, obtaining representation rights and contracts requires a thorough target selection process.

FOOTNOTES

[1] Derek C. Bok and John T. Dunlop. *Labor and the American Community* (New York: Simon and Schuster, 1970), p. 54.

[2] Shortly after this was written, the afternoon paper "merged" with the morning paper.

[3] Myron Roomkin and Hervey Juris. "The Changing Character of Unionism in Traditionally Organized Sectors," *Monthly Labor Review,* February 1979, p. 37.

[4] Jeanne M. Brett, "Why Employees Want Unions," *Organizational Dynamics,* Spring 1980, pp. 47–59.

[5] Julius G. Getman, Stephen B. Goldberg, and Jeanne B. Herman. *Union Representation Elections: Law and Reality* (New York: Russell Sage Foundation, 1976).

[6] W. Clay Hammer and Frank J. Smith. "Worker Attitudes as Predictors of Unionization Activity," *Journal of Applied Psychology,* August 1978, pp. 415–421.

[7] Chester A. Schreisheim. "Job Satisfaction, Attitudes Toward Unions, and Voting in a Union Representation Election," *Journal of Applied Psychology,* October 1978, pp. 548–552.

[8] Brett, "Why Employees Want Unions," pp. 47–59.

[9] "Poll Finds Love for Labor, Hate for Its Leaders," *The Minneapolis Star,* February 8, 1982, p. 16A.

[10] Kenneth S. Warner et al. "Motives for Unionization Among State Social Service Employees," *Public Personnel Management,* May–June 1978, pp. 181–191.

[11] Markley Roberts and William E. Bittle. "The Union Contract: A Solid Investment," *The AFL-CIO American Federationist,* May 1981, pp. 5–8. The article also presents evidence that organized employers can afford to pay higher wages, because unionized workers are more productive than unorganized workers.

[12] Industrial Union Department, AFL-CIO, *Labor and Investments,* Vol. 1, No. 2.

[13] Available from U.S. Department of Labor, Office of Wages and Industrial Relations, Room 1286, General Accounting Office Building, 441 G Street, N.W., Washington, D.C. 20212, Telephone 202/523-1597.

[14] At the time of this writing, the U.S. Department of Labor announced plans to drop the "Area Wage Surveys" due to budget cuts. Because of their importance to unorganized employers in setting wage rates, it is doubtful that this data series will be discontinued permanently.

[15] At the time of this writing, plans to drop this data service have also been announced.

[16] Obtain U.S. Internal Revenue Service Form 5500, "Annual Return/ Report of Employee Benefit Plan" for health plans covering 100 or more participants, or Form 5500C for plans with less than 100 participants. Address inquiries to U.S. Department of Labor, Pension and Welfare Room N4677, Labor-Management Services Administration, 200 Constitution Ave., N.W., Washington, D.C. 20216.

[17] *1980–83 Agreement between FMC Corporation, Northern Ordinance Division, and Local 683, International Union United Automobile, Aerospace & Agricultural Implement Workers of America,* pp. 61–64.

[18] Securities and Exchange Commission, 1100 L Street, N.W., Washington, D.C. 20549, Telephone 202/523-5506.

[19] The Information Bank, Mt. Pleasant Office Park, 1719A Route 10, Parsippany, N.J. 07054, Telephone 201/539-5850.

[20] Richard Prosten. "The Rise in NLRB Election Delays: Measuring Business' New Resistance," *Monthly Labor Review,* February 1979, pp. 38–39.

[21] "An Acid Test at Dupont," *Business Week,* December 14, 1981, pp. 123–124.

[22] Alma Herbst. *The Negro in the Slaughtering and Meat Packing Industry in Chicago* (New York: Houghton Mifflin Co., 1932).

5

Organizing by the Unorganized

The organizer must come face to face with his or her role. By definition an organizer is an aggressive person—a person who wants to achieve. Often, aggressive, achievement-oriented people live by the credo, "If you want to get a job done right, do it yourself." Adopting this attitude toward organizing will not succeed. Instead, the organizer must follow Saul Alinsky's "Iron Rule of Organizing": "Never do for others what they can do for themselves." The reasons for Alinsky's Iron Rule are very practical:

1. Because union treasuries are limited, unions cannot ever hope to place enough full-time staff in the field to do all of the work involved in successful organizing drives. Therefore, the workers themselves must do most of the hard work necessary for organizing unions.

2. Outside union organizers are prohibited by law from gaining access to the private property of employers. While organizers can contact workers outside workplaces, often the most convenient and perhaps the most effective contacts occur at the workplace by workers committed to promoting unionization.

3. Organizers must help develop local unions, which can function by themselves after the organizing campaign succeeds. Organizing's goal is not merely union membership and collective bargaining rights, but the development of local unions capable

of taking charge. If organizers do all of the work of the campaign, local union leaders will not be developed and the local union will falter. Furthermore, workers who do not organize themselves cannot achieve solidarity. With solidarity comes power.

In this chapter, one may be struck by the lack of unanimity among organizers on the most effective organizing tactics. There is no agreement, for example, on the importance of housecalls and where there is agreement that housecalls should be included, there is no agreement on the most effective way of making them. This lack of agreement indicates that no formula for successful organizing has been developed and that each organizer must develop an approach—through experimentation and trial and error—which best suits his or her individual talents, the industry in which organizing occurs, and the individual characteristics of each organizing target. Ideally, experimentation would occur on a larger scale so that some "principles of organizing" similar to "principles of economics," for example, would be developed. The difficulty with "principles" in social sciences such as economics and, to extend the term further, labor union organizing is that one cannot control all of the variables determining outcomes in individual cases so that truly universal principles do not exist. The value of this chapter to the experienced organizer is that it may suggest some different approaches and new experiments to be conducted. To the inexperienced organizer, the chapter provides a wide range of alternatives from which to choose.

PLANNING THE CAMPAIGN

In theory, at the time the organizer selects a target, he or she would be able to plan the entire campaign through the date of the authorization election victory. This is not possible, because the dates at which various phases of the campaign occur are not predictable. Essentially, each campaign consists of three phases:

1. The period preceding the filing of the election petition.
2. The period of delay preceding the election date announcement when jostling occurs between the employer, the union, and the Board over such issues as the composition of the election unit and unfair labor practice charges.
3. The period preceding the election date.

While winning the election is the overall objective of the planning process, each phase also has its own objective. During the first phase, the organizer is concerned with obtaining signed authorization cards from at least 30 percent of the desired election unit. During the second phase when campaigns often seem to run out of gas because of long delays, the organizer is concerned with maintaining interest and momentum. During the third phase, the campaign should peak so that interest and support of the union are at their highest.

During the first phase, some organizers allow a set amount of time to achieve a signed authorization card majority. If a majority is not attained within that time—sometimes as short as a week or two—the organizers pull out. The rationale is that signing authorization cards costs workers very little, because the union can ultimately be rejected through the election. This minimal commitment of a card majority is necessary in order to justify further expenditures of time and money by the union. In addition, by setting a time limit the organizers impose discipline upon themselves to conduct as intensive a campaign as possible and avoid the temptation of "giving it another week" when the possibility of attaining a majority is realistically very slim. Other organizers believe that time limits cannot be set for this first phase of the campaign, because each group of workers is different and some groups require more cultivation than others.

Regardless of whether one sets a time limit for achieving a 30 percent or 50 percent or 75 percent ratio of signed authorization cards, the planning process is essentially the same, although the actual plan of each organizer will be markedly different. The planning process involves three decisions: (1) a choice of organizing media (e.g., housecalls, mass meetings, formation of a workplace organizing committee); (2) a choice of organizing messages (e.g., "The employer has the ability to provide the higher pensions stipulated in union contracts," "The truth about strikes"); (3) a choice of when to use the chosen media and messages. A plan for achieving a 60 percent signed authorization card majority within one week at a twenty-five-employee target might be as follows:

- **Day 1.** Introduce the union by passing out the leaflet "What is the International Worker's Union" as workers enter the office. Announce meeting through leaflet passed out as workers leave the office.

- **Day 2.** Hold meeting at Local Motel at 7 p.m. Announce need for 60 percent authorization card majority and form organizing committee. Educate committee on law, employer campaign, and issues. Seek information on other issues.

- **Day 3.** Have organizing committee distribute the leaflet, "A fair share," during the lunch break. Stay by the telephone and answer questions from the committee. Distribute the leaflet, "A legal right to organize," as workers leave the workplace. Meet with committee at 7 p.m. to determine appropriate unit.

- **Day 4.** Have committee distribute the leaflet, "What to expect from the employer," during lunch break. Distribute leaflet, "You and the IWU," as workers leave. Housecall fence sitters with committee members.

- **Day 5.** Hold rally right after work at Local Park. Announce that petition for election will be filed.

Each organizer will have his or her own plan, because each organizer will prefer certain media and messages. Also, organizers differ as to the sequencing or timing of media and messages. Regardless of these differences, the planning process itself—the three choices that must be made—is the same for all organizers during each of the three phases of the campaign.

The second phase of the campaign preceding the announcement of the election date is usually the most difficult to plan for because of its uncertain duration. Yet the organizer should be able to approximate minimum and maximum times for this phase and develop an "optimistic" plan and a "pessimistic" plan. Ways of attempting to maintain interest and support during this difficult phase are discussed later in this chapter.

The third phase that occurs after the announcement of the election date is the easiest and, at the same time, often the most difficult to plan. It is the easiest because the time frame is well established and hardest because the employer will launch its maximum effort during this period. An example of an actual employer's plan for the final two weeks of a campaign is contained in Exhibit 3–1. In a later section of this chapter, ways of peaking the union's campaign during this final phase are examined.

As with any plan, the organizer's campaign plan should be flexible, so that changes can be made as circumstances change. Yet flexibility does not excuse failure to plan. If many aspects of employers' anti-union campaigns are predictable, the only way the the organizer can assure that he or she has developed the offensive weapons to counter the anti-union campaign is through planning.

RECRUITING IN-THE-WORKPLACE ORGANIZING COMMITTEES

The primary vehicle for workers organizing themselves into labor unions is the in-the-workplace organizing committee. Experienced organizers generally agree that the committee is the key to success and without sufficient interest to form a committee, it is best to drop an organizing campaign. A number of strategies for identifying potential members of the committee can be followed.

Unions that learn of potential organizing targets through unsolicited contacts from workers interested in unionization or through contacts stimulated by radio, television, and newspaper advertisements have an obvious person around whom a committee can be formed. The contact person may also be able to identify other potential committee members.

Some unions have organizers hire into targeted workplaces. From the inside, organizers are able to build an organizing committee. This process can be quite effective but securing employment and maintaining it may be difficult even when the organizer falsifies application forms, because employers are more conscientious about checking credentials and references than they were in the pre-World War II era when this was a widely used tactic.

The organizer can follow workers as they leave the job in order to identify local taverns and restaurants where workers congregate. If there are no gathering places or the workers meeting there are not interested in organizing, the organizer can follow workers to their homes. This procedure calls for fast talking by the organizer, because workers tend to become anxious about unannounced visits to their homes, particularly when they are aware that someone has followed them. If these contacts are successful, they can be the source of information on other workers who may be interested in union representation.

Another method for identifying potential committee members is to contact other unions in the locality of the target. Spouses, relatives, and friends of union members may be employed at the

target and may be more predisposed toward organizing than the
workers one contacts through the hit and miss approaches of conversing with workers at bars and restaurants and following workers
home. By networking through local unions, the organizer also might
discover other information useful to the campaign. For example, if
the organizer is unfamiliar with the community, inquiries should be
made regarding religious and ethnic organizations and other citizen
groups which are sympathetic toward organized labor and which
might be the source of information on potential union activists.

Sometimes organizers attempt to conduct a "silent campaign,"
whereby the personalized approach is used to contact a handful of
union supporters who then individually contact other workers. The
committee never campaigns openly at the workplace and concen-
trates its activities on individual and small group discussions outside
the workplace. If successful, the first notification the employer has
of union activity comes from the Board announcing the filing of an
election petition. The employer may not learn the identity of organizing committee members until the union wins the ensuing election. The silent campaign can be successful provided that all employees respect the confidentiality of the campaign and do not disclose
information to the employer.

Some organizers distribute leaflets to workers as they leave or
enter the targeted workplace. The leaflet cites some advantages of
unionization and information on how to contact the organizer. An
authorization card may also be included. Rather than asking workers
to contact the organizer on an individual basis, some organizers announce the time and place of a meeting through the leaflet. This
approach tends to be used by organizers who conduct a number of
campaigns simultaneously, often for unions with wide jurisdictions.
It is a quick and relatively easy way to gauge the sentiment of the
work force toward unionization and to identify potential organizing
committee members.

Organizers attempt to recruit workers for the committee who
are well respected by their fellow employees. Because the organizer
is dealing with a group of strangers at this early stage of the campaign,
identifying these workers is not an easy task. Certain worker types
are highly visible in most workplaces and the organizer will naturally
be attracted to them. Most workplaces have consumer affairs experts
who give advice on where to shop, what to buy, and how to invest
savings. Then there are the dealers who provide hot and cool mer-

chandise at a good price. There are bookies, loan sharks, health experts, and opinion providers in the fields of religion, bigotry, and politics. There are also intellectuals, comedians, studs, and strutters. These highly visible workers might be right for the committee because they have a following among factions of the work force, but they may also turn off other workers. Campaigns have been lost when committee leadership roles were assumed by highly visible workers with ardent followers but a larger number of relatively silent workers who disapproved of the individuals on the committee. The composition of the committee, not unionization, became the deciding issue in these campaigns.

There is no formula. Chronic complainers can be identified by the reasonableness of the issues they view unionization as resolving. If their primary issues are the types that usually come under the "management's rights" clause of contracts or are not normally considered to be grievances, the organizer should be wary of recruiting these workers for the committee, because they are likely to turn against the union as the campaign progresses and make it the object of their complaints. Likewise, the organizer should avoid workers with poor work records. Employees with good work records may resent them and view the union as primarily benefiting employees who are viewed as lazy and irresponsible. In addition, employees with poor work records are the most likely to be discharged or otherwise disciplined during the campaign, so that the organizer is confronted with the difficult task of proving that the employer's action was in fact motivated by the employee's union activity. Aside from these sparse guidelines and the ideal that the committee represent all departments or sections at the workplace and be representative of the racial, ethnic, religious, sex, and skill composition of the work force, organizers generally attribute the selection of an effective committee to a combination of experience, intuition, and luck.

Some organizers do not trust their experience, intuition, and luck and do not attempt to select committee members. Instead, they invite all workers who are interested in unionization to join the committee and attempt to create a mass movement. Their logic is that selecting an effective committee is too unsure of a process and the more people involved in doing committee work, the more effective the campaign is likely to be. In addition, there is "safety in numbers" so that workers are less inclined to be intimidated by the employer when engaged in committee work. The invitation to join the committee may be issued at a meeting which was announced to workers through leaflets distributed outside the workplace.

Real differences of opinion exist among organizers on the best way to recruit in-the-workplace organizing committee members. Essentially, there are two methods:

1. Personally contacting individual workers and slowly building the committee.

2. Contacting workers in mass and inviting all who are interested in unionization to join the committee.

Part of the difference may depend on the personal style of the organizer. Some organizers feel better working with people on a one-by-one basis. Others are very comfortable on a platform in front of large groups of people. But more than personal style affects the choice of approach. The individual approach is more likely in situations where the union views the target as essential to maintaining or enhancing its collective bargaining power by reducing non-union competition. A commitment of money and personnel to a long organizing drive may be made. In these instances, distributing a leaflet that announces a union organizing meeting involves the considerable risk that few if any of the workers at the target will attend. What does the union do for an encore after announcing its intention to organize and failing to attract sufficient support at a meeting? There is no guarantee, of course, that contacting workers on an individual basis will necessarily result in more support than the mass approach.

The mass approach to contacting workers allows the organizer to gauge the sentiment of workers very quickly and to move on to another target if the effort fails to attract support. A danger is that the organizer may not make the effort to carefully select targets at which the union is likely to secure contracts and instead substitutes the relatively quick and easy method of announcing organizational meetings for careful target selection. The result may be that the union organizes workplaces where it cannot secure contracts, so that any effort saved in organizing is lost when attempting to negotiate the first contract.

Proponents of the mass approach contend that workers are already predisposed one way or the other toward unionization and that a softer sell, more personalized approach accomplishes little. To the criticism that the employer is alerted at a very early stage to the union's intentions and the identity of union supporters, proponents of the mass approach counter that the employer is bound to learn of the union's presence through the more personalized approaches and that in-the-workplace organizing committee members will be identified eventually during the long course of the campaign.

One's choice of method should be based upon which of the two methods is most successful. However, there is no factual evidence on a large-scale basis to demonstrate the effectiveness of one method over the other. Ultimately, the choice of method may be best determined by the personal style of the organizer and the amount of time and money allocated for the campaign.

Whether the personal or mass approach to contacting potential committee members is used, the means for interesting workers in joining the committee is essentially the same. If workers organize into unions over issues and the belief that group action will improve wages, benefits, and working conditions, the same may be said about why workers join organizing committees. What prevents them from joining is fear of the reactions of employers, spouses, relatives, friends, and community institutions such as churches and fraternal organizations and the hope or wishful thought that the employer will improve conditions without unionization. The organizer must address the issues, the fears, and the wishful thinking of potential committee members and demonstrate that unionization is the action they must take if they are to achieve improvement. By carefully researching the target in advance, the organizer is better prepared to make this presentation.

LIQUOR, DRUGS, SEX, AND ORGANIZING

Because an organizer is often transient, living in a motel far from home, with irregular hours, late night meetings, and lulls of inactivity, liquor, drugs, and sex sometimes pose a great temptation. Close contact with workers at the organizing target is a necessary and important ingredient of successful campaigns. The temptation to include liquor, drugs, and sex in the process can be strong.

Whether liquor, drugs, and sex are vices or virtues lies with the beholder and that is the problem. Some workers employed at organizing targets view them as vices and a reputation as a "boozer," "doper," or "quick fly" or "spread artist" can ruin organizing drives. Organizers' codes of conduct include "don't fall in love" and "open the bottle in the motel room." If liquor, drugs, and sex are viewed as virtues by the organizer, fine. Just make sure they are kept out of the campaign.

DIAGRAMMING THE WORKPLACE

Whether the organizer takes the personalized approach or the mass approach to forming the organizing committee, detailed diagrams of the workplace must be constructed. The only difference is timing. With the personalized approach, the diagrams will be constructed slowly as the organizer contacts individual workers. With the mass approach, the organizer will begin constructing the diagrams at the first meeting of workers interested in unionization and will continue the process through contacts with representatives of individual departments or sections.

Diagramming the workplace has three primary objectives:

1. Preparing for the election unit determination made by the Board. (See chapter 2 for a fuller discussion of the issues involved in this process.)

2. Assuring that committee members are able to contact workers in all departments or sections of the workplace.

3. Identifying all eligible voters so that support of unionization can be tracked throughout the organizing drive.

The initial step is to construct an overall diagram of the workplace, paying particular attention to employee entrances and public access sidewalks and roads in the event that the organizer chooses to distribute leaflets. Exhibit 5–1 is an overall diagram for a mortgage company's regional branch office with a potentially organizable work force of approximately fifty employees. The diagram discloses that the targeted employees, except for administrative secretaries, enter and exit from a single parking lot off of a main highway with a narrow shoulder. If leafleting is to occur safely with a minimum of inconvenience to employees, it is best conducted on the employer's premises by organizing committee members.

EXHIBIT 5–1. Diagram of Work Site

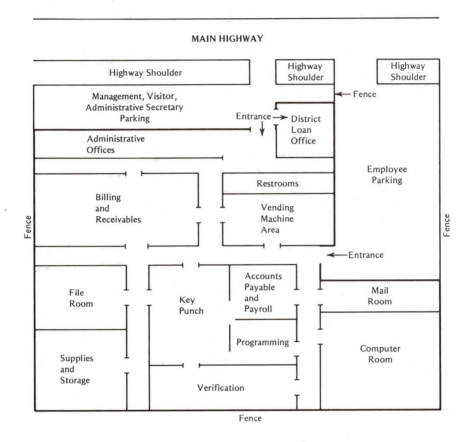

Starting times:	Keypunch and Computer Room at 8 a.m. All others at 9 a.m.	
Quitting times:	Keypunch and Computer Room at 4:30 p.m. All others at 5:30 p.m.	
Rest Periods:	Fifteen minutes in the morning and afternoon. No set schedule as to when taken.	
Lunch Periods:	Noon to 12:30 p.m. Employees allowed to leave workplace. Some do. Usually go to fast-food restaurant next door.	
Number of shifts:	One	

Starting times, quitting times, rest breaks, and lunch periods for each department or section should also be noted, because these are times when organizing committee members can communicate with other workers. If employees leave the workplace during the workday, this should be noted. If there is more than one shift, this should be determined, because diagrams should be constructed for each shift.

The Board's determination of the overall election unit, specifically whether certain departments will be excluded from the election unit and whether this workplace will be coupled with other workplaces operated by the employer, depends upon the "community of interest" between departments and the employer's workplaces. The greater the interrelationship between departments and workplaces, the more likely the Board will include them in the election unit. Because the Board decides each case on its own merits, there is no set of criteria that govern the determination. As a consequence the organizer should gather as much information as possible on the employer's production process in order to make a strong case for the targeted unit.

In the particular case of the mortgage company's regional office, it is one of ten regional offices operated by the employer. Each regional office bills and collects money on loans granted by district loan offices within its region. This regional office services eighteen district loan offices in a five-state area. One of the district loan offices is located in the same building as the targeted regional office. The regional offices also pay bills incurred by the district loan offices and their payrolls. The region's personnel office is also housed at the facility. Its functions are to maintain personnel records, set salary rates for the district offices and the regional office, and approve appointments and promotions.

The organizer desires to organize all nonmanagerial and non-confidential employees at the facility. Possible objections by the employer should be anticipated and evidence gathered to support the union's position. The employer may argue that the district loan office should be excluded from the election unit because it is a separate entity even though it is located in the same building as the regional office. The organizer should cite the common parking lot, restroom, and food and beverage facilities and the centralized personnel office as evidence supporting the union's position.

The employer might argue that the establishment of personnel policies at the regional office level for both the district loan offices and the regional office establishes a community of interest which requires the union to organize all of the district offices within the region. The organizer must now demonstrate the differences between workplaces. The lack of common facilities and the wide geographical dispersion of offices can be used to substantiate the union's position.

Gathering information on the employer's operations and anticipating the employer's position are the keys to providing the Board wth information which may lead it to granting the union its desired election unit. As with unfair labor practice charges, the organizer should not expect the Board to do the union's work.

By identifying the departments within the workplace through an overall diagram of the target, the organizer is prepared to move on to the more difficult task of constructing a detailed diagram of each department. These detailed diagrams of each department or section will provide the basis for the union's position in the determination of eligible voters in the election unit, its objective of having an organizing committee member with access to each employee, and its tracking of support for and against unionization among the targeted workers. The largest department within the mortgage company's regional office is Billing and Accounts Receivable, which is diagrammed in Exhibit 5–2.

A schematic view of the department identifying the physical location and job title of each position is provided in Exhibit 5-2. A reference number for each position—1, 2, 3, etc.—is also included. The reference numbers are indexed to cards compiled on each worker. An example of a card is provided in Exhibit 5-3.

The cards are intended to personalize the organizing campaign as much as possible. Provision for the workers' names, addresses, and phone numbers is made. While the "Excelsior list" will provide this information at a later stage of the campaign, it is important to determine the identity and residence of each worker at an earlier stage, particularly if housecalls are planned. Switchboard operators, Christmas card lists, and a judicious use of the phone book can often provide this information.

The organizer, by asking the right questions of committee members representing the various departments, should determine the eligibility of each worker to vote in the election. Close relatives of the employer, professional and confidential employees, and supervisors are ineligible for Board-conducted elections. The most com-

EXHIBIT 5–2. Diagram of Billing and Accounts Receivable Department

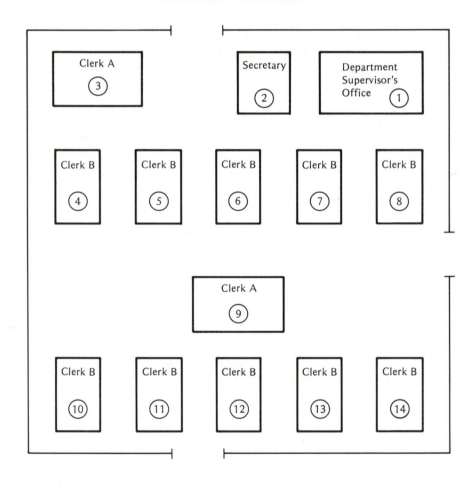

BILLING AND ACCOUNTS
RECEIVABLE DEPARTMENT

EXHIBIT 5–3. Card for Recording Employee Eligibility Data

Department: Reference No:

Name:

Address:

Phone Number:

In unit sought?   Why?

Assigned To:

Issues:

(Reverse Side)

Date:											
Prounion											
Antiunion											
Undecided											

Comments:

mon problem confronted by organizers is determining whether workers perform supervisory functions. Any worker who hires, transfers, suspends, lays off, recalls, promotes, discharges, assigns, rewards, or disciplines other workers or who has the power to do so may be viewed as a supervisor. The use of these powers must go beyond simple routine and require the exercise of "independent judgment." If the person in question exercises these powers and has his or her decisions reviewed by a supervisor, the extent of the review becomes important. If approval is merely routine, the person will be considered to be exercising supervisory powers. However, if the approving authority conducts its own independent investigation of the matter before granting approval, then the person does not exercise supervisory powers. The 4" × 6" card depicted in Exhibit 5–3 provides space for indicating the worker's eligibility for the election unit being sought.

An examination of Exhibit 5–2 indicates that there are two Clerk A positions in the Billing and Accounts Receivable Department. These workers may be functioning as supervisors, so the organizer should obtain information to resolve the issue. The view that these two employees have of unionization will naturally affect how the organizer and the employer will view their status in presentations to the Board.

The card in Exhibit 5–3 provides space for noting the organizing committee member to whom the worker is assigned and for a description of the workplace issues that this employee views as being particularly important. By discovering the concerns of workers through individual discussions with organizing committee members, the campaign can be geared to the issues most likely to gain a positive response toward unionization.

Through periodic and frequent polls of the election unit—sometimes as often as twice a week—the organizer should be able to predict the outcome of the election rather accurately. If the election looks like a loss, the campaign may be intensified in order to alter the trend, or the organizer may decide to withdraw the election petition and move on to another campaign. The reverse side of the card in Exhibit 5–3 provides space for tracking each worker's view toward unionization. Some organizers rely on signed authorization cards as the primary indication of support. This is a mistake. Workers change their positions during the course of campaigns and the organizer should be aware of these changes.

While the procedure described is time consuming, it is important to the success of the campaign and can be simplified somewhat by the use of an automated data processing system or "the computer." The AFL-CIO Department of Organization has used the computer in its Houston organizing campaign to keep track of eligible voters and can provide further information on how to implement the procedure.

EDUCATING THE COMMITTEE

Upon forming the committee, the organizer must educate its members. The only knowledge of unions and how to organize them possessed by nearly all unorganized workers is fragments of information, often inaccurate, which they have received from personal acquaintances and the media. It is best to assume that workers know nothing about unions and how to organize them.

A goal of the initial organizing committee meetings is to prepare workers to obtain authorization cards. Some organizers tell committee members at the very first meeting that they must return within a week with cards signed by a majority of employees if the campaign is to continue. Their view is that most workers are already predisposed for or against union organization and that it is important to build momentum. Also, they believe that the employer may be caught off guard. Other organizers will hold a series of meetings before asking the committee to obtain authorization cards and not impose a time limit on the committee to obtain a majority. Again, the question arises of what the organizer does for an encore if the timetable is not met and the union is committed to launching a full-scale campaign.

Organizing committee members should receive general survey information on the laws regulating organizing and very specific instructions on legal aspects which they may confront directly. They must know what they and the employer can and cannot do under the law. They must be trained to identify and, more important, to document unfair labor practices, particularly those involving discharge or other discipline for union activity. (Chapter 2 of this book should be of assistance.) Because workers cannot be expected to be legal experts, if it is at all practical, arrangements should be made for workers to have access to the organizer throughout the workday either by use of the telephone or in face-to-face meetings during breaks. Evidence supporting unfair labor practice charges should be gathered as soon as it is feasible.

The organizer should not shy away from informing committee members of the weaknesses of the law. The discharge of union supporters for union activity and the long delays encountered during Board procedures should not come as surprises. The odds are that these obstacles will be incurred; committee members should be prepared for them.

Committee members should be acquainted with the union's history and aspects of its constitution and bylaws such as dues, fines, assessments, election of officers, contract ratification, and strike authorization. Committee members themselves and the workers they contact in the process of securing authorization cards will have questions about these matters. Their interest will increase as the employer makes an issue of the union's governance system. If the union has prepared itself for these attacks by clarifying its constitution and bylaws, the task of the organizer and the committee will be easier.

The committee should be prepared for the tactics the employer will use during the campaign. Very likely, the employer's initial communications will attempt to stop the authorization card-signing drive. Committee members should be prepared to confront the threats and inaccuracies conveyed by the employer. (See the discussion in chapter 3.) Beyond this initial confrontation over authorization cards, the committee should learn about the carrot and stick tactics likely to occur throughout the campaign, efforts intended to instill loyalty and fear in workers.

After carefully selecting this target, the organizer should have identified economic and noneconomic issues which should give workers a reason to organize. In addition to conveying these issues to the organizing committee, the organizer should present an assessment of the employer's ability to pay and the likelihood that it will in fact pay. Additional issues will probably be raised by the committee and the organizer should discuss honestly the union's ability to resolve these issues.

The committee should also function as the eyes and ears of the organizer at the workplace by reporting the employer's anti-union tactics to the organizer. Copies of written materials and the essence of oral communications from supervisors should be conveyed to the organizer.

As the campaign progresses, committee members must assess the support for unionization among workers in their departments or other assigned units. They may also be asked to make house calls and distribute literature.

All of these facets of organizing committee work require education. The task of educating the committee continues throughout the entire campaign as new problems arise, fundamentals are forgotten, and mistakes are repeated. Education is a major aspect of assisting workers to organize themselves. Like the school teacher, the organizer is preparing workers to stand on their own and confront the obstacles before them. From this point on the local union is being built and its leadership developed.

CAMPAIGN MEDIA

A number of oral and written communication techniques are available to organizers. While some organizers use all of the available media, others use only one or two techniques exclusively. At least one effective organizer, for example, never issues any written communications except for a leaflet announcing the initial meeting and confines the union's campaign to meetings. Regardless of the number of techniques used, organizers generally agree that oral communication is more effective than written communication as expressed in the adage "You can't organize by leafleting at the plant gate." Within the broad categories of oral and written communications, however, there is less agreement among organizers on which specific techniques are the most effective.

Communications at the Workplace by the Organizing Committee As discussed in chapter 3, employers rely heavily upon frequent, face-to-face communications by first-line supervisors to convey anti-union messages. The in-the-workplace organizing committee can perform a similar function for the union. Two factors determine the effectiveness of this technique.

Some workplaces are more conducive to communications among workers than others. If conversations among workers while on the job are a normal part of each work day, the organizing committee has an excellent opportunity to talk union. If supervisors tend to take rest breaks and lunch with the workers whom the committee is attempting to organize, there may be little opportunity for frank discussions about unionization. The committee must contact workers at other times and places, if face-to-face communications are difficult to conduct at the workplace. Above all, the committee must be instructed not to break work rules in an attempt to converse on the job.

Employers and union avoidance consultants spend considerable time and effort training first-line supervisors to convey anti-union messages. Likewise, if the organizer is to utilize the committee effectively, its members must be trained to conduct face-to-face communications with prospective union supporters. This training is well worth the effort, because face-to-face communications by organizing committee members may be the most effective technique available to the organizer.

In addition to educating the committee about the law, the union, campaign issues, and union avoidance tactics of the employer, the organizer should assist committee members with the communication process they will use when persuading their fellow workers to support unionization. Simply telling committee members that they should be good listeners, not become belligerent when encountering resistance, and be friendly yet assertive in their approach is fine, but a more effective way of teaching these skills is to have organizing committee members practice their approach through role playing. Organizing committee members can alternate between the roles of union advocate and prospective union supporter, thereby sharpening their communication skills in a simulated environment before actually going about their task.

Some organizers demonstrate wrong ways of communicating. Demonstrations of the "shy approach" and the "hostile approach" not only entertain workers, they assist organizing committee members in developing a style with which they are comfortable and which is likely to be effective.

Housecalls are sometimes the only way to achieve face-to-face communications with potential union supporters because of a lack of opportunity to conduct such conversations at the workplace. Even when communication at the workplace is possible, visits to workers' homes are a routine part of some organizers' campaigns. Housecalls demonstrate the concern of the union for the individual worker and his or her views. A free discussion can occur in an environment where the worker does not feel threatened. The organizing campaign is individualized and each worker's particular issues and concerns are addressed.

Other organizers never include housecalls in campaigns, regardless of the degree of personal communications at the workplace. They cite a variety of reasons. Housecalls are time consuming, likely to be resented by some workers who view them as an intrusion on their personal lives and an invitation to spouses and other household residents to become involved in a personal decision, and may be a source of unnecessary controversy and social pressure in close-knit communities, particularly where the race and/or sex of the house-callers differs from that of the potential union supporters. A few organizers admit that they do not make housecalls because they do not feel comfortable entering a stranger's home. Others simply state that housecalls do not make a difference; time is better spent on other forms of communication.

If housecalls are to be part of a campaign, a decision must be made upon whom to call. Some organizers attempt to reach all workers in an election unit. Others wait for an initial indication of support for the drive as demonstrated by signed authorization cards or surveys conducted by the organizing committee. Then, if a majority of the unit indicates its support, housecalls will be restricted to union supporters in order to reinforce their support; if less than a majority is indicated, workers classified as "undecided" are also included. Some organizers restrict housecalls to workers who appear undecided about their support, so-called "fence-sitters."

Some organizers will make all housecalls by themselves or in the company of organizing committee members, while others will train and encourage committee members to make the visits on their own. While many organizers attempt to match housecallers and potential supporters on the bases of age, race, national origin, and sex, others contend that such match-ups are unnecessary and may even be self-defeating. As evidence, they will cite instances of opposites attracting, men being more effective with women than women, blacks being more effective with whites than whites, and the exact opposites of these relationships.

Where activists from other locals of the union reside in the same geographic area as workers at the organizing target, some organizers have the union activists make housecalls. Often, the union activists and the targeted workers have children in the same schools or similar community concerns. These "neighborly chats" can evolve into discussions of union organizing.

No agreement exists on whether appointments for housecalls should be made by telephoning in advance or whether housecalls should be made without advance notice. By calling in advance, potential supporters have the opportunity to say "no," which can spare the caller from unpleasant confrontations on the front porch. In addition, by calling in advance, potential supporters are more likely to make provisions for children and television sets to be quiet so that purposeful discussions can occur. Setting up appointments also saves time that would be lost by calling on potential supporters who are not home. On the other hand, a major reason for not making appointments is that workers may be more inclined to say "no" to someone on the telephone than to a person at their front doors.

Regardless of whether or not appointments are made, calls upon complete strangers should be avoided. If the worker has signed an authorization card or has been contacted by an organizing committee member at work, there is a premise for the call—"discuss further" or "got your name from"—and a greater likelihood that the housecall will be well received.

The rule for actual conduct of housecalls is "bright, brief, and begone." While an exchange of small talk (sports, weather, etc.) might be necessary to get the conversation rolling, get to the point of the visit. Be prepared to address issues of particular concern to this worker and to answer questions. Where a union is conducting housecalls simultaneously by a number of organizers or committee members, some organizers will station experienced union officials at a telephone bank so that answers to unanticipated questions can be provided quickly. This is an especially good tactic in large unit campaigns during the time immediately preceding an authorization election.

Do not get into arguments. If a worker is against the union, arguing probably will not change his or her mind and can turn a rather quiet opponent into a vocal adversary of unionization who may cause a great deal of damage.

If a worker is leaning toward support of the union, but not entirely committed, a follow-up call is usually made. In addition to asking union supporters to sign authorization cards, they are often invited to join the organizing committee. Working with the committee can solidify a worker's support. Having been bright and brief, it is time to begone.

Mass Meetings can be an effective technique for persuading workers to support unionization. Union supporters can be energized by the demonstration of numerical strength and enthusiasm and become more resolute in their support. Likewise, workers who are undecided about supporting unionization may be moved by the demonstration of strength and enthusiasm to get on the bandwagon, their fears of employer retaliation and negative consequences of unionization allayed. These are the desired effects of mass meetings.

However, mass meetings can have an opposite effect and impede the momentum of the campaign. Attendance may be sparse with the consequence of conveying the impression to workers at the meeting and those who hear about it the next day that the union has little support. The meeting can consist of boring, long-winded speeches which fail to engender the desired enthusiasm and fail to answer the questions workers have about this bold action of forming a union. Achieving the desired results and avoiding the negative consequences requires careful preparation.

The organizer should assure that the meeting is well attended. Simply passing out a leaflet announcing the meeting is not as effective as personal, face-to-face invitations from organizing committee members who can then report the anticipated attendance to the organizer. The day, time, and place of the meeting should be planned with the organizing committee. The meeting should not conflict with bowling night, the opening day of smelt fishing season, or a favorite television show and should not be held at a location such as a tavern, fraternal club, or church which some workers might be hesitant about entering. Sometimes a meeting right after work at a public park with a picnic pavilion, in case of rain, and a large parking lot is the best choice.

The size of the meeting place should fit the anticipated crowd with the guideline being that it is better for the room to be too small than too large, because a respectable turnout can look small in too large of a room. Some organizers schedule meetings in rooms with portable dividers so that they can make last-minute changes in the room size as the crowd develops. The sound system and ventilation should be adequate as should be the parking.

Serving refreshments can be a good idea, but alcoholic beverages might offend some people. In addition, some organizers have had bad experiences where workers got into fights after a few drinks and the organizing drives never fully recovered. It is best to avoid serving alcohol.

The organizer should consider attempting to get coverage of the meeting by local television and radio stations and newspapers. In some communities, the meeting will be viewed as newsworthy. Media coverage can add legitimacy to the campaign and contribute to the bandwagon effect. If media coverage will be attempted, it is advisable to put signs and banners around the meeting place so that photographers and television camera operators have some good visuals with which to enliven pictures.

Getting the media to cover the event is not always successful and depends on such factors as competing news stories and media managements' views of unions. If media coverage is desired, a press release should be issued about a week before the meeting. The press release should be about a page in length and include the five W's—who, what, when, where, and why—and the name and phone number of a person to be contacted for further information. About a day before the meeting, follow up the press release with a phone call to each radio and television station and newspaper. It is best not to exaggerate the size of the crowd, because while exaggeration may get coverage for the event, the media will be reluctant to cover future events.

Before the media arrives, it is best to designate a few union supporters as spokespersons. Have them rehearse what they will say about the purpose of the meeting. As soon as reporters arrive, introduce them to the spokespersons.

The agenda for the meeting should serve the purposes of solidifying the support of workers already in favor of unionization and gaining the support of workers who are undecided. Speakers at the meeting might include members of the organizing committee, the organizer, officials of the international union, a local union, or an AFL-CIO body, and community supporters such as well respected clergy and politicians. Speeches should be short and to the point so that sufficient time is available for questions and answers.

To get the question and answer period going, it is a good idea to have union supporters ask questions that are likely to be bothersome to workers who are undecided about their support. "What about stikes and strikebreakers replacing us?" "What about fines and assessments?" Do not be squeamish. The employer is likely to raise these issues, if it has not already. The mass meeting is a good time to address these difficult issues head-on for all to hear.

Small Group Meetings lie somewhere between mass meetings and house calls as an organizing campaign communication tool. They are often held at workers' homes, hence, they are sometimes referred to as "house parties." The meetings are often limited to a specific group of workers with particular concerns. Black, Hispanic, or Oriental workers, women, and certain occupational groups or departments within a workplace may have particular concerns such as discrimination, health and safety, skilled wage differentials, and occupational mobility which are best addressed by a small group meeting format.

A danger of small group meetings is that the organizer and the organizing committee may be accused of making secret deals with factions of the work force. It is best to make no secret of the small group meeting, to assume that everything discussed at the meeting will be learned by the employer and members of the election unit not in attendance, and to make no commitments that the union is unlikely to fulfill.

Telephone Calls are the least personal form of oral communication but can be an effective technique. They are most effective when the caller and the person called know each other. If the campaign is being conducted by a relatively large organizing committee which is fairly representative of the work force, telephone calls can be conducted rather easily and can be a good substitute for communications at workplaces where face-to-face conversations are difficult to conduct.

Because telephone calls intrude upon workers' personal lives, discretion should be exercised. As with housecalls and other forms of communication conducted by the organizing committee, the organizer should provide training on how to be bright, brief, and be-gone.

Advertising on radio and television and in newspapers is used during organizing campaigns under special circumstances. Where a union or coalition of unions is interested in organizing extensively within a geographic area, advertising about unions and their accomplishments can be a good way of educating and influencing workers. However, if workers at the organizing target comprise a small portion of the total work force in a geographic region, advertising is a very inefficient way of reaching workers at the target, because advertising rates are established on the basis of the total audience reached and the union is in effect paying for its message being received by a large number of people who are not involved in the campaign.

In small communities, radio ads are relatively cheap. If there are only a couple of stations in town, ads at the morning and afternoon "drive times" can reach a large portion of the electorate. Advertisements in the media should be used with discretion.

Leaflets or Handbills are a quick and relatively easy way to communicate with many workers at the same time. Whether they are an effective form of communication, however, is not as certain among organizers. Some organizers who regularly handbill say that leaflets are not an effective way of communicating the union's messages and are used only to demonstrate to workers that the union is actively working to win the election. Between the extremes of organizers who never distribute a leaflet and those who handbill nearly every day of the campaign, there are organizers who selectively handbill only certain "news" such as unfair labor practice charges and Board decisions. Others use handbills only in conjunction with direct oral communication techniques like housecalls and contacts by organizing committee members on the job. The leaflets provide a script for the direct contacts and make the task of inexperienced organizing committee members a bit easier.

There are basically two types of leaflets. Many international unions have "canned" leaflets which tend to be rather general in their messages, yet very eye appealing because they appear to have been composed by graphic arts professionals. They require little work by the organizer other than duplication and distribution. Some organizers view these as too general in content and "too slick" in appearance and never use them. Others confine their use to initial leaflet distributions during each campaign, as an introduction to the union.

Most organizers who handbill extensively prefer the second type, leaflets that they develop themselves for each campaign. These leaflets address issues specific to a campaign and while carefully planned, tend to be amateurish in appearance—what one would expect from an organizing committee comprised of workers.

If extensive leafleting is planned, arrangements should be made with a union printer, so that the "union bug" can be affixed to the printed material. Make sure to ask for the union label, because the printer may not automatically include it. Failure to use a union printer can weaken efforts to gain the assistance of other unions and central labor bodies during the campaign and ensuing contract negotiations. Calls to local printing unions will yield the names of organized printers and can sometimes result in a discount price. In addition to a union contract, select one that will guarantee a rapid turnaround time, because important developments in the campaign become stale news when leaflets are delayed by the printer. One way of cutting costs is to ask the printer if he has any unused paper stock he is willing to sell at a discount.

Leaflets should be short, to the point, and easy to comprehend. A guideline used by some organizers is a message that can be read in fifteen seconds while the recipient is walking. Anything longer is viewed as unlikely to be read. Other organizers aim for simply a "reasonable" length.

A leaflet should be appealing to the eye. Pictures, particularly of organizing committee members, cartoons, and other graphics are a good idea. Stationery and office supply stores can provide stencils and transfers with which to make the handbills clear, neat, and interesting. Make the print large enough for workers with vision problems to read. Also, using colored paper can help make the recipient want to read the handbill.

The message of the leaflet should not be complicated, or if it is complicated, it should be simple. Use short sentences. Remember that an estimated one out of every five adult Americans is functionally illiterate. If a substantial portion of the work force has a native tongue other than English, do the handbill in English on one side and in the foreign language on the other side. The leaflet should inform, explain, and convince the audience. Do not rely on emotional appeals; state the facts which the survey of wages, benefits, and working conditions demonstrate. Emphasize the issues and the path toward improvement. Limit the message to one or at most two issues, because the message is to be read and digested in a short time span.

Bad leaflets are sloppy, inaccurate, or overly complicated. Copies of union contract provisions distributed as handbills tend to be

overly complicated. Amateurish drawings, poor grammar, obscenities, and reproduction on second class printing equipment make a
bad impression. Failure to proofread might result in a leaflet with
the slogan, "You can live with the (union) but not as well."

A simple guideline for composing leaflets is to view the process
in five parts:

1. **Open Space.** The leaflet should not be crowded in appearance.
   Crowding might make it seem too formidable to the recipient
   to read in a short time span. Open space makes the leaflet more
   eye appealing.

2. **Headline.** Summarize the leaflet's message in a few words and
   put the headline in bold print. Some examples: WATCH OUT
   FOR ILLEGAL TACTICS, FIRING ILLEGAL—WORKER
   REINSTATED, COMPANY'S WAGES LAG, WHAT IF WE
   HAD A UNION, VOTE TOMORROW. The headline should
   catch the reader's attention. In addition to the headline, or
   instead of a headline, a GRAPHIC—photograph, cartoon, line
   drawing—can be used to catch the reader's attention.

3. **Message.** This is the heart of the leaflet. Try it out on organizing
   committee members before having it printed. If they have questions, miss the point, or are not persuaded by it, go back to the
   drawing board and try again. Address only one or two issues,
   and make it simple.

4. **Action.** What do you want the reader to do? VOTE UNION,
   SIGN AN AUTHORIZATION CARD TODAY, and RE-
   PORT VIOLATIONS OF THE LAW are examples of actions
   that leaflets urge workers to take. The action being urged gives
   the leaflet a purpose.

5. **Authorship.** From whom does the leaflet come? Early in the
   campaign, the organizer may be the source. Later, the organizing
   committee, "we," should be the source of handbills. Making
   the transition from "you" to "we" is important, if workers are
   to organize themselves.

In planning the layout for a handbill, one can assign space to
the five parts in a manner similar to that in Exhibit 5–4. From the
top of the page to the bottom, the five parts follow in sequence. To
give variety to leaflets, the order in which the parts are presented
can be altered. For example, the authorship might be at the top of

EXHIBIT 5–4. Sample Union Leaflet

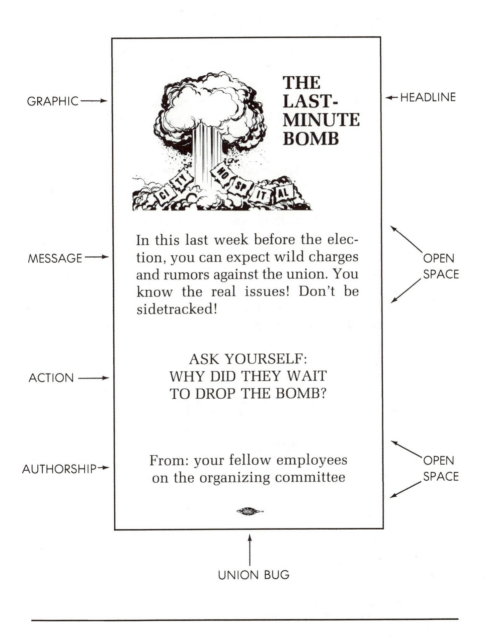

the page (e.g., From the Organizing Committee), followed by the action, followed by the message and headline. The important point is to include the four parts and plenty of open space.

Organizers differ as to when is the best time to distribute leaflets. Some prefer distributing leaflets as employees enter the workplace on the premise that they can discuss its message among themselves. Others believe that some workers do not take leaflets into the workplace, because they fear retaliation by the employer and, therefore, prefer to handbill as workers leave for home. Still others distribute leaflets at both times, often distributing the intial leaflets of the campaign as workers leave the job and, after the campaign builds momentum, handbilling as workers enter the job.

Surveys are used to communicate with unorganized workers for a number of reasons. Surveys can communicate that unions operate on democratic principles by seeking the views of the workers they represent and those whom they attempt to represent. In addition, a survey can force unorganized workers to examine the wages, benefits and working conditions at their places of employment and may lead them to conclude that the only path to improvement is unionization. Also, surveys can provide information on workplace issues to organizers and organizing committees. These issues can in turn provide the basis for organizing campaigns.

Exhibit 5–5 is a sample survey which addresses issues thought to be important at an early stage of the campaign. Not only does the survey seek the views of workers, it is intended to inform workers of conditions with which they may be unaware, such as the employer's compensation policy and average pension benefits.

Surveys can be distributed as workers leave the workplace for home. The results of the survey should be reported to workers. As additional issues surface during the campaign, they can also be communicated by the survey technique.

Letters to the homes of election unit members are sometimes used in campaigns. If the campaign progresses as planned, the names and addresses of workers will be obtained far in advance of the "Excelsior list" so that housecalls and letters can be an integral part of the drive shortly after its initiation. Sometimes letters are sent that simply thank workers for signing authorization cards. In other cases, letters include messages that are longer and more complicated than those

EXHIBIT 5–5. Union Survey

This survey is intended to measure the attitudes of XYZ Company employees toward their working conditions. Based upon the results of this survey, the union will develop a platform of proposed changes which will be negotiated with the employer. Replies are strictly confidential. Please enclose the completed survey in the attached stamped, self-addressed envelope and mail today.

1. Does the employer "play favorites" when disciplining workers for the violation of work rules?
   _____ Almost Always   _____ Sometimes   _____ Never

2. Are promotions made without due regard to merit and on the basis of "office politics"?
   _____ Almost Always   _____ Sometimes   _____ Never

3. Do you think that some employees are afraid to use the company's grievance procedure because they will be branded as "troublemakers"?
   _____ Yes   _____ No

4. Are workers sometimes afraid to admit that they cannot complete a task in the allocated time and to ask for overtime with the result that they skip breaks and take work home? _____ Yes   _____ No

5. Do you believe that the company could fire you through no fault of your own and for no good reason? _____ Yes   _____ No

6. Do you believe that the company's "merit pay adjustment" system has treated you fairly? _____ Yes   _____ No

7. Do you believe that XYZ Company employees deserve higher wages than those provided by other Twin City employers (XYZ's acknowledged compensation policy), because XYZ employees are more productive and XYZ is more profitable than other Twin City companies? _____ Yes   _____ No

8. Do you believe that the $200 deductible for each family member under the medical insurance plan is fair? _____ Yes   _____ No

9. Do you believe that the $150 per month average pension benefit after twenty years of service will allow you to live your retirement years in dignity?
   _____ Yes   _____ No

10. Do you believe that there are health and safety problems in a modern office like that at XYZ, which are not being corrected? _____ Yes   _____ No

in leaflets on the premise that workers have more time to read and digest material arriving at their homes than that contained in leaflets distributed at the workplace.

Some unions like to involve spouses and other household residents in the worker's decision to organize and send letters for this purpose. Other unions and organizers do not send letters for precisely this reason. They believe that there is a body of workers who does not care to get involved in long, sometimes emotional discussions with spouses and other family members about unionization. Avoiding the "nag effect" can be a good reason not to send letters to the home.

Union Buttons, T-Shirts, Bumper Stickers and other insignia do not lend themselves to extensive messages because of space limitations, yet they can be important forms of communication. They can convey a sense of safety in numbers to union supporters and can become fashionable, "the thing to do," with the effect of transforming a group of workers with little in common except for their employment at a particular workplace into a mass movement with a common goal.

While the Board prohibits employers from limiting the right of workers to wear union insignia except in cases where the insignia pose a safety hazard, the organizer should exercise discretion. Distributing large buttons or T-shirts to workers who normally wear dress shirts and blouses, for example, is not appropriate. Small, tasteful buttons are more appropriate.

THE UNION MESSAGE

Upon identifying or targeting the audience most likely to be receptive to the product being offered, good salespeople convey to potential customers a message with two parts. Naturally, they tell customers about the positive aspects of the product in relation to other products—cleaner, faster, more economical, etc., than the competition. Second, they try to anticipate and neutralize the doubts that customers may have about purchasing the product. This is the function of cancellation provisions, warranties, and money-back guarantees.

When selling newspaper subscriptions, for example, I start my telephone sales pitch by emphasizing the glories of a two-week free subscription, particularly the money that can be saved by reading the advertisements and clipping the coupons, because in these hard economic times most consumers are concerned about their budgets and clip coupons. Appealing to the person's need to know the news is not too effective, because television, radio, and magazines can do as good or a better job than newspapers. But they cannot provide the wide array of advertisements and money-saving coupons available in newspapers.

Before the potential subscriber has a chance to utter a word, I anticipate and attempt to neutralize the doubts he or she may have about this wonderful deal. Initially, I told people that they were under no obligation to continue the subscription. That message worked some of the time. Then, I thought to myself about how one cancels the subscription after the two-week free trial. I started telling people that they could write on their bill that they did not wish to continue and mail the bill back to the company. That message improved sales, but then I thought about the bother of writing on the bill, getting a stamp, and making sure that the letter is mailed.

Most subscriptions to the *Minneapolis Star* and *Tribune* are prepaid, meaning that one pays in advance for the newspapers one will receive. At today's rates, the newspaper collects hefty interest on these prepayments and carriers like myself are spared the problems of collecting. So, the message became, "If you don't want to continue, all you have to do is disregard the bill and the *Star-Tribune* won't deliver after two weeks, because subscriptions are prepaid and they won't deliver to anyone who hasn't paid." This message neutralizes doubts most effectively; sales improved dramatically.

Convincing workers to form a union is much more complicated and involves a more serious decision than the process of selling newspaper subscriptions, but the principle is the same. Union organizing campaigns must convey two types of messages: (1) They must demonstrate that workers will be better able to resolve workplace issues of wages, benefits, and working conditions by forming a union and (2) they must anticipate and neutralize the doubts that workers have about forming unions before these fears and loyalties to the status quo are kindled by the employer.

Getman, Goldberg, and Herman's study of thirty-three union organizing drives discloses that unions did a good job of presenting the reasons why workers should organize and a mediocre job of anticipating and neutralizing the objections to unionization. In nearly all of the campaigns, unions said that they would prevent unfairness by setting up a grievance procedure and seniority system and would improve wages and fringe benefits. Unions substantiated these claims in about 70 percent of the campaigns by demonstrating the gains that they had made in negotiated contracts. However, in only about one half of the campaigns did unions tell workers that the employer would attempt to frighten them from supporting the union, that union leaders are selected by the members, and that strikes can only be authorized by a vote of the membership. Likewise, in only about half the campaigns were workers advised of their legal rights to engage in union activity and of the illegal actions that employers might take against them. Also, the issue of plant closings was seldom addressed even though this was one of the most potent messages conveyed by employers.[1]

Failure to address issues like strikes and plant closings ignores the realities of organizing campaigns in the 1980s. There are enough books published and enough lawyers and consultants available to know that any employer worth organizing knows or can easily find out about anti-union tactics. Certainly the same themes recur in campaign after campaign; seldom is there a surprise. Addressing and neutralizing anti-union messages before they are voiced by the employer puts the union on the offensive and in the position of making the employer's campaign appear stale and without substance. The union's image as an honest and forthright organization is also enhanced. Also, workers have greater confidence and a feeling of power if they know what will occur during the campaign.

The rest of this section consists of messages which unions should communicate during campaigns. By no means is it intended to be a comprehensive guide, because campaigns differ. In some campaigns the same messages will have to be repeated over and over again in varying forms before they are received by workers. For example, workers sometimes find it difficult to believe that their wages, benefits, and working conditions are so much less than those of organized workers that the organizer must go so far as arranging for on-site inspections by influential workers among the group of skeptics. In other campaigns, the key issues of the campaign are so readily understood that buzz words like "dignity," "respect," and "a voice" are sufficient to convey the union's message without a thorough discussion of specifics. Likewise, in some campaigns the employer is viewed by workers as so lacking in credibility that all anti-union messages are received with great skepticism, while in others the employer's views are carefully weighed. Despite these differences, the basic thrust of every campaign should be to demonstrate the advantages of organizing and to neutralize the objections likely to be raised by the employer.

Improvements in Wages, Benefits, and Working Conditions Are Dependent upon Unionization The most frequently used message by employers and the message remembered most by workers in the thirty-three organizing campaigns studies by Getman, Goldberg, and Herman is that improvements in wages, fringe benefits, and working conditions are not dependent upon unionization. A major thrust of the union's campaign must be to dispel this proposition. The extensive information gathered on the target by the process examined in chapter 4 provides both the basis for launching the campaign and the rationale for convincing workers that unionization is the path, indeed the only path, to resolving workplace issues.

The next two messages most frequently used by employers are that wages are good and equal to or better than under union contracts and that the cost of union dues outweighs the benefits to be gained. Again, the information provided by the target selection process provides the rationale for persuading workers that wages and other aspects of employment are indeed better in a union organized workplace than in one remaining unorganized and that union dues yield a significant return on "investment."

The union's messages on the advantages of unionization should go beyond a mere comparison of union and non-union conditions of employment in order to be most effective. Union organizers and employers know that workers are likely to organize if two conditions exist: (1) workers are dissatisfied with wages, fringe benefits, and working conditions, and (2) workers believe that unionization can resolve these issues. The organizer should anticipate that if the existence of the issues is indisputable, the employer will concentrate on demonstrating that unionization will not resolve the issues through claims of inability to pay. The consequences of inability to pay and "excessive" union demands—layoffs and plant closures—will at least be implied. Also, the employer is likely to convey another often used message: "Unionization may lead to a loss of current benefits."

Where a thorough examination of the target as outlined in the previous chapter has been conducted, the issues of the campaign are identified and the employer's ability to pay is assessed. Communications of organizing issues should include three factors:

1. **The issue.** "Pensions are only $50 per month after 25 years of service." "The grievance procedure is ineffective as demonstrated by . . . ."

2. **The union comparison.** "Pensions in Local 75's contract are $100 per month after 25 years of service." "Local 75's contract has a grievance procedure with a last step of final and binding arbitration by a neutral third party."

3. **The employer's ability to pay.** "Our employer has a return on its investment that is among the top 25 percent for firms in the industry according to Standard and Poor's." "Would the Last National Bank loan money for plant expansion if they did not believe the firm is profitable? Would the employer borrow money at 15 percent interest to expand and hire new employees if it did not believe that this plant is profitable?"

Discussions with union organizers and examinations of leaflets distributed in organizing campaigns indicate that nearly all organizers include the first two of the three factors—the issue and the union comparison. Inclusion of the third factor—ability to pay—is not nearly as frequent with the result that employers can and often do persuade workers that substandard wages, benefits, and working conditions exist because of inability to pay. By their own admission, many organizers do not assess ability to pay.

The Law Protects the Worker's Right to Organize   The workers should be informed of their right to organize and be advised of actions by the employer which are prohibited under the law. Because the law is very complicated, it is impossible to relate all of the possible configurations these violations might take. Above all else, workers should be advised to promptly contact members of the organizing committee or the organizer whenever they have any indication of a possible violation by the employer. This message may take the form of an "Unorganized Worker's Bill of Rights," shown in Exhibit 5–6.

"Don't Be Surprised, If . . ."   Workers at the organizing target should be prepared for the media which the employer is likely to

---

EXHIBIT 5–6. Unorganized Worker's Bill of Rights

1. Workers have the right to talk about forming a union during rest periods and lunch breaks.

2. Workers have the right to refuse to tell their supervisor, another manager, or a lawyer or consultant hired by the employer whether they support the union.

3. Workers who support the union cannot be punished because of their support. Examples of unlawful punishment are denial of a promotion, denial of overtime, transfer to an undesirable job or one that isolates the supporter from other workers, discharge, and any other action that is based on the worker's union support.

4. Supervisors, other managers, lawyers, and consultants cannot *threaten* to punish workers because they support the union.

5. Workers cannot be *promised* that they will receive some benefit like a promotion or raise if they do not support the union.

6. Members of management, lawyers, and consultants cannot spy on union meetings or observe who attends union meetings.

7. Workers cannot be asked to work against the union.

---

use during the campaign. They should know that

1. Top management or a lawyer or consultant hired by the employer will probably instruct first-line supervisors to conduct face-to-face conversations with an anti-union theme on a regular basis with employees. These anti-union messages do not necessarily represent the actual views of supervisors, because they have their orders and can be disciplined for not following instructions.

2. The employer will probably conduct meetings during working hours for the purpose of convincing workers not to support the union. Just before the election, one of these meetings is quite likely to be held. A "big bomb" might be dropped in the form of some issue not previously addressed during the campaign. The reason for the last-minute "big bomb" is that the union has limited time to respond. Workers should be prepared for the "big bomb."

3. Meetings outside the workplace might also be held. Attendance at these meetings is "voluntary." Dinner, refreshments, or other

inducements to attend might be offered. Spouses and special friends might also be invited. Workers should think about just how "voluntary" their attendance is at employer-conducted meetings relative to meetings conducted by the union.

4.   The employer may send "personal" letters to employees' homes. Sometimes it takes a union organizing campaign for the employer to demonstrate its "personal" concern for the welfare of employees.

5.   In addition to the personal letters, there will probably be pamphlets, leaflets, articles in the employer's newspaper, posters, and bulletin board postings conveying anti-union messages. During the election campaign, the employer's communications will focus on the union and little else.

6.   Gimmicks may be used to convey the anti-union message. Play money representing union dues, two paychecks (one for union dues), raffles, and other devices may be used to divert attention from the real issues in the campaign.

7.   In addition to these types of communications from the employer, these same devices may be used by a "vote-no committee," a "committee of loyal employees" or a "concerned citizens committee" from the community. Their concern will be so great that they will spend money out of their own pockets to convey anti-union messages.

8.   Rumors may be started. While it may be difficult to determine just who started them, workers should not keep rumors to themselves or pass them on to fellow workers, but should be encouraged to bring them to the attention of union organizers and organizing committee members.

Neutralizing Supervisors   Workers should be alerted that the anti-union statements of first-line supervisors are the most potent communication tool available to employers and that these statements are orchestrated by top management and do not necessarily represent the true views of supervisors. Inform workers that supervisors can be fired for failing to make anti-union statements. By questioning the commitment of supervisors to preventing unionization, workers may be more inclined to disregard these communications, particularly from supervisors whose leadership is respected by workers.

Organizing committee members should also consider confronting supervisors directly in an effort to undermine their enthusiasm for the anti-union campaign. Supervisors lack job security, and are subject to dismissal for no reason. Some unions negotiate contracts that maintain the seniority rights of supervisors and provide them with the right to reenter the bargaining unit if they are forced or choose to leave management. Confronted with this possiblity, some supervisors may view unionization to be to their advantage.

If fringe benefits are an important campaign issue and the benefits received by supervisors are similar to those received by election unit members, it should not be difficult to convince supervisors that they will share in improvements gained by the union. If supervisors have expressed discontent about their salaries or salary increases, they should be able to perceive that union-negotiated wage increases will ultimately benefit them as the employer attempts to maintain a differential between supervisory and nonsupervisory personnel so as to retain the loyalty and morale of supervisors and provide an incentive for workers to enter supervision.

Along with the threat of dismissal for failure to actively pursue the anti-union campaign, the employer will attempt to convince supervisors that they will lose the power to manage. Because there is no penalty imposed by the law for top management lying to supervisors, they may be told that they will be unable to discipline workers, that good relationships with workers will necessarily become hostile, that they will lose flexibility, and that they will find it more difficult to attain production standards. The organizing committee should consider showing supervisors the "management's rights clauses" in contracts negotiated by the union at other workplaces and explaining the true nature of the steward system and grievance procedure in most collective bargaining relationships. The thoughtful and fair supervisor loses little power when unionization occurs and may gain improved wages, benefits, and job security.

Portraying supervisors, particularly well-respected ones, as having their "orders" when they conduct anti-union conversations, and selling supervisors on the benefits that may accrue to them through unionization can be effective ways of neutralizing the employer's most effective communication tool. Some organizers go a step further and contact supervisors away from the workplace. In fact, these are the only housecalls one organizer makes. No threats are made. Supervisors are simply asked to stop pushing workers against the union. Some comply with the request. Rather than simply reacting to the daily anti-union activities of first-line supervisors, the union should take the initiative by attempting to neutralize supervisors at an early stage of the campaign.

The Nature of Collective Bargaining   The employer is likely to emphasize that collective bargaining does not require it to agree to the union's demands and that a contract specifying a reduction in current wages and benefits may indeed be negotiated. The union should emphasize its analysis of wages and benefits at the target compared with those in union contracts and the employer's ability to pay higher wages and benefits. Without collective bargaining, the employer has been able to shortchange workers, while a substantial improvement in wages and benefits is likely with collective bargaining. Would employees ratify a contract calling for a reduction in wages and benefits without the employer demonstrating to their satisfaction that cuts are necessary?

The Truth About Strikes   The strike issue should be diffused by educating workers about the following facts:

1.   The employer will probably attempt to scare workers by stressing strikes as a reason for not supporting the union.

2.   The media focuses attention on strikes but seldom views the preponderance of contracts settled without a strike as newsworthy.

3.   There are approximately 195,000 union contracts in the United States. Ninety-eight percent of contract negotiations are settled without a strike.

4.   Union members vote on whether or not to strike. In order to strike, a proportion of the voting membership stipulated in the union's constitution and bylaws must vote to strike. A strike may also require approval of the international union. A strike is not taken lightly and no one can force workers to strike.

The Arbitration Offer   In order to counteract use of the strike issue by employers, some organizers offer to submit the initial contract negotiation to binding arbitration by a third party neutral. If the target has been selected by the comprehensive target selection process outlined in chapter 4, the union should have a high degree of certainty that if the offer is accepted, the resolution of organizing issues will occur. The offer will not be accepted, but the union can dramatize the point that strikes often occur because of unreasonableness by employers.

Members Elect Union Representatives Employers depict unions as "outsiders" and as undemocratic. Workers should know that union representatives are elected by the membership and, therefore, have a motivation to be responsive to those whom they represent.

Members Decide Contract Proposals and Ratify Contracts Unions provide workers with a voice at the workplace. First of all, the union's program in collective bargaining is determined by the membership through meetings and surveys. Second, members of the local union are elected to the bargaining committee to assure that the will of the membership is carried out. Third, all union members have a vote in ratifying the contract or electing representatives who ratify the contract. With this participation of each union member at each of the three steps of the collective bargaining process, how can unions be viewed as outsiders?

Plant Closing Unlikely Where a plant closing is rumored or hinted at by the employer, some organizers challenge the employer to "guarantee" this outcome, knowing that such a threat would constitute a serious unfair labor practice. Whether this is the most effective way of reducing the fears of employees over a plant closure is uncertain. If the organizer determines that the employer is profitable through the information gathered during the target selection process, a more assertive approach to the issue may be appropriate.

Plant closings are costly, not only to workers, but to employers. The organizer should consider tackling the issue head-on by informing workers at the outset of the campaign that the threat of a plant closing may be an issue in the campaign but that the evidence indicates that a closing is unlikely because of the costs that would be borne by the employer. These costs include building a new facility and training inexperienced workers. Where the union has succeeded at organizing runaway shops, the organizer should use these examples to demonstrate that the employer does not necessarily escape unionization. So why not pay workers fair wages and benefits and provide reasonable working conditions at the present location?

Dues and Initiation Fees Waived The employer is likely to make an issue of dues and initiation fees. Some unions waive initiation fees for all workers at newly organized workplaces and do not require dues to be paid until a contract is negotiated. Dues are portrayed as an investment upon which workers will draw "interest" in the form of higher wages and better fringe benefits. "You will only have to make your dues investment when you start drawing interest."

Purpose of Dues Many organizers inform workers how dues income is spent by the union. The portion received by the international union is spent on full-time union representatives who help local unions negotiate contracts and settle grievances, on lawyers who represent the union in court cases, on researchers who assist the union in negotiations, on a newspaper which keeps members informed, and on a strike fund. The portion received by the local is spent in a manner determined by the local's membership. These expenditures may include the cost of arbitration, education of union officers and members, and the cost of conducting meetings.

Employer Dues Where wages and benefits are less than those at union organized workplaces, the differences can be portrayed as "employer dues"—what workers are paying to the employer for being unorganized. These "employer dues" are usually far more than the union dues.

Fines and Assessments Employers too often give the impression that workers will be fined and assessed to death. Some unions have never had fines or assessments during their entire histories, while in most others these additional costs of union membership have occurred infrequently and for very justifiable reasons. Rather than waiting for the employer to make an issue of fines and assessments and then defending the union's record, the credibility of the union will be enhanced by frankly discussing the issue and diffusing it before the employer has the opportunity to create doubts.

Union Corruption Employers often use a broad brush stroke to paint all unions as corrupt and, by association, the specific union conducting the organizing drive. The union should not get into a mud-slinging foray with the employer and should announce its intention early in the campaign to keep its messages factual and above board. A simple admission of some rotten apples existing in labor unions, as in any other organization, might be appropriate as long as emphasis is placed upon factual evidence demonstrating that the particular union doing the organizing has an unblemished record of conduct. Where individuals within particular international unions have received widespread publicity for corruption, organizers for these unions have diffused the issue by citing the record of their particular region, district, or local.

"Outsiders"   Union avoidance consultants and the employers who hire them are required to file reports with the U.S. Department of Labor.[2] These reports contain details of the activities performed by consultants and the costs of the consulting arrangements. If the organizer is aware of a consulting relationship and the reports are not filed, the Department of Labor should be advised. Regardless of whether the reports are filed, members of the election unit should be told of the consulting relationship. If the cost of the arrangement is known, demonstrating the price that the employer is willing to pay to avoid unionization should be publicized. This message has been very effective in campaigns.[3]

Unions Preserve Individual Freedom   The employer is likely to tell workers that they will lose individual freedom by forming a union. Some organizers anticipate the issue and neutralize it by telling workers that it will not stand in the way of their negotiating higher wages and benefits than that prescribed in the union contract. Baseball players and movie and television performers are union members. Their unions negotiate minimum salaries for their members. Bob Hope, Mike Wallace, Reggie Jackson, and other stars do not work for the minimum wage; they negotiate higher wages and benefits for themselves. Also, by law organized workers have the right to pursue their individual grievances with their employer without union representation. When the boss says "no, take it or leave," how much freedom does the individual have then?

Why Make Promises to Improve Now?   Workers should know that the employer is likely to admit that problems exist and will often imply that conditions will improve if the workers reject unionization. If information is available on employee turnover or formal and informal grievances filed by employees prior to the organizing campaign, it should be conveyed to workers. In addition, workers should be asked the question heading this subsection along with another set of questions: If employees accept the implied promises and reject unionization, what guarantee do they have that the promises will be kept? Will this union or another union come running and incur the expense of another organizing campaign if the promises are not kept?

Unions Cooperate With Employers Over Common Problems   The employer is likely to paint a picture of labor-management relations as unfriendly, stressful, and uncooperative. To workers who have a good working relationship with their immediate supervisor and fellow employees, this charge is likely to be unsettling. Probably the only way of dispelling this notion is to cite examples of labor-management cooperation with which the union has been involved. If it has not been in this position, cooperative efforts to solve common problems can be cited in other industries such as automobiles, steel, meatpacking, and long-shoring.

Offer to Debate   Many organizers make it a standard practice in each campaign of challenging the employer to a debate on the premise that workers who are undecided regarding their support of the union will often be persuaded by this offer, because employers nearly always decline the challenge. The union portrays the employer as afraid to be confronted with the facts in the campaign, instead relying on its advantage of being able to conduct captive audience presentations at the workplace.

"Housekeeping"   The organizer must be aware of allegations that the employer is likely to bring against his or her particular union, often during the final moments of the campaign. Some possibilities are criminal charges leveled against union officers including the organizers themselves, plant closings or drastic reductions in the work force at plants represented by the union, overall declines in the union's membership, decertifications of plants once represented by the union, violent strikes, charges of undemocratic procedures by dissident factions within the union, union officers' salaries including those of the organizers themselves, long strikes, and unusual aspects of the organizer's personal lives. Organizing campaigns have been lost due to charges of these types, particularly when made during the final moments of campaigns.

In addition to warning workers to be wary of the "big bomb"

at the last minute of a campaign, some organizers try to second guess the opposition. For example, one organizer issued a leaflet shortly before an election informing workers that the officers of another local within his international union had recently been indicted by a grand jury. The leaflet also asked why the employer had not revealed this information earlier and speculated that the employer may have been planning to drop the "big bomb" just prior to the election. The organizer succeeded in diffusing the issue.

Some issues are difficult, if not impossible to diffuse. A former organizer, for example, could never find a way of diffusing the fact that he had been married seven times.

The important point to remember is that the union and the individual organizer's personal life are open books. With the wide array of information retrieval systems available today—some of them illegal—there is virtually nothing that can be hidden. Everything is fair game during a campaign and hoping that the employer will not discover or will choose to ignore some aspect of the union or the organizer's personal life is not just risky; it is fatal. This means that the organizer should investigate the runaway shop, the plant being phased out, the decertified unit, and his or her credit, criminal, and medical files and prepare as factual and logical an explanation as possible. Not for defense, but as part of the overall strategy of anticipating and neutralizing the opposition.

Rumors   Regardless of how well the organizer anticipates and neutralizes the employer's campaign, there is a strong likelihood that unanticipated allegations against the union will arise. Some of these allegations may be preposterous. In addition to being told they will need a union steward's permission to use the restroom and will have to pay for the use of company parking lots, workers have been told that female spouses and other relatives of the first-hired male worker would be dismissed, maintenance workers would be unable to assist one another with unusually heavy or difficult work, members of minority groups would dominate the union in workplaces where they comprise a small portion of the work force, the union's only goal in collective bargaining is a union shop and dues check-off and it would "fix" the ratification vote, women would need the "approval" of male union officials to keep their jobs and receive promotions, and industry-wide seniority would prevail so that workers laid off at another company could bump workers at the target. Given the poor education about labor unions that workers receive while in school and the media's distortions of unions, such wild allegations cannot be dismissed as ridiculous and totally unbelievable.

The organizer must warn workers to be wary of rumors and encourage them to ask the organizer and the workplace committee about their validity. In addition, members of the organizing committee should be asked to report unanticipated charges against the union to the organizer. The organizer must then develop a strategy to combat the rumor. In a well-planned, aggressive campaign of anticipating and neutralizing the employer's anti-union messages, instances where the organizer is placed in a defensive posture should seldom occur.

Fears of Workers About the Election Procedure   The employer is likely to mount a "get-out-the-vote" campaign prior to the election. However, the employer is unlikely to address the fears that workers may have about voting. Instead, it may encourage rumors or the natural pessimism of some workers that the election is not really a secret ballot election.

Workers should be assured that they will mark their ballots secretly in a voting booth. Their names will not appear on the ballot. They will fold the ballot and personally place it in a sealed ballot box. After everyone has voted, the ballots will be mixed up while still in the box. Then an agent of the Board will open the box and tally the vote.

KEEPING THE MOMENTUM

Each organizer has his or her personal yardstick for determining when to file an election petition with the Board. Even though only a 30 percent demonstration of interest is required by the Board, some organizers will only file a petition if 75 percent of the desired election unit signs authorization cards. Others wait until 50 percent have signed, while some will file with 30 percent if they believe that majority support will eventually be achieved.

Regardless of when an election petition is filed, all organizers encounter the problem of how to maintain interest in the campaign during the long interval of time that elapses between the date the election petition is filed and the actual election. While no sure-fire formula exists, there are some tactics that organizers use to maintain campaign momentum:

1. Keep workers posted on what is occurring at the Board.

Let them know that the employer is attempting to postpone the inevitable by engaging in delaying tactics including spurious unfair labor practice charges and challenges of the election unit's composition. Be on the offensive with a frank discussion of the law's weaknesses. Where workers are discharged or otherwise disciplined for union activity, demonstrate through messages communicated by the organizing committee, meetings, housecalls, and leaflets how the union protects workers. Testimonials by the affected workers can be particularly effective.

2. Continue to hammer away at the issues.

Convey new versions of the same message used earlier in the campaign which demonstrate that the union is the only means for resolving workplace issues. Continue messages that anticipate and neutralize employer tactics. Bring in union members from other locations to testify to the union's effectiveness. A change in faces can add interest and spark to the campaign. Picnics, concerts by labor-oriented performers, a screening of *Norma Rae* along with an appearance by the real "Norma Rae," Crystal Lee Sutton, and other social events have been used to convey the union's messages in new ways.

3. Keep the organizing committee active by expanding its role in the campaign.

While at the pre-petition stage of the campaign the primary functions of the organizing committee may have been to identify workplace issues and to convey messages to other workers, now is an excellent time to have the committee function more like the local union will function after the election. The organizer must increasingly step aside and permit workers to develop their leadership skills at the three primary functions of a local union—contract negotiations, grievance handling, and internal organizing.

While an election of union officers is inadvisable, because such an election may inject a divisive issue into the campaign, the committee can proceed with many of the other functions of a local union.

Drafting of a preliminary constitution and bylaws for the local union can occur with the understanding that it will not be acted upon until the union is authorized. By soliciting the views of members of the election unit, the internal organizing process occurs and the concept of union democracy is elevated from a somewhat abstract concept, perhaps viewed by workers as a part of the campaign's rhetoric, to a process in which they participate. In addition to preparing for the union's internal governance, meetings and surveys can be conducted to determine the union's position when negotiating the initial contract.

If the employer has a grievance procedure, the committee can attempt to resolve workplace issues through the procedure. If grievances are won, the value of organizing can be demonstrated. If lost, the need for a legitimate grievance procedure may be demonstrated. If the employer does not have a grievance procedure, the committee can demonstrate its strength and unity by acting as an ad hoc grievance committee. In addition to gaining experience at handling grievances, the committee is performing the internal organizing function that should assist in the maintenance of union support.

PEAKING THE CAMPAIGN

All too often, employers hold captive audience speeches and drop a "big bomb" on workers just prior to authorization elections. The objective is to peak the campaign just before workers enter the voting booths. In addition to warning workers in advance about the employer's tactics, it is advsable for unions to also mount a last-minute scoring drive.

Some organizers purposely hold back information which is particularly damaging to the employer's position until just prior to the election. Examples are recent reports of the employer's financial prosperity, announcements of workers discharged for union activity being reinstated with back pay, recently issued citations by government health and safety agencies, company concessions in response to grievances filed by the organizing committee, recent contract settlements by organized plants with characteristics similar to those of the target, and evidence of illegal activities conducted by the employer.

Also, some organizers hold rallies just prior to the election to solidify support. Properly planned, pre-election rallies can convey an image of strength and unity. Now might be the time to hold that "debate" with the employer (who will not be in attendance, of course) or to schedule that speech by a celebrity sympathetic to the union.

The advantages for peaking the campaign are with the employer. However, the union should not be passive and in the position of defending itself against the employer's attacks. Be on the offensive until the end of the campaign.

ELECTION DAY

In addition to allaying the fears of workers regarding the secrecy of the election (discussed above), the organizer should engage in permissible campaigning until the time that the polls close. Remember that the "twenty-four hour rule" only applies to employer campaign speeches and, under certain circumstances, to union-amplified sound devices aimed at workers. While campaigning is not allowed around the polls, it is permissible at other locations of the workplace.

The organizing committee should function like precinct captains in Mayor Richard Daley's Chicago. The union position should be reiterated and all union supporters should vote. If union supporters are absent from work, their absences should be reported to the organizer who has made arrangements with retirees from the union or other union activists to assure that supporters make it to the polls. Child care and transportation may be necessary. Laid-off workers should be told that the employer is likely to challenge their right to vote.

The organizing committee should select as election observers those workers whom they believe are the most likely to have the respect of their fellow workers and the most likely to understand the guidelines for authorization elections and to enforce the procedures. Observers should represent the composition of the unit in regard to age, race, sex, job classification, etc. With a structured, well planned approach to getting out the pro-union vote and attempting to sway "fence-sitters" at the last minute, the organizer can say with confidence that "nothing more could be done."

LOSING THE ELECTION
IS NOT THE END

If the union loses the election, the organizing campaign should not be considered over, because the union has an excellent chance of winning a succeeding election. Overall, unions have much higher win rates in NLRB-conducted second and third elections than in initial elections. The reasons are not hard to identify. The employer goes all out to win the initial election; its tactics are not likely to be different in a second election. The organizer and union supporters are unlikely to encounter surprises and will be better prepared to meet challenges posed by the employer. Also, during the first election, the employer may have explicitly or implicitly promised to resolve the workplace issues upon which the campaign focused. If the issues still exist, workers are not likely to believe that the employer will resolve them without the assistance of a union.

The pace of the campaign naturally changes after the union loses an election, but its objective is the same—the support of union adherents should be kept and the support of workers who did not vote for the union should be gained. A properly trained organizing committee with periodic coaching by the organizer can accomplish this objective. The organizing committee can function as a grievance committee during the interlude between elections. Periodically, meetings can be conducted and leaflets distributed. The first leaflet can be as early as the day after the election, announcing that the union is not quitting.[4]

Union supporters must proceed carefully, because they are vulnerable to discipline and discharge for union activity if the employer is determined to reduce the union's chances of winning a second election. The organizing committee should continue to gather evidence supporting unfair labor practice charges and, with the assistance of the organizer, assure that the rights of workers are protected.

CONCLUSION

The overriding theme of this chapter is preparation: preparation for the three phases of the campaign, preparation of workers for the anti-union campaign, and preparation of the organizing committee to organize and to develop the leadership skills for functioning as a local union. The key to workers organizing themselves is the preparation made by the organizer.

FOOTNOTES

[1] Julius G. Getman, Stephen B. Goldberg, and Jeanne B. Herman. *Union Representation Elections: Law and Reality* (New York: Russel Sage Foundation, 1976).

[2] For employer reports, request Form LM-10, and for consultant reports, ask for Form LM-20 and Form LM-21. Available from Office of Labor-Management, Standards Enforcement, U.S. Department of Labor, Washington, D.C. 20216, Telephone 202/523-7393.

[3] Kinsey Wilson and Steve Askin. "Secrets of a Union Buster," *The Nation,* June 13, 1981, pp. 725–728.

[4] American Labor Education Center, "Organizing the Unorganized: Ten Ways You Can Win," *American Labor,* July 1980, No. 9, p. 5.

Kicking Unions Out

6

Since the passage of the Taft-Hartley Act which established the procedures for union decertifications, the number of decertification elections has increased from 97 in 1947 to 849 in 1977[1] with unions consistently losing about 75 percent of the elections. The number of deauthorization elections in which workers determine whether or not to continue the union shop or another type of union security provision in their contracts has increased from 74 in 1968 to 140 in 1978. One union avoidance consultant estimates that only one out of four managers and one out of ten workers knows about the decertification process, while the deauthorization procedure is known by only about one percent of each group. By conducting seminars and writing books on "deunionization," union avoidance consultants have helped to close the information gap that may exist among managers and workers and have contributed to the rapid growth in decertification and deauthorization elections. It is prudent for every union activist to assume that his or her employer knows or is likely to know about the "process of deunionization."

This chapter examines three aspects of "deunionization." First, the law governing decertifications and deauthorizations is examined. Second, employer tactics for fostering union decertifications and deauthorizations are described. Finally, tactics that unions may find useful during decertification and deauthorization campaigns are explored.

The succeeding two chapters, chapter 7 and chapter 8, examine "preventive maintenance" procedures so that unions can avoid finding themselves thrust into the midst of decertification and deauthorization campaigns. Chapter 7 explores the strike situation during which many union decertifications occur. Chapter 8 looks at the ways in which unions can maintain membership solidarity through the process of internal organizing.

THE LEGAL FRAMEWORK FOR DEAUTHORIZATIONS AND DECERTIFICATIONS

The deauthorization provision of Taft-Hartley applies to the union security clauses in collective bargaining agreements. The most common type of union security clause is the union shop, but the deauthorization provision also applies to less frequently used types of union security clauses such as the modified union shop, maintenance of membership provisions, and the agency shop. Because the union shop is prohibited in so-called "right-to-work" states, the deauthorization procedure is applicable only in those states that allow the union shop and other forms of union security.

The NLRB procedures for deauthorizations are similar to the procedures that unions must follow when seeking to gain certification as bargaining agents for groups of workers. A request for a deauthorization election must be filed with the NLRB by an employee or group of employees; the employer cannot file the petition. The request must be supported by at least a 30 percent demonstration of interest, usually in the form of a petition signed by workers in the unit. The deauthorization election request can be filed at any time during the life of the contract, but only one deauthorization election can be held in a twelve-month period.

Elections to decide the issue of whether or not to continue the union security clause in contracts follow the same procedures used by the Board in union certification elections. In determining the winner, however, the votes to remove the union security clause must represent a majority of the workers eligible to vote, not the actual votes cast as in union certification elections. As a consequence, workers who do not cast ballots in deauthorization elections are in effect supporting the continuation of the union security provision. If the union loses the election, it continues to be the exclusive bargaining agent, but no longer has the benefit of the union security clause.

Decertification—revocation of a union's certification as exclusive bargaining agent for a group of workers—can occur in two ways. The most frequent way is through a decertification election, which again closely parallels the union certification process and the union deauthorization process. A request for a decertification election must be filed by an employee or group of employees—not by the employer—with the NLRB. The request must be supported by at least a 30 percent demonstration of interest.

A decertification election cannot be held within one year after a union is initially certified by the Board as bargaining agent. If the employer is found by the Board to have committed unfair labor practices while bargaining for the first contract, the twelve-month period in which a decertification election cannot occur will begin at the time when the Board views the employer as having begun to "bargain in good faith." If a petition is filed prior to sixty days before the lapse of the twelve-month period, the request for a decertification election will not be honored by the Board.

Where a union has negotiated a contract, a decertification is barred during the life of the contract provided that the contract is not for a period of time over three years. This is the Board's so-called "contract-bar doctrine." There is, however, an exception. The Board will receive a petition for a decertification election during a thirty-day "window period" which is defined as being no sooner than ninety days before the expiration of a contract and no later than sixty days prior to a contract's expiration date. For hospitals and health care institutions, the thirty-day period falls between ninety and 120 days prior to the contract's expiration. If a valid petition for a decertification election is received during the thirty-day period the employer's obligation to negotiate a new contract is removed until the decertification election is held and the issue of union representation is settled.

Where a union has negotiated a contract with an employer, but the contract expires without a new contract being negotiated, the Board will accept a petition for a decertification election. Often the expiration of a contract without a new contract being negotiated results in a strike. The Board has special rules regarding the rights of strikers and strikebreakers in decertification elections. These rules are examined in chapter 7 where the strike–decertification strategy is examined.

Regardless of the circumstances under which a petition for a decertification election is filed, the Board will conduct only one decertification election in a twelve-month period. The actual election procedure is the same as that for the other Board-conducted elections discussed previously. In determining a winner, the Board looks at the actual number of votes cast as in union certification elections with the union losing tie votes.

The second way a union can be decertified is through a petition filed by the employer with the Board claiming that the union no longer represents the workers in the unit that the union is certified to represent. The employer must support its petition with "objective evidence" demonstrating that the union no longer represents the majority of employees. The Board examines each case on its own merits in determining whether a sufficient "good faith doubt" exists, so that guidelines are somewhat vague.

A petition calling for the union to be ousted, signed by a majority of workers and presented to the employer, would be an example of objective evidence the Board would probably consider as substantiating a "good faith doubt." Dissatisfaction with the union expressed orally by a large number of workers, a large turnover of employees so that few of the workers who originally supported the union are currently employed, and a majority of workers crossing the union's picket line during a strike are when taken by themselves considered by the Board to be insufficient evidence to support a "good faith doubt." When taken together, the Board might find that substantial evidence exists supporting the employer's request for withdrawal of certification. Failure of the union to conduct regular membership meetings or to process grievances, no appointments or elections of shop stewards, workers choosing to revoke their dues check-off authorizations, and employee-filed petitions for deauthorization and decertification elections are other sources of evidence that might substantiate an employer's "good faith doubt." Again, however, the Board decides each case on its own merits.

In order to obtain "objective evidence" supporting a "good faith doubt," the Board allows employers to conduct polls of employees. The following conditions must be met for the Board to consider the poll as "objective evidence":

1. The only purpose of the poll is to determine whether the union represents a majority of employees and employees are told that this is the sole purpose.

2. Employees are assured that no reprisals will occur as a result of the poll.

3.   Responses to the poll are confidential.

4.   The employer has not engaged in unfair labor practices which would create a coercive atmosphere.

In order to substantiate the employer's claim, the results of the poll must clearly demonstrate that a majority of employees no longer desire to be represented by the union.[2]

The same time limits which apply to employee-filed petitions for decertification elections apply to employer requests for Board removal of union certification, namely the initial contract, "contract-bar," and expired contract rules.

The law recognizes that it would be naive to assume that employee petitions for deauthorization and decertification elections and "objective evidence" supporting employer requests for withdrawal of union certification occur in a vacuum without influence by employers. However, Taft-Hartley's provision of "freedom of speech" for employers hampers the Board's ability to distinguish between coercive and noncoercive employer behavior and makes the regulation of the "deunionization" process weak and arbitrary. Virtually the same prohibitions apply to "deunionizations" as apply to union certifications. Employers are not allowed to threaten, promise, or enact punishments or rewards which influence worker support for the union. However, employers retain the right of "free speech" and all that this right entails. While an employer cannot initiate or sponsor a drive to deauthorize or decertify a union, it can tell its employees that they have a right to deauthorize or decertify. It can tell employees who are interested in deauthorizing or decertifying what to say and how to say it during the campaign. It can offer its own opinions on the issues at hand, its support for the "deunionization" effort, as long as it is not "coercive" support.

While the Board has repeatedly held that providing information is permissible, other activities may not receive its approval. Employers who give "deunionization" committees their company letterhead stationery for decertification or deauthorization petitions and who arrange transportation for a petition instigator to deliver the petition to the Board may cross the thin line between sponsorship (illegal) and support (legal). Employers who allow employees to use company time to work on the decertification and company property such as meeting rooms, typewriters, and printing equipment may also cross the line. Asking employees to initiate a decertification petition is illegal, but helping them to word the petition is legal. The Board decides each case on its own merits, so that when taken by itself an action may be legal but when taken together with other actions, the Board may find that the employer has engaged in illegal sponsorship.

Because the Board decides each case on its own merits and looks at the "totality" of employer conduct, it is important for unions to gather evidence supporting any action that may be interpreted to be employer sponsorship. A systematic approach to monitoring the anti-union campaign is necessary. Exhibit 6–1 is a check list of actions which may provide sufficient evidence of employer interference. The union must document its charges with the five W's: who, what, where, when, and witnesses.

Employers have violated the law by contacting workers in private and asking them to instigate decertification campaigns. The only sure ways that an employer can be caught engaging in this illegal activity are if it contacts workers who are sympathetic to the union and they, in turn, tell the union of the employer's action, or if leaders of the decertification effort let it be known that the employer asked them to instigate the campaign. Usually, union activists believe that the employer has crossed the fine line between supporting and sponsoring the decertification. Proving it, however, is another matter. Union activists must attempt to build a case for the Board, which is usually based on circumstantial evidence. The check list in Exhibit 6-1 may assist in building such a case.

If a union loses a decertification or deauthorization election, it must strive to demonstrate to the Board that "serious" or "pervasive" unfair labor practices were committed by the employer and/or employees leading the campaign. The Board will then overturn the election and either order another election or continue the union's certification on the basis of a fair election being impractical.

EMPLOYER TACTICS

The union deauthorization procedure does not rid employers of unions, but is viewed by some union avoidance consultants as a good prelude to decertifying a union, because a deauthorization election can be held any time during the life of a contract, unlike union decertifications. The object is to hit the union in the pocketbook by

EXHIBIT 6–1. Employer Interference Checklist

1. Are workers opposed to the union allowed to campaign against the union during working hours other than rest breaks and lunch periods? Is this a departure from work rules? Do union supporters have the same right?

2. Have workers opposed to the union been recently transferred to jobs that allow them to move around or otherwise gain greater access to other workers?

3. Have union opponents been allowed to use the employer's property for meetings? Are meetings conducted during work hours?

4. Are union opponents meeting production standards? Have they received any privileges not normally given other workers?

5. How did union opponents get the idea to undermine the union? Did the employer ask them? Were they threatened or promised something?

6. Have union opponents been meeting with management more often than usual? Have they met with outside lawyers or consultants?

7. Have union opponents used the employer's typewriters, copying machines, postage machines, in-the-workplace mail system, bulletin boards, or any other company property for the decertification campaign?

8. Has the employer made any threats or promises?

9. Have union supporters been disciplined or otherwise discriminated against?

10. Has the employer "tightened-up" so that the union finds itself processing more grievances than is normal? Are more grievances than usual being deferred to arbitration?

11. Has the employer abandoned its contractual obligation to follow basic provisions of the contract in regard to matters such as seniority and dues check-off?

12. Have supervisors asked bargaining unit members about their support of the union?

13. Has the employer made improvements in the terms of employment, by-passed the union in the process, and attempted to demonstrate that workers do not need the union?

reducing its dues income. This reduction in income may, in turn, make the union less receptive to serving the needs of the unit, which if it occurs, will have the effect of increasing worker dissatisfaction with the union.[3]

A way for employers to set the stage for a deauthorization

campaign is through hard bargaining for the initial contract. Full-time union staff usually play the key role in negotiating the first contract for a newly organized local union, because local union activists tend to be inexperienced at collective bargaining. Major goals of full-time staff are the negotiation of a union shop clause and a dues check-off clause, whereby the employer deducts dues from employee paychecks and remits the dues to the union. A full-time union staff person may view an initial contract as a "good" settlement, if it includes the union shop, the dues check-off, a written obligation by the employer to continue current wages, benefits, and working conditions, and slight improvements in the terms of employment, particularly if he or she views the newly organized local's bargaining power as somewhat weak. The first contract may be viewed as a starting point upon which succeeding contracts will be built. If the expectations of bargaining unit members were unrealistically inflated during the organizing campaign, the first contract may be a big disappointment. Not much of a suggestion may be necessary from the employer to influence some members into believing that the union's only reason for organizing and negotiating a contract was to extract dues income from their paychecks.[4]

Employers have sent letters to workers' homes, distributed leaflets at the workplace, and enclosed slips in pay envelopes informing workers of the procedures for eliminating the necessity of paying union dues. Exhibit 6–2 is an example of such a letter. While this letter seems to be advocating the filing of a petition and is very close to the employer actually launching a deauthorization campaign, it is, in the strict interpretation of the law, perfectly legal. Employees are told of their rights under the law and steps are provided to facilitate the action. Yet employees must initiate the procedure. To a group of recently "organized" but not yet "unionized" workers, this action may be very appealing.

Some employers convey information on the decertification process during organizing campaigns. Ostensibly, the purpose of this message is to inform employees of just how difficult it is to remove a union once it is authorized, but it also serves to lay the groundwork for a decertification should the union win the authorization election. Exhibit 6-3 is an example of such a communication. It was issued in a campaign won by a union; subsequently, the union was decertified.

Employers who are squeamish about "informing" workers about deauthorization and decertification procedures can leave the "edu-

EXHIBIT 6–2 Anti-union Letter to Employees Regarding Union Dues

To All Employees:

As you know the recent union contract requires all employees to pay union dues. For most of you this means a monthly deduction of $11.64 (about the price of a couple of bags of groceries). Failure to pay these dues would result in discharge according to federal law.

Some employees have asked whether there is a way to stop this required payment of dues to the union. Yes, there is!

The National Labor Relations Board, which governs these matters, has a procedure entitled a "deauthorization petition," which can remove compulsory union dues. All that is required is that one or more employees draw up a petition requesting that the union dues requirement be revoked. This petition must then be signed by at least 30% of the employees who are required to pay union dues. The NLRB will then conduct a secret ballot election where you and your fellow workers would decide in secret whether or not to require the payment of union dues in order to hold on to your jobs. The union would still be here if it loses this election, but the payment of dues would be strictly voluntary. *All other provisions of the contract (wages, hours, pension, health care, vacations, etc.) would not change! The only change would be that union membership and union dues would be strictly voluntary!*

As your employer, management cannot initiate or sign this petition. You, the employees, must do so. If you are interested in further information, either contact the NLRB at (612) 725-2611 or stop by the Personnel Office during your lunch break. We have copies of petitions which employes have used at other companies.

The choice of whether or not to be forced to pay union dues can be yours! Remember that the decision is made by a secret ballot election. No one will know how you vote and under federal law no one can force you to belong or to pay dues.

Sincerely,

The Management

cation" to groups like the Southern Employees Education Fund whose purposes are to

assist employees in the exercise of their right to refrain from engaging in labor union activities and affiliation, assist employees

EXHIBIT 6–3 Anti-union Letter to Employees Regarding Decertification

To All Employees:

A question raised more frequently of late by some employees is what is entailed in getting rid of the union—if it wins the election and doesn't work out.

If a union is certified as your sole and exclusive bargaining agent, removing the union—which is called decertification—is a very difficult task.

1. On your own you would have to gather signatures of approximately 30 percent of your fellow employees and file a petition with the National Labor Relations Board. The company would be prohibited, by law, from helping you in any way. You would have to pay with your own money the fees for an attorney to help you.

2. It is very difficult to have the National Labor Relations Board order a decertification election. In 1975 less than 50 percent of the approximately 1,100 decertification petitions filed went to election. *Any* involvement by the employer is reason for the National Labor Relations Board to deny such an election.

3. If an election were directed, you would have to run a campaign—against the union—without any aid from the company. As in the upcoming certification election, you would have to get a *majority of those who actually vote*, not a majority of those eligible to vote.

4. Finally, a decertification petition could not be filed for one year after a union was certified. If a contract were negotiated, no decertification action could be taken for the life of the contract or for three years, whichever was sooner.

If the union suggests that you give it a try—and remove it if you don't like the results—keep in mind that decertification is by no means an easy task.

Throughout this campaign I will lawfully provide factual information. Please review the material. Consider the practicalities and realities of union representation. I hope that you will then make your decision based on fact—not on emotion or some unrealizable union predictions.

I want to clear up one more important point. I am not interested in recriminations. You have my personal word that no one will lose his or her job or suffer any harm because he or she was for the union. To resolve our problems here, we need ideas, help, and support from all of you.

If you have any questions on the union issue, please ask your supervisor or me.

Sincerely,

Signature

in opposing representation by a labor union, assist employees in bargaining units represented by labor unions freely to decide whether to continue representation . . . assist in the procurement of decertification. . .[5]

Employer associations like the non-union Master Printers of America issue pamphlets which provide detailed information on deauthorizations and decertifications. The MPA's pamphlet concludes on the following note:

"More and more individuals are concluding that unions are too powerful and that they have lost touch with the individual members actually working in a plant. Many union members are fed up with increasing dues, fees, strikes and the loss of individual freedom. Unions are no longer needed in most modern printing plants."[6]

In addition to written information on the deauthorization and decertification procedures, the employer may use the "troops," first-line supervisors, to convey the message. Captive audience presentations may also be used and are, if management watches its "p's and q's," perfectly legal. The advantage of a face-to-face, supervisor-to-employee, campaign is that management can step over the legal boundaries with less chance of detection than in a written campaign.

In all likelihood, the employer identified workers opposed to unionization during the organizing campaign; they may have already formed a "loyal employees" or "vote-no" committee. Management may secretly assist in the reactivation of the anti-union committee so that it can make threats and promises that would be illegal if made by the employer. When made by the committee, which is technically a step removed from management, these same threats and promises may be viewed as permissible campaign rhetoric by the Board.

Once the union mounts an active campaign against deunionization, the employer's right of "free speech" enables it to legally argue against the union. For example, it is permissible for the employer to state

It is my belief that all employees can be treated fairly and equitably without union representation, and that present policies of improving wages and upgrading benefits will continue as they have in the past.[7]

When the election date is established by the Board, the employer is likely to mount a spirited "get out the vote" campaign. Within the letter of the law, the employer may hold raffles and contests as an inducement for workers to vote.

The messages to be conveyed during a deauthorization or decertification campaign are likely to be determined in two ways—purposeful discussions with bargaining unit members by the "troops" and attitude surveys conducted by the employer. In addition to identifying the issues in a campaign, these two methods provide management with a measure of the sentiment against the union.

The employer is likely to use the information gathered through informal interviews and surveys to reduce objections which employees have to its personnel policies. Unpopular supervisors may be terminated, rest areas may be modernized, and employer-sponsored social activities may be expanded. Employees may be encouraged to by-pass the grievance procedure and take problems directly to management because the "open-door" is faster and yields equal or better results. The purpose is to demonstrate that improvements are not dependent upon the union and are granted willingly by the employer. This is the "carrot" side of the employer's campaign.

The "stick" side of the campaign will also be revealed by the informal interviews and surveys. The full-time union representative may appear to be lazy or self-centered, the last bargaining session may have brought few improvements, the local's officers may seem more interested in taking care of themselves, or members "just don't know what they're getting in return for their dues." Whatever the objections, true or false, the theme is that these conditions will continue unless employees "deunionize."[8,9]

Continuing the tradition of spies and agent provocateurs which precedes the passage of the Wagner Act, one modern day consultant advises employers to hire people who will pose as ordinary employees but whose real purpose is to instigate a decertification. The prescription:

> The employer hires a management consultant, one who is a specialist in labor relations as an employee. He would be the counterpart of the union "plant," and he will give you a reading on the potential success of decertification. The employer can generally improve his chances of decertification by hiring a few new employees in the unit who would know how, or would learn

how, to spread the gospel to create an uprising and oust the union. They could even start the petition to decertify and file the petition with the NLRB.[10]

Workers may be pawns in the decertification process. Rather than relying on workers to follow Board procedures and successfully launch a decertification, the employer may simply use workers who are disaffected from the union to launch a petition drive and then use this petition as supporting evidence for its own withdrawal of recognition of the union. The procedure is then taken out of the hands of amateurs and placed into those of professionals, the employer's legal staff or law firm.[11]

Instead of filing a petition with the Board claiming that "objective evidence" exists to substantiate the employer's "good faith doubt" that the union represents employees, the employer may simply refuse to deal with the union. The union must then file unfair labor practice charges with the Board. According to one union avoidance consultant, this may be the preferred method, "because it is a time-consuming procedure and allows the employer more managerial freedom (and the absence of bargaining) during the time the charges are being processed by hearings and appeals."[12]

The anti-union Taft-Hartley Act was passed in 1947 and remains nearly intact to this day despite intense political activity by organized labor, particularly against Section 14B, the so-called "right-to-work" provision. Progressive labor union activists might acknowledge the need for the decertification and deauthorization provisions of the Act on the grounds that in a democratic society the workers who have formed a union should also have the right to dissolve that union or to at least eliminate its right to compel membership when that union no longer serves their needs. This is fine in theory, but when the law's provisions for decertification and deauthorization can be twisted in ways which imperil freedom of choice, one must question whether the law really allows workers to exercise control.

UNION TACTICS

While chapters 7 and 8 will examine strategies that prevent deauthorizations and decertifications from getting off the ground, this chapter is concerned with the short-run, the period when a "deunionization" effort is launched by the employer. This period does not necessarily coincide with the time an actual petition is filed with the Board, for as one union avoidance consultant advises: "A decertification is not done easily and should be planned a couple of years in advance."[13]

The union must be aware of tip-offs to a decertification or deauthorization effort. It must develop an "early-warning system" similar to the one employers use to detect the likelihood of a union organizing drive. In addition to the strike as a prelude to a decertification effort (to be discussed in chapter 7), a number of other actions may occur and may tip-off the union that the employer is attempting to either have workers petition for a decertification election or set the stage for "objective evidence" which will substantiate that the employer has a "good faith doubt."

For a union to rely on the warning signs enumerated in this section is a very passive approach to combating decertifications. The old saying in sports that the best defense is a good offense also applies to unions. Rather than waiting for the employer to tip its hand, it is better for the union to take the initiative and to determine just how likely a successful decertification may be (more on that in chapter 8).

The warning signs:[14]

1.   Acquisition of new operations.

The employer may acquire new operations capable of producing the product your bargaining unit produces, thereby giving it the opportunity of playing your bargaining unit off against the workers at other locations. If your bargaining unit does not go along with the employer's contract proposals, it may threaten to shift production to the other locations. (What is it telling workers at other locations?) If the other locations are not organized, the employer has greater latitude to make threats than if they are organized. But, even where the same international union has contracts at all locations, the employer may be able to play one off against the others, because contract expiration dates are often not the same and the employer can shift production from one organized plant to another organized plant to weaken each local union's collective bargaining power. The employer vehemently opposes common contract expiration dates of consolidated bargaining with all units. Bargaining units resisting the play-off face the possibility of extinction through long-term shifts of production to other units. Ultimately, a decertification may occur as the employer promotes the "law of the jungle," which in this version means survival of the weakest bargaining unit.

2. Threats to close down or move.

Similarly, rumors may be circulated or the employer may come right out and say that it is shutting down the facility and either going out of business completely or moving elsewhere. "Labor costs are too high! The only possible solution is for the union to make substantial concessions on the contract." The union is in a bind. If the union is convinced that the employer is not bluffing and makes concessions, some bargaining unit members may be convinced that the union is ineffective and may promote a decertification effort. If the union is convinced that the employer is bluffing, some bargaining unit members may disagree with the union's assessment and, because of the fear of losing their jobs, may push for a decertification.

3. Provision of union wages and benefits in non-union locations.

If the employer maintains non-union locations, it may provide the same or higher wages and fringe benefits there as at union organized locations. The message conveyed to unorganized workers is that they should feel no need to form a union. Likewise, the employer may convey the impression to organized workers that they would be as well off or better off without union representation. Keep an eye on wages and benefits at the employer's unorganized facilities and particularly on efforts by the employer to make these comparisons known to members of the bargaining unit.

4. Hiring of new legal counsel.

Some law firms do business with both unions and employers. These law firms are probably less inclined to engage in union decertification efforts than those that deal with employers exclusively. However, there are law firms that bust unions and continue to represent other unions. Some law firms have gained notoriety for their union busting activities. If a change in law firms occurs, contact the AFL-CIO Department of Organization which has compiled a list of law firms notorious for their union busting activities.

5.   Change in management.

A change in personnel directors or other top managers may indicate a change in the treatment the union will receive. Personnel directors and other top managers are not alike. Some view union representation as necessary to balance competing interests in the workplace. They may prefer working under the rules and regulations of a union contract to being in a position where employee discipline and other personnel matters are left somewhat up in the air. They may be sympathetic toward unions because of their own employment experiences or because of their political ideology. Other personnel directors and top managers view unions with disdain and would like nothing better than to break them.

Where a new manager has worked before is important, because previous employment experiences color attitudes and, more important, expectations of the new workplace. The new manager has been hired because he or she is viewed as successful by your employer. If the new manager worked in a non-union or an aggressively anti-union environment, he or she will probably view that personnel policy as a precondition for success at the new workplace. He or she is likely to impose that personnel policy on your workplace. Information on previous employment will probably be included in a biographical sketch in the employer's newsletter to employees. If not, bring it up in conversation with the new manager. If the manager's previous employers are union organized, check out their personnel policies through the appropriate unions. If they are not organized, check with unions in their geographic areas. They may have tried to organize the employers. Your international union or the AFL-CIO Department of Organization should be able to assist you.

6.   New ownership.

This is a sure sign of a change in personnel policies. Often, a small family-owned company is sold to a large company, a "multinational conglomerate." "Multinational" because it has operations in many countries, and "conglomerate" because it produces many different goods and services. The new owners will most likely have a standardized corporate personnel policy, which they will attempt to impose on your workplace. They may push to change the pension plan and health care package to bring them into conformity with the rest of the company. In some cases, these changes will benefit workers.

Prior to the sale, the union may have negotiated contracts solely with management from the workplace. Now, the union may bargain with people out of corporate headquarters whose sole responsibility is to negotiate contracts and who travel from one company location to another performing that function. The interests of local management may take a back seat to the interests of corporate headquarters. Whether the new owners will attempt to break the union depends upon corporate policy. Again, your international union and the AFL-CIO should be able to assist you in obtaining this information.

7. Attempts to withdraw from multi-employer agreement.

This may indicate an attempt to decertify. Otherwise, the entire bargaining unit comprised of all employers must be decertified as a whole. Decertifying all of the units represented by a multi-employer agreement is much more difficult to accomplish than a decertification of a single unit.

8. Increased involvement by supervisors.

The foremen and other first-line supervisors who normally come in contact with workers on a daily basis are the first-string offense in a union avoidance campaign. Be wary if they begin to take an interest in the "feelings" of their subordinates. Management may be attempting to take over the role of stewards and other union leaders. The implication is "You don't need the union. Management will take care of your needs." Couple the supervisor's sudden interest with a substantial increase in the number of meetings attended by them and the evidence of an effort to break the union expands. The meetings may be in the form of training classes on "communications," "human relations," or "labor relations."

9. Harassment of union leaders.

Harassing and disciplining union leaders in clear violation of the contract indicates that management is attempting to undermine the authority of the union. Given the deficiencies of National Labor Relations Board procedures for handling cases of unlawful discipline for union activity, the likelihood of at least a partial victory by the employer is great. The union must be conscientious in its efforts to obtain full reinstatement and must be prepared to demonstrate that the unlawful discipline for union activity is sufficient grounds for nullifying a decertification effort.

10. Delay of grievance settlements.

Rather than settling most grievances at the first and second steps of the grievance procedure as in the past, management begins to drag out settlements to higher steps. A higher step of the procedure may require participation by a full-time union staff person. He or she has many bargaining units to service. Delays occur. The union staff person finds that management is unwilling to settle. More and more grievances are going to arbitration. The union wins nearly all of the arbitrations, but finds that its meager treasury is being drained in the process. Members of the bargaining unit are frustrated by the delays and find that management is more willing to listen to their complaints if they sidestep their stewards. The seed is planted—why bother with the union? Recall the discussion in chapter 1 of the decertification effort at Clinton Corn. Foot-dragging over grievances is a preview of what will occur in contract negotiations and ultimately may be a preview of a decertification effort.

11. Change in composition of bargaining unit.

If the composition of the bargaining unit has changed substantially in recent years so that a significant portion of the unit is comprised of young workers, management may attempt to drive a wedge into the union's ranks by attacking the seniority system. Advocacy of the "merit principle" in lay-off, promotion, and pay increase decisions strikes at a fundamental tenet of unionization. Not that unions are against merit, but history demonstrates that prejudice, nepotism, sexual favors, and other factors unrelated to productivity have been applied in employment decisions under the guise of "merit." Informing new bargaining unit members of management's abuse of the "merit principle" prior to the formation of the union becomes increasingly difficult as the original union members retire. But, the union must be diligent and strive to inform recent members of exactly what a *return* to the "merit principle" entails.

12. Change in union leadership.

If long-time union officers retire or are defeated for reelection, management may attempt to test the new leadership. This is particularly true if the new leadership lacks experience and does not demonstrate knowledge of the fundamentals of labor relations and union administration. Couple a change in leadership with a substantial change in the composition of the bargaining unit and it becomes an even more inviting target for a decertification.

13. Attempts to take credit for wages, fringe benefits, and working conditions.

Management may distribute to employees a new handbook describing all the benefits *provided by the employer*. Nowhere is the union mentioned or the employer's resistance to granting the benefits during collective bargaining. The employer is trying to imply to employees that they would be as well off or better off without the union.

14. Surplus of labor.

A labor surplus as a result of high unemployment generally or layoffs by a competitor may provide the employer with scabs if a strike occurs.

15. Recruitment of bargaining unit members for supervision.

Be wary of management efforts to establish special classes, meetings, or training for bargaining unit members who desire to eventually go into supervision or who are identified by management as having the potential for supervision. Management has an excellent opportunity to plant the seeds for a decertification. Bargaining unit members desiring supervision also have an excellent opportunity to demonstrate their "loyalty" to management and their "leadership potential" by guiding a decertification effort.

16. Creation of an employee organization.

A nearly certain sign of a decertification effort is the appearance of an "independent union" at the workplace. It may be called an "employees' association," but whatever its name, the purpose is to subvert the legitimate union. Creation of such an organization by the employer or consultants hired by it is illegal but may be difficult to prove. Usually, these organizations appear during and after strikes when outsiders and bargaining unit members scab on union members.

17.   Training supervisors to do employees' work.

A concerted effort by management to train supervisors to do bargaining unit members' work indicates that the employer is preparing to operate during a strike. Where the employer has shut down operations during previous strikes, this may indicate plans to hire strikebreakers and ultimately to push for a decertification.

18.   Attitude surveys and questionnaires.

A favorite tactic of management consultants is to measure the susceptibility of bargaining units to decertifications through attitude surveys. The questionnaires are usually administered on company time. The answers to certain questions can help consultants gauge whether or not the bargaining unit is ripe for a decertification. Some consultants also advise management to hold gripe sessions with small groups of workers. Managers or consultants ask certain leading questions which attempt to measure receptivity to a decertification and to plant the seed for a decertification.

19.   Sudden increase in work force.

The union should be wary of a dramatic increase in the work force shortly before the time periods when the Board will receive a decertification petition, because a large increase in employment may represent an attempt by the employer to stack the vote against the union should a decertification election be held. The union must be diligent in its effort to "unionize" workers added to the bargaining unit. Also, be wary of a dramatic increase in the number of supervisors or other employees outside the bargaining unit. The employer may be building a strikebreaking force.

20.   Resistance to additional stewards.

Strong resistance by management to an increase in the number of stewards where the contract stipulates a prescribed number of union representatives indicates that the employer is attempting to prevent the union from improving its service to the membership. A plan to decertify the union may be indicated.

21.   Increase in employee services.

The employer may initiate "quality circles," a "work enrichment" committee or a "family service" committee. Ostensibly, the purposes of the respective committees are to produce a better product, to give workers greater satisfaction with their jobs, and to provide workers with rehabilitative services for problems such as alcohol, drug, and child abuse. Whatever their name and function, these new approaches to workplace and family problems can provide very real benefits to members of the bargaining unit. However, they may have an additional purpose. The employer may seek to use the programs as a way of weakening the union. Be wary of efforts to exclude the union from participating in the committees. Also, keep a close eye on committee discussions and recommendations that infringe upon the contract and cast the union into the role of "the obstacle to 'progress.'" Weakening the seniority system, subcontracting, and supervisors doing bargaining unit work are examples of the "progress" desired by some employers. In addition, the union should be alert to efforts to reduce its role at the workplace, including tampering with the grievance procedure by encouraging workers to bypass stewards and any other efforts that are designed to "make the union unnecessary."

Perhaps the most important factor in determining whether the employer will succeed at "deunionization" is the emergence of an individual in the bargaining unit who will take charge of the anti-union campaign.[15] The employer may hire someone specifically for this purpose. If the union suspects that this is the case, it should conduct a background investigation on the individual or individuals in order to determine if evidence exists that would substantiate its suspicion.

The employer may also attempt to recruit members of the bargaining unit to lead the anti-union campaign. The union should consider having some union supporters take an undercover role. They could periodically "bitch" to the "troops" about the union. Set them up as the people the employer is likely to contact when it decides to launch a decertification. The "troops" may be asked to identify workers who might be willing to launch a decertification; provide those people! Catch the employer at its game!

If the union has workers who are willing to testify to the Board that the employer contacted them about launching a decertification campaign or engaged in any other illegal activity, it should be cautious about blowing the whistle on the infractions too soon. It is best to have the employer dig itself in deeper by having the informants play along with the employer even to the point when the decertification campaign is to be launched. The employer's credibility with the Board could be so severely damaged that no decertification election is ever conducted.

If the employer hires a labor law firm or union avoidance consulting firm to direct the decertification campaign, the union should be sure to name both the employer and the outside firm in its charges to the Board. The Board may issue a cease and desist order against the employer as well as the outsider. This can prevent the outsider from selling its wares elsewhere to the benefit of your union and other unions.[16]

Inform the membership of their rights under the law. One union distributed a leaflet with the following message:

HOW CAN WE STOP THE HARASSMENT OF UNION SUPPORTERS?

It is against Federal Law for the company to discriminate against Union supporters. As always, we do not intend to let them get away with breaking the law at your expense. We are asking Union supporters to start keeping diaries of the break time, talking time, etc., of company supporters. We will be able to use this as evidence before the National Labor Relations Board to prove that the company is discriminating against and trying to set up Union supporters. Please call us immediately if you think you have an unfair practice charge to file. We will continue to back you 100%.

In addition to the message conveyed by this leaflet, the union trained union supporters to keep "diaries" recounting the who, what, when, where, and witness aspects of incidents at the workplace. Similar training of union organizing committee members during organizing drives is an important ingredient of "deunionization" campaigns.

Likewise, the union should use the same media it uses during organizing drives. Housecalls, workplace conversations, leaflets, letters, and meetings are all appropriate ways of conveying the union's messages, with oral, face-to-face discussions probably being the most effective:

Finally, it is clear that the most effective tactic involved direct contact between trustworthy, credible individuals and the members of the bargaining unit. One-to-one contact allows the development of trust and the commitment of employees to work in the campaign or vote in the desired way. It also allows problems and issues to be dealt with directly rather than avoided.[17]

The most difficult aspect of "deunionization" campaigns is determining the messages to be conveyed. A good starting point is to recognize that the union has a problem that it created. Certainly the law, the employer, or outside consultants bear part of the responsibility, but the union has a track record on which it must run. Campaigns that concentrate on attacking the employer tend to be unsuccessful—either the attacks are not believed or they arouse sympathy for the employer and backfire on the union.[18]

The union must determine the issues in the campaign and the reasons why some employees want to "deunionize." Chapter 8 discusses the identification of issues as part of the internal organizing process. Basically, it is a matter of surveys and interviews, the same tools that employers use to identify employee dissatisfaction with unions.

If the union's performance is lacking, it must develop a plan for improving its performance. A shift in the focus of the union's demands in the upcoming contract negotiations or a change in the full-time union staff assigned to the bargaining unit may be part of the plan. In addition, the union should emphasize its accomplishments. Overall, the union's campaign should be positive in tone. "Mistakes will be corrected and the gains made by the union will be retained" should be its motto.

Ultimately, the best way to stay unionized is to avoid "deunionization" campaigns altogether. This is the subject of the next two chapters.

FOOTNOTES

[1] John C. Anderson, Gloria Busman, and Charles A. O'Reilly, III, "The Decertification Process: Evidence from California," *Industrial Relations,* Vol. 21, No. 2, Spring 1982, p. 178.

[2] Alfred T. De Maria, *The Process of Deunionization* (New York: Executive Enterprise Publications Co., Inc., 1979), p. 49.

[3] De Maria, *The Process of Deunionization,* pp. 8–9.

[4] De Maria, *The Process of Deunionization,* pp. 32–33.

[5] AFL-CIO Department of Organization, *Report on Union Busters,* May 1979, Issue No. 4, p. 5.

[6] De Maria, *The Process of Deunionization,* p. 132.

[7] De Maria, *The Process of Deunionization,* p. 87.

[8] AFL-CIO Department of Organization, "Decertification—Matthew Goodfellow," *Report on Union Busters,* Issue No. 1, February 1979, pp. 11–12.

[9] AFL-CIO Department of Organization, "Decertification Without a Strike," *Report on Union Busters,* Issue No. 13, February 1980, pp. 5–6.

[10] AFL-CIO Department of Organization, *Report on Union Busters,* Issue No. 18, July 1980, p. 5.

[11] AFL-CIO Department of Organization, *RUB Sheet,* February 1980, Issue No. 13, pp. 11–12.

[12] De Maria, *The Process of Deunionization,* p. 40.

[13] AFL-CIO Department of Organization, *Report on Union Busters,* Issue No. 18, July 1980, p. 6.

[14] AFL-CIO Department of Organization, "Warning Signs," *RUB Sheet,* No. 13, February 1980, pp. 6–8.

[15] Anderson, Busman, and O'Reilly, "The Decertification Process," p. 193.

[16] "How to Bust a Union Buster: West Coast Industrial Relations Association," AFL-CIO Department of Organization, *RUB Sheet,* October 1980, Issue No. 21, pp. 5–7.

[17] Anderson, Busman, and O'Reilly, "The Decertification Process," p. 194.

[18] Anderson, Busman, and O'Reilly, "The Decertification Process," p. 194.

ADDITIONAL RESOURCES

Anderson, John C., Busman, Gloria, and O'Reilly, Charles A., III. "What Factors Influence the Outcome of Decertification Elections," *Monthly Labor Review,* November 1979, pp. 32–36.

Chafetz, I., and Fraser, C. R. P. "Union Decertification: An Exploratory Analysis," *Industrial Relations,* Winter 1979, pp. 59–69.

Dworkin, J. B., and Extejt, M. M. "Why Workers Decertify Their Unions? A Preliminary Investigation," *Proceedings,* 39th Annual Academy of Management Meetings, August 1979.

Fulmer, William E. "When Employees Want to Ouster Their Unions," *Harvard Business Review,* March–April 1978, pp. 163–70.

Krupman, W. A., and Rasin, G. I. "Decertification: Removing the Shroud," *Labor Law Journal,* April 1979, pp. 231–41.

7

Combating the Strike-Decertification Scenario

The largest, most publicized "deunionization" in U.S. history occurred in 1981 when the Professional Air Traffic Controllers Organization struck and was subsequently decertified by the federal government. A scenario for ousting unions became well known, perhaps inducing more employers to try it and certainly making unions more aware of the need to combat it. The PATCO strike-decertification is not unique, for it has happened to other unions. What was different was that the decertified union was large and it seemed to have the power to win the strike.

An integral part of the collective bargaining classes I teach is the "Power Exercise" where we examine various factors in an attempt to determine the relative strengths of unions and employers in the respective industries of class participants. One of the objectives of the "Power Exercise" is to assess the likelihood of unions conducting successful strikes. While never having had a PATCO member in a class, but based upon my passing knowledge of their situation, I would have had to conclude—as the leadership and most of the membership of PATCO did—that it was virtually impossible for the air traffic controllers to lose the strike they launched in August 1981.

Given the state of current technology, controllers are necessary to insure safe air travel; computers cannot do the job. Controllers go through long training periods and apprenticeships so that strike-breakers cannot be recruited easily. Most major airlines were already losing money or earning meager profits at the time of the strike; a cutback in flights would have been devastating. Other unions, particularly the Airline Pilots Association, might have honored the strike on the basis that safety was threatened. PATCO had publicized the stressful working conditions of controllers since its founding in 1968. Coupled with the public's concern about air safety, public support of the strike seemed likely. Even more important than the other factors, PATCO had endorsed Ronald Reagan, their boss, for the presidency in 1980 and had received a "pledge to you that my administration will work very closely with you to bring about a spirit of cooperation between the President and the air traffic controllers." Furthermore, about 11,400 out of a possible 16,300 controllers walked out; membership solidarity did not appear to be a problem despite the illegality of the strike. PATCO had successfully increased wages through walkouts in 1970. This was not some small local union in Clinton, Iowa, or Minneapolis, Minnesota, but a national union of 12,000 members with the power evidently in its pocket. What went wrong?

Playing "Monday morning quarterback" is easy and there is probably no way that PATCO could have known about all of the factors undermining its seemingly unpenetrable position, but its president at the time of the strike, Robert Poli, does admit some strategic errors. PATCO telegraphed its intent to strike years before the actual strike. Contingency plans were made by the federal government during the Carter administration nearly two years before the actual strike.[1]

There is strong evidence that the federal government built itself a cadre of strikebreakers in anticipation of a PATCO walkout. The military lent about 800 controllers, 10 percent of its total. In 1969, the military had 6,500 controllers handling about 8.7 million military flight hours, while in 1980, largely in an effort to conserve fuel, it reduced flight hours down to 3.2 million but still retained 5,500 controllers. Also, during the late 1970s, the government hired three times as many supervisors as controllers, thereby building an internal strikebreaking force. In addition, the government called back recently retired controllers and, according to PATCO, threatened controllers on disability income with a cutback in benefits if they did not return to work. The slump in the airline industry provided 700 furloughed airline pilots who did clerical jobs previously done by the controllers.[2]

Another reason why the system continued to operate was a change in daily flight schedules. Rather than allowing airlines and private planes to schedule flights whenever they desired with peak flight concentrations during the morning and evening rush hours, flights were spread throughout each day.

The strike had a substantial economic impact on the airlines. Immediately after the walkout, 18,000 airline employees were laid off and the airlines lost an estimated $2.2 billion in gross revenues in 1981. Yet the airlines maintained their support of the federal government's actions of firing striking controllers, refusing to bargain with PATCO after the strike, and decertifying the union. A reason for the support may be that the major airlines, eg., Eastern, United, American, viewed the freeze on additional routes and the cutback in existing routes as an effective way of reducing the competition from new airlines such as New York Air and Midway. By operating essentially non-union and concentrating their flights during peak passenger rush hours, the new airlines cut prices below those of the majors and made substantial dents in their revenues. The strike reduced competition in the airline industry.[3]

Robert Poli contends that some unions actually encouraged the decertification of PATCO:

> Stories about how we didn't cooperate with the AFL-CIO before we struck and how various union presidents were miffed that we didn't ask their blessing started to circulate from day one. Their comments sent a clear message to the Administration that there would be no real support for us.

Poli acknowledges that some union leaders did provide support, "but by and large the national union leaders tried to put as much distance between us and them as possible."[4] As a relatively new union with a recent change in national officers, PATCO probably did little to encourage the support of other unions. No instance of workers refusing to cross PATCO's picket lines were reported in the national media, probably because PATCO members had crossed other unions' picket lines in previous strikes and PATCO did a poor job of public relations.

PATCO members were among the highest paid of unionized

workers with an average salary of $30,000, with some members earning $50,000. Couple this salary schedule with a demand for a $10,000 yearly increase and a thirty-two-hour work week and the controllers received little public sympathy. The government's primary message, however, was that the strike was illegal and the controllers had taken an oath not to strike. The no-strike oath was particularly effective when paired with the salary and hour demand. Only after the strike was launched did the union emphasize that the real issue was job-related stress created by management, the Federal Aviation Administration.[5]

In 1970 (after the first PATCO strike), in 1978, and again in 1982, the federal government commissioned studies of the air traffic control system. All three studies reached essentially the same conclusion: Unless the Federal Aviation Administration changes the way it treats its workers, the strikes and work slowdowns that have characterized labor-management relations since the mid-1960s will continue.[6]

In April 1982, one of the three authors of the 1982 study, Samuel Bowers, a professor at the University of Michigan, urged the government to rehire the fired controllers, citing the major reason for the strike as bad management with half of the FAA's managers classified as "very bad." Bowers predicted that controllers currently on the job would be on the verge of a strike in three years, if the FAA's management does not improve.[7]

Nearly a year after the strike, Art Barrett, a controller at the Atlanta airport and a member of a new union called the United States Air Traffic Controllers Organization, appeared on network television with a petition urging the government to rehire the fired controllers. Barrett, a controller with fifteen years of experience, was reassigned to a desk job and ordered to take medical and psychiatric examinations by the FAA.[8]

Publicizing the poor management in the control towers rather than the wage and hour demands could have changed the public's image of the PATCO strikers. Whether the outcome of the strike would have been different, however, is anybody's guess. What is certain, however, is that the PATCO strike-decertification demonstrates the difficulty of predicting the outcome of a strike. Yet it is precisely this prediction—this prediction of the power relationship between labor and management—that a union must make before embarking on a strike.

THE STRIKE-DECERTIFICATION FRAMEWORK

> . . . a historic shift appears to be looming in the balance of power between labor and management. It is a shift that favors management by making strikes less likely to be called, more costly for workers who do elect to walk out, and in general less effective as a means of pressuring management to make concessions.[9]

Is the preceding passage merely rhetoric of the order one might expect in a magazine directed at business executives or a realistic assessment of collective bargaining in the 1980s? Herbert Meyer, the author of the article from which the quote is excerpted, supports his statement by emphasizing the decline in the number of strikes over approximately the last twenty years. In 1981, the number of "major strikes," which the U.S. Department of Labor defines as involving at least 10,000 workers, declined to its lowest level since 1963. In addition, he points out that two major strikes in the 1980s did not accomplish what union members had hoped. The strike by the Oil, Chemical, and Atomic Workers in 1980 against the oil refining industry had little impact upon production even though strikes against some refiners lasted as long as twelve weeks. And, of course, Meyer cites the PATCO strike as support for his thesis.

Meyer presents a number of reasons why strike activity has declined and why management presumably has an upper hand when dealing with strikes. Strikers are no longer eligible for the federal government's food stamp program. High unemployment in the 1980s makes unionized workers more concerned about being able to find other jobs during strikes and if strikes are broken. Also, high unemployment increases the ranks of potential strikebreakers. "The Chrysler lesson" of large, previously profitable firms on the verge of bankruptcy is cited as another reason why workers are less inclined to walk off their jobs.

The two most important structural factors altering the power relationship according to Meyer are results of changes in production processes. As part of the long-term union avoidance strategy, employers are phasing out production centers with large numbers of workers and decentralizing production among large numbers of geographically dispersed workplaces. It is unlikely, for example, that there will ever be an industrial complex on the scale of the Ford Motor Company's Rouge plant located in Dearborn, Michigan. In the 1950s, UAW Local 600 had as many as 60,000 members. By dispersing production geographically, often to non-union plants, and where organized, by resisting common contract expiration dates, employers can reduce the impact of strikes by shifting production to nonstruck plants. Also, small plants are easier to operate with strikebreakers than a large plant.

The second factor is common to many industries. Increased mechanization and automation have made the task of shutting down an employer's production during a strike more difficult than in earlier periods when production processes were more labor intensive. Where production processes are highly automated, managers and other un-organized personnel are likely to be able to continue producing for extended periods of time.

What makes Meyer's view of declining union power important is that it appears to reflect a popular and growing view in management circles. Unions should expect employers to test increasingly their ability to strike successfully, because power is the crux of collective bargaining and employers seem to think that they have more power than unions. In Meyer's words: "Managers are discovering that strikes can be broken, that the cost of breaking them is often lower than the cost of taking them, and that strikebreaking (assuming it to be legal and nonviolent) doesn't have to be a dirty word."[10]

While nowhere in the law is it explicitly stated, the law views collective bargaining as a power struggle. The legal requirements are set forth in section 8(d) of the National Labor Relations Act as

> ... the performance of the mutual obligation of the employer and the representative of the employees to meet at reasonable times and confer in good faith with respect to wages, hours, and other terms and conditions of employment, or the negotiations of an agreement, or any question arising thereunder, and the execution of a written contract incorporating any agreement reached. ...

The law does not require employers or unions to agree to change wages, hours, or working conditions. All that the parties must do is "meet at reasonable times and confer in good faith." Neither party is required to agree to a proposal or to make a concession as long as it seems to have the intent—the "good faith"—of reaching an agreement. Failure to reach agreement—an "impasse"—and a subsequent strike or lockout do not necessarily violate the good faith requirement.

There is no requirement that the agreement be "fair" or "just." If the union has greater bargaining power than the employer, it can use the power to have the employer accurately conclude that it has been "taken to the cleaners." The same holds true for employers with greater bargaining power than unions. Likewise, the union and the employer may be "unfair" or "unjust" in their demands, thereby forcing an impasse and a strike or lockout and still remain within the law as long as they demonstrate the intent of reaching an agreement. For example, an employer with record high profits can force an impasse by demanding takeaways from the union and still remain within the law.

Violations of the requirements for good faith bargaining are reported to the NLRB as "unfair labor practice charges."[11] As with charges filed in connection with union authorizations and decertifications, unfair labor practice charges filed because of violations of the good faith bargaining requirement may take years to resolve. Likewise, the Board's resolution of bargaining violations is unsatisfactory and encourages employers to violate the law. If an employer fails to bargain in good faith, the Board should order the employer to sign a contract providing bargaining unit members with what they would have received if the employer had not broken the law. Agreements reached with employers elsewhere in the industry are a basis on which this determination could be made. Instead, possibly after years of delay, all that the Board does is order the employer back to negotiations and another try at "good faith bargaining." Yet there is an important reason for unions to pursue violations by the employer of the good faith bargaining requirement.

The Board differentiates between two types of strikes—"economic strikes" and "unfair labor practices strikes." An economic strike occurs when a contract expires or before a first contract is negotiated and is over collective bargaining issues such as wages, benefits, job posting, grievance procedure, discipline policy, health and safety, and discrimination. An unfair labor practice strike is a protest against unfair labor practices committed by the employer in collective bargaining. The Board views unfair labor practice strikes as a protected action against the employer's illegal activities and provides certain safeguards to workers who engage in these strikes.

Unfair labor practice strikers can be replaced by the employer, but they cannot be replaced "permanently." The Board allows unfair labor practice strikers to return to work at a time they offer to return with the effect of forcing the employer to discharge their replacements. Unfair labor practice strikers can vote in a decertification election, but their replacements cannot vote.

"Permanent" replacements can be hired to take the jobs of economic strikers with the result that economic strikers lose the right to return to their jobs even when a strike is settled. Unless the union is able to negotiate the reinstatement of economic strikers, the law only entitles them to being recalled when job openings occur. Economic strikers and their permanent replacements are allowed to vote in union decertification elections, provided that the election occurs within twelve months after the start of the strike. After that period, economic strikers are not entitled to vote in decertification elections and the election unit is limited to their permanent replacements and members of the bargaining unit who did not join the strike or returned to work. Hire more permanent replacements than economic strikers during the first twelve months of a strike or delay the election until after twelve months elapse, and the outcome of a decertification election is virtually assured.[12]

Supervisors and other nonbargaining unit workers who do bargining unit work during a strike and students intending to return to school are considered to be "temporary replacements" and are not eligible to vote. Strikers, regardless of whether they are protesting economic issues or unfair labor practices committed by the employer, are not allowed to vote if they have taken a "permanent" job elsewhere. The deciding factor in determining the eligibility to vote of strikers who have taken other jobs is whether they intend to return after the strike is settled.

A striker may lose his or her eligibility to vote in a decertification election if discharged by the employer for "serious" misconduct during the strike. Abusive language directed at scabs is usually not considered serious by the Board. Destroying property of the employer or scabs and physical violence against scabs is considered serious. For this reason, some union activists maintain decorum on picket lines and confine their persuasion of scabs to times and places away from the workplace. Threats of violence and actual violence away from the workplace are also prohibited by the Board, but the union can legitimately make housecalls of a non-coercive nature.

In this power struggle termed "collective bargaining," the law provides only one safeguard to unions that attempt to resolve impasses through strikes and at the same time desire to assure that they are not decertified in the process. This safeguard is the unfair labor practice strike. Some unions which determine that they do not have the power to strike without losing through the strike-decertification scenario attempt to confine their strikes to the unfair labor practice type. This can be a risky strategy unless the union is certain that it can prove to the Board's satisfaction that the employer has indeed committed unfair labor practices in collective bargaining. Unions considering defending themselves against decertifications by this strategy definitely need the assistance of good legal counsel.

Blend the view that the employer is more powerful than the union with the law's provision allowing decertifications when contracts expire and a rationale for provoking collective bargaining impasses is provided. Stir in an economic strike, scabs, and their right to vote in decertification elections and a recipe for busting unions develops. As one union avoidance consultant puts it: "Strikes often present the employer with opportunities to deunionize."[13]

SURVIVAL STEPS—WHEN AND HOW TO STRIKE

The time to beat the strike-decertification scenario is before taking the strike vote and walking out. There are four steps every union can take to improve its chances for survival.

First, the union should gather as much information as possible on the factors determining its power and the power of the employer. Many of these factors were discussed earlier in the book. Ability to pay, ability of outsiders to do bargaining unit work, ability of the employer to shift production elsewhere, and a number of other conditions affect the power relationship. Do not be blind-sided; know what the employer is capable of doing and what the union is capable of doing.

Second, do not trust your own judgment completely. While the recommendation to the membership to strike rests with local union activists, they can be too close to the situation to make an impartial judgment of the local's ability to withstand decertification. Consulting with trusted outsiders, the proverbial "second opinion," can be helpful.

Third, if a strike is called, the union must control the factors that can give it power. Maintaining the solidarity of the membership is the most important factor. Under this broad category there are many specific things that the union can do to exercise the power it has.

Fourth, if a strike is likely to result in a decertification, the union should look at alternatives to striking before accepting the employer's last offer. Sometimes the union can pressure the employer into a more favorable settlement without a strike.

These four survival steps are discussed in detail in the rest of the chapter.[14]

THE STRIKE DECISION

The power of the union to beat the strike-decertification scenario needs to be studied carefully each time negotiations are pending, because it can change over time. The employer may acquire the capacity to produce elsewhere or the number of potential strikebreakers may increase substantially, for example, during the usual three-year time span between contracts. Likewise, the power of the union may improve between contracts because, for example, the employer may now suffer a permanent loss of customers from a strike. Information on these and other factors can be gathered by observing management in action on the job, by doing the basic library-type research described in chapter 4, and by consulting with other locals, the international union, other unions, and the AFL-CIO. The more pertinent information you gather, the more likely you are to make an accurate prediction.

Here are the factors affecting the outcome of a strike. They are phrased as questions so that you can go through them one by one and provide the appropriate answers:

1. Does management appear to have the ability to pay higher wages and benefits, but yet is adamant about obtaining takeaways or providing only minor improvements? Does management seem to be encouraging a strike?

2. Can management continue to supply customers during a strike by shifting production to other locations?

3. Has management indicated or are there rumors of a plant shutdown?

4. Does the employer match or surpass the provisions of the union contract at its non-union locations?

5. Has the employer hired a law firm with an anti-union record?

6. Have managers with an anti-union background been employed recently?

7. Has a change in ownership occurred? What is the record of the new owners toward unions?

8. Has the employer withdrawn from a multi-employer agreement?

9. Has a change in union leadership occurred recently? Has the employer attempted to test the new leadership?

10. Will the employer have little difficulty recruiting scabs because of high unemployment in the local economy or lay-offs by a competitor? Are bargaining unit members too skilled to be replaced?

11. Has the employer trained relatively large numbers of bargaining unit members for supervisory positions? Are they likely to support a strike?

12. Have supervisors been trained to do bargaining unit work?

13. Has the work force been increased substantially prior to the contract's expiration and before the union has a chance to "organize" the new hirees into the union?

14. Has management vehemently opposed an increase in union stewards and other representatives in an apparent attempt to reduce the union's effectiveness?

15. If your union operates in the public sector, does the applicable law allow unions to strike? Is the public likely to support a strike and pressure government officials to settle on the union's terms?

16. Are most other firms in the industry organized? Would the union's demands put the employer at a disadvantage relative to the competition in the industry so that it might have an incentive to try the strike-decertification scenario?

17. Would the employer settle without a strike or after a short strike, because it may suffer a permanent loss of customers?

18. Could the employer shut down the plant and run away to another location, because the investment in plant and equipment

is low or the capital equipment is quite portable or the location of the production point is relatively unimportant?

19. Has the employer stockpiled inventory in anticipation of a strike?

20. Is this plant a supplier of a product for other plants operated by the employer? Is the employer able to obtain this product elsewhere?

21. Could the employer change the production process during a strike by bringing in more automated equipment which would reduce its dependency on labor and make it easier for supervisors and scabs to meet production?

22. Does the employer attempt to take credit for all improvements in wages, benefits, and working conditions? Has the union managed to set the record straight with the union membership?

23. Have supervisors attempted to take over the role of union stewards by encouraging workers to by-pass the grievance procedure? Has the union aggressively challenged management's tactic and received the support of bargaining unit members?

24. Are grievances being deferred increasingly to arbitration for settlement?

25. Have union leaders been harassed and disciplined unjustly by management? In addition to filing charges of discrimination against union activity with the Board, has the union succeeded at stopping the practice by applying other pressures?

26. Has the employer introduced "participatory management" programs and attempted to keep the union out of their direction? Has the union succeeded at attaining full union participation?

27. How have the police, local politicians, community leaders, and the media reacted to other strikes? Do they have the power to influence the outcome? Would their intervention tend to favor the union?

28. Has the bargaining unit ever been involved in a strike? What was the outcome? What changes, if any, have occurred since that time? Do the changes favor the union?

29. If there are other unions at the workplace, are their members likely to honor the union's picket lines? What about transport unions?

30. What percentage of the bargaining unit is likely to honor a strike? Are there workers in key jobs who are unlikely to support a strike?

THE SECOND OPINION

Sometimes local union activists are too close to the heat of negotiations, daily troubles at the workplace, local union politics, and management personalities to make an impartial judgment of the local's ability to withstand a decertification effort. Many union constitutions recognize this possibility and require the approval of the international union before a strike by a local union can be launched. Largely because of the mix of local union and international union politics in the strike approval process, the constitution's provision may not be an effective safeguard against ill-advised strikes.

Regardless of whether the union's constitution requires the approval of strikes by the international union, the local union should at its own initiative seek the opinions of trusted individuals outside the local. Unionists from the international staff, other locals within the international union, and other unions may be able to point out aspects of the power relationship that local activists have overlooked. With the decision still firmly in the hands of the local union, the union has reached out to other unionists for valuable advice and possibly acquired their support should a strike be launched. The advice of labor lawyers, particularly when there is the possibility of an "unfair labor practice strike," can be sought. Local politicians conditioned to power plays within the political arena are another source of advice. Again, this serves a dual purpose; by consulting with local politicians before a strike, their cooperation should be easier to enlist if a strike is launched.

Two purposes are served by "second opinions." The local union has enlisted the aid of important parties seemingly outside the direct power struggle between the employer and the union, but who may in fact constitute the deciding forces should a strike be launched. Also, the local union introduces an impartial, objective view of the power struggle.

Consumer advocates advise getting a second opinion before making a major purchase or undergoing a major medical treatment. Certainly, the decision to strike is as crucial.

EXERCISING POWER

The immediate objective of a strike is to halt production and thereby impose costs upon the employer. In order to achieve this objective, the union must have the power to keep bargaining unit members from working and the power to prevent outsiders from doing bargaining unit work. This exercise of power during a strike requires detailed planning before the walkout actually occurs. In chapter 5, ways of systematically conducting a union organizing campaign were discussed; planning for a strike entails many of these same procedures.

A *strike committee* should be formed which is representative of the various departments or sections of the workplace. Where the union has an adequate number of stewards or other departmental representatives to service the membership, the composition of the strike committee can be established along representational lines. If there is an insufficient number of stewards, union activists from the various departments or sections of the workplace should be recruited for the committee.

Members of the committee participate in planning overall strike activities and operating a *control center* which can be contacted by strikers when questions arise. In addition, strike committee members are responsible for maintaining the solidarity of strikers in the departments they represent. As with organizing campaigns, committee members should keep a *file card* on each striker in their units. At least once per week, committee members should have a face-to-face *conversation* with each striker. These conversations have two purposes, *maintaining morale* of strikers and *measuring support* for the strike. At strike committee meetings, the committee should be able to gauge support for the strike so that tactical changes can be made if support is waning.

A way of assuring that each striker is connected with a strike committee member is to construct a *diagram of the workplace* similar to that discussed in chapter 5 for organizing campaigns. In addition, the diagram includes entrances to the workplace and the sites of picketing activity during the strike.

Picketing is a primary way of persuading the public, members of other unions, workers outside the unit, and members of the bargaining unit from undermining the power of the union to stop production during a strike. The strike committee should determine the following matters:

1. **The number of pickets** to be assigned to each entrance. The union might like to assign enough pickets to physically intimidate outsiders from entering; however, the employer will then seek a court injunction limiting the number of pickets. In order to reduce the likelihood of having the courts decide the issue and hiring a lawyer to represent the union at the proceedings, the union can check with other unions in the locality when deciding on an appropriate number of pickets, if it has not struck before.

2. **Picket line hours.** A general rule is to maintain a picket line whenever there is movement in and out of the workplace. In many cases, this means maintaining the picket line around the clock with at least token representation during off-peak hours.

3. **Picket signs** should have a short message which can be read in a few seconds. If the union is picketing retail establishments in addition to the workplace in order to conduct a consumer boycott, it must be certain that its picket signs convey that the dispute is not with the retailer so that it does not violate Taft-Hartley's secondary boycott prohibition. A member of the international union or a labor lawyer with experience in these matters should be consulted if any doubts exist. The signs should be printed by a unionized firm and the "union bug" affixed.

4. **Refreshments, heat, and shelter** may need to be provided for the pickets.

5. **Picket line captains** should be appointed. They should be individuals with the leadership skills to maintain discipline among strikers while on picket line duty, to handle relations with the media when their representatives arrive at the strike scene, and to make decisions in coordination with the control center when emergencies occur. "Emergencies" include the arrival of scabs, filming by the employer, and police surveillance.

Strike committee members and picket line captains must continuously stress the need for strikers to avoid *picket line misconduct* which could result in the termination of their employment and their disqualification from voting in a decertification election. Strikers should be aware of the employer's ability to film and record their activities on the picket line and that these films and recordings can be introduced as evidence in court and Board proceedings.

Likewise, the union should be prepared to record instances where management and strikebreakers provoke incidents on the picket line. While cameras and recording devices may not be too practical, picket line captains should immediately record "The Five W's" of such incidents, because this evidence may be crucial at court and Board proceedings.

Because the police and employer surveillance can limit the effectiveness of the picket line, the strike committee should be prepared to extend its persuasion of strikebreakers beyond the confines of the picket line. As with the initial stages of organizing campaigns, strikebreakers can be followed to taverns, restaurants, or home. Violence and threats of violence are illegal and can result in the same sanctions as those for picket line misconduct, but a noncoercive appeal is within the law.

Public support can affect the strike and is paramount if a consumer boycott is staged. Therefore, good relationships with the *news media* are important. Pickets must be told to refer media representatives to strike captains who, with the assistance of the strike committee, should develop a succinct and convincing explanation for the strike. Strikers should also be warned against staging demonstrations at the urging of media representatives, because these staged demonstrations serve only the interests of the media and can be damaging to the union.

The attention of the news media can boost the morale of strikers if the attention is positive. The union should not simply react to charges leveled by the employer or wait for the media to arrive at the picket line. Instead, *news bulletins* and *press conferences* objectively stating the reasons for the walkout should be initiated at the beginning of the strike and periodically thereafter as the strike proceeds and as newsworthy items evolve.

Other unions should be contacted far in advance of the strike and asked for their support. Unions whose members are in the position of having to decide whether to cross picket lines should receive special attention. While their leaders may not be in a position to formally instruct their members not to cross, because of no-strike provisions in their contracts, they may informally support such action. As the strike progresses, other unions may be asked to attend rallies and contribute money to the strikers. Sometimes a respected leader of another union may intervene with the employer as an informal mediator of the dispute. These types of support are easier to obtain prior to a strike than after the walkout occurs. Participation in the area's AFL-CIO Central Labor Union provides an established channel for obtaining the support of other unions.

Where a picket line is ineffective and the strike-decertification scenario is being enacted before the eyes of strikers, the union must make some difficult choices. *Politicians and the police* can make or break the effectiveness of a picket line. Historically, unions have won some strikes because law enforcement officials did not enforce the law. The founding of United Auto Workers Local 3 at "Dodge Main," for example, was facilitated by the refusal of the Hamtramck police to allow boxcar loads of strikebreakers to enter the struck plant. Governor Frank Murphy's reluctance to order the National Guard to oust sitdown strikers from General Motors plants in Flint, Michigan, in 1937 is another example.

In the broad scope, however, these are exceptions. While politicians and the police are more tolerant of picket line activities in some communities than in others, it is usually a mistake to anticipate that they will tolerate picket line violence or other illegal activities for long, even if the union has maintained excellent relations with them. If local authorities do not enforce the law, state and eventually federal authorities may be enlisted. I am unaware of strikes in recent years that have been won because law enforcement officials did not enforce the law.

If scabs are crossing the picket lines daily and the workplace is approaching normal production, the union is left with few alternatives. One is to attempt to reach a contract settlement with the employer which includes the reinstatement of all strikers including those subject to discharge for infractions during the strike. Because the employer has the upper hand at this point, the contract will presumably be settled on terms close to its last offer. Gaining the reinstatement of all strikers becomes a crucial issue. In recent years, some unions have been in the position of accepting the employer's last offer with only the right of reinstatement for strikers as job openings occur, meaning that the scabs stayed on the job.

Another alternative is to continue the strike in the hope of eventually persuading the employer to reach a settlement close to that of the union's position. Sometimes this approach is futile; a year elapses and strikers are prevented from even voting in a decertification election. Before a year has elapsed, the employer may stack the unit so that the union cannot win the decertification election.

The last alternative is to attempt to stop scabs from crossing picket lines through illegal means, without the cooperation of the police. Scabs will not be deterred from entering the workplace because law enforcement agencies have greater resources than the strikers. However, the illegal activities will gain a great deal of media attention, which may ultimately force the employer and government officials to resolve this source of unfavorable publicity and threat to public safety.

Many observers conclude, for example, that it was the Roosevelt administration's threat to cut off government loans which forced employers to sign an agreement ending the 1934 Minneapolis Teamster's strike in which four people were killed and hundreds were injured. In 1982, Minneapolis was the scene of another strike settled in a similar fashion. On April 1, the 750-member Local 1B of the Graphic Arts International Union struck the Bureau of Engraving (a privately owned firm without government affiliation). On May 24, nearly two months after the strike began, the employer began hiring an estimated 200 scabs. For the next month, picket line violence and violence away from the workplace occurred resulting in about 40 people being arrested. The mayor's office intervened and appointed a mediator, shortly after the violence culminated with a scab on a motorcycle being trailed and shot on his way from work. The strike was settled three days later, a month after the employer started hiring scabs and three months after the strike began.

The union gave up its COLA provision and accepted a two-year wage freeze. The employer granted amnesty to workers accused of misconduct during the strike, and agreed to discharge all but about fifteen skilled workers among the scabs. While the union hardly won a victory, it did beat the strike-decertification scenario. As Lawrence Olson, president of Local 1B, is quoted as saying: "When we went out, there weren't any scabs and no charge of reprisals. Today there was. It's a whole different ball game. It's not just what we wanted, but it's the best we could get."[15]

Violating the law can beat the strike-decertification scenario, but at no small cost and with absolutely no guarantee of success. It is a dangerous sort of brinkmanship, and should not be undertaken lightly.

While the union's ability to prevent outsiders from doing bargaining unit work is tenuous when the employer is determined to hire scabs, the union is in a better position to keep its own members from entering the workplace and breaking the strike.

A major reason why workers abandon strikes is the financial losses incurred. Union strike funds and donations from the public and other unions can provide some help. Because of recent cuts in social services, little government assistance is available to strikers. Where the union operates a credit union or has influence with banks or other financial institutions because of its association with pension funds, loans to strikers should be arranged.

A traditional source of income to strikers is another job. When skilled workers such as airplane mechanics, printers, tool and die makers, and construction workers strike and the economy is bustling, some take other jobs within their respective industries. When the economy is dragging, skilled and unskilled workers alike are sometimes able to find lower paying jobs. Even airline pilots who regularly make over $50,000 per year join me in delivering newspapers on the tundra when they are on strike. The union should assist workers in finding other jobs during strikes.

In addition to the direct income loss, strikers feel the pinch from the loss of one particular fringe benefit—medical care. While there is no way that the union can reasonably compensate for major medical procedures, which can often be postponed, it can ease the minds of strikers and their families by providing free or low-cost medical care for minor emergencies. There may be a physician or a nurse practitioner in the community who will volunteer free or low-cost medical assistance for strikers in the hope of securing their business when the strike is over. Pharmacies may also help for the same reason. Unions have done their members a great service by providing medical coverage in union contracts, but they have also created a dependency. To assume that this dependency ends during a strike or to pass it off as "not the union's job" is a mistake.

Many workers with children at home incur child care expenses in order to be able to work. When they strike, they are faced with taking care of their children entirely by themselves in order to save money. This can be a strain on workers accustomed to regular work. The union can establish a child drop-in center on a low-cost basis or a reciprocal hours basis—an hour's child care for an hour's work at the center or some fraction thereof. Most states strictly regulate child care centers, but it is often possible to get a temporary permit should the authorities intervene.

In addition to financial losses, strikers may return to work during a strike because they become isolated from the union. So-called "rugged individualism" is a much praised American virtue, while a strike requires workers to act as a group. Strikers must place their individual welfare—what they might gain by breaking the strike—second to the harm inflicted on the group. Therefore, the union must strive for group cohesiveness or solidarity.

It is important for the union to impress upon workers, particularly those with limited union experience, that crossing picket lines is unacceptable. The media often portray scabs as "rugged individuals" who are upholding the law, particularly when they are escorted across picket lines by the police, while the union view is seldom expressed. By stressing the injustice of scabs benefiting from the hardships endured by others, in Jack London's words, people who "steal from blind men's cups," strikers will know that strikebreaking is unacceptable to the group and will bring social sanctions after the strike is settled.

In addition, workers must be reminded continually of the strike's purpose, because after a few weeks, the employer, the media, spouses, or friends may reinforce a thought that has already crossed the minds of some strikers: "Union members will never get back what they have lost during the strike." While outsiders and recent members of the bargaining unit are likely to evaluate strikes strictly in terms of dollars and cents, the cause of a strike is often deepseated and approaches the intangible, despite the prominence given to the economic package by the union itself. Dignity and self-respect, and the way management treats workers daily on the job may be more important than the publicly acknowledged reasons for the strike. Emphasizing that a return to work will give the employer cause to challenge workers and their union even more than before the strike can be very persuading.

The threats of social ostracism and management reprisals, however, are not sufficient to achieve solidarity during a strike. The union must also provide purposeful activities for each striker and communicate with them regularly.

By being immersed in strike activities and thereby feeling that they are part of the action, strikers are less likely to think about returning to work than if they are bored like school children during the last days of summer vacation. The union should assign regular picket line duty to strikers. Daily picket duty for short stretches of time is preferrable to assignments on the line for long hours, a couple of days per week. Strike headquarters should be an accessible gathering spot for strikers. Low-cost refreshments and recreational activities can be provided. Sports competitions, parties, picnics, songfests, concerts, and other activities can break the tedium and keep workers together.

In addition to regular face-to-face conversations between strike committee members and strikers in their units, the union can communicate through newsletters, leaflets, and group meetings. Strikers are naturally interested in the progress of negotiations. If there is no progress, they should know this. Rumors abound during strikes; by regularly communicating with strikers, the strike committee will learn of the rumors and be able to combat them.

Potentially, the greatest power a union has during a strike is the solidarity of its membership. Nurture it! Do not lose it!

ALTERNATIVES TO THE STRIKE

If the union is certain that the employer may attempt to enact the strike-decertification scenario, it can sign an agreement on the employer's terms. Unsatisfactory as it is, this may be the only solution in some cases. In other situations, the union may be able to forgo signing a new agreement and remain at the workplace, pressuring the employer to make a more acceptable offer. A United Auto Worker's local recently used this tactic of working without a contract successfully.

In September 1981, Moog Automotive Inc., part of a foreign-based multi-national, offered members of UAW Local 282 at its St. Louis plant a takeaway contract which would have reduced wages by about $3 per hour. Previously, however, the company had boasted of record sales. The union interpreted the situation as indicating a possible strike-decertification. Unemployment in the St. Louis area was high; company executives boasted having 3,000 job applications on file. A new chief officer had been brought in from an anti-union company, and lawyers from an anti-union firm were also hired. The union was faced with accepting an apparently unjustified takeaway contract or launching a strike, which could lead to a decertification. It did neither.

Instead, the union's leadership asked members to report to work after the contract expired and to apply pressure on the employer. Workers were asked to "work to rule," meaning, for example, not to work out of their classifications, to refuse overtime, and to engage in collective actions at the workplace. Among these collective actions were "taking complaints as a group to supervisors, holding union meetings on the plant floor during lunch, and directly confronting health, safety, and production problems on the spot."[16]

The union formed a "Solidarity Committee" to coordinate the campaign which included collecting money to help workers who might be suspended or fired. On three occasions, the committee called plant-wide meetings at the union hall in the middle of the day; over 80 percent of the members walked out to attend these meetings. Within individual departments, workers turned off their machines and walked into supervisors' offices to present grievances.

The company retaliated by firing seven workers, suspending forty-three others, and issuing 231 written reprimands, but the union did not back off. For example, a worker who received a written reprimand taped it to the back of his shirt. The foreman complained and almost immediately 70 percent of the workers in the department taped reprimand forms to their shirts. The next day, the foreman was transferred.

On Martin Luther King's birthday, a holiday demand of the union, nearly all the workers stayed away from the plant. On another occasion, an entire department walked out in protest over health hazards, after repeatedly asking management to make changes.

In March, nearly six months after the old contract expired, a new three-year contract calling for a 36 percent increase in wages and benefits was signed. In addition, the union won reinstatement with full back pay for all workers who were fired or suspended during the dispute; reprimands were also rescinded. The union beat the strike-decertification scenario.[17]

The purpose of this strategy is to buy time for the union to pressure the employer into a more favorable contract without striking and risking a decertification. There is no guarantee that the final settlement will be better, because the employer may not submit to the pressure. In Local 282's case, the final settlement was perhaps what might be expected from a company producing automobile replacement parts and benefiting from the 1981-82 slump in new car sales. If 30 percent of Local 282's members were laid off, the final settlement might have been a takeaway contract despite use of the tactic.

Once the contract expires, it is extremely important for the union to continue to bargain in "good faith" and to avoid reaching an "impasse." If an impasse is not reached, the terms and conditions of the old contract continue. In planning its strategy, the union should be very careful if it is considering having union members engage in actions that violate the contract. Union members can be disciplined for breaking work rules such as refusing overtime if it is mandatory, protesting safety conditions by walking off the job, or sabotaging machinery. Ultimately, these job actions could result in the discharge of union activists and their replacement by employees whom the employer believes will support a decertification. Certain other activities such as conducting union meetings during lunch hours and protests made during nonwork hours would probably be considered protected union activities by the Board.

Could this tactic have worked in the PATCO strike? Possibly. By returning to work but refusing to sign the agreement on the government's terms, the union could have saved face and served notice to the FAA that it was not returning to "business as usual." If poor management was the real issue, the union may have been able to exert enough pressure internally and from the public to resolve the issue favorably.

There is nothing new about working without a contract and pressuring the employer in the meantime, but as UAW Local 282 has demonstrated, it can be a good way of beating the strike-decertification strategy.

Many unions achieved recognition from employers in the 1930s through sitdown strikes. It was a popular though illegal tactic which at times and places spread like wildfire; in April 1937, for example, an estimated 25 percent of Detroit's labor force was involved in sitdowns. Workers in manufacturing, transportation, retailing, food service, and virtually every other industry occupied their places of employment around the clock until their unions were recognized. Two factors made the sitdowns successful. Law enforcement officials were often reluctant to oust the sitdown strikers, because they wanted to avoid bloodshed and, in some cases, sympathized with the strikers. Another factor was that some employers feared that valuable machinery and other equipment would be destroyed if the police and national guard stormed the plants, stores, and offices.

During the summer of 1980, UAW members in Ontario, Canada, used this old tactic when their employer, Houdaille Co., announced that the plant would be closed. The sitdowners won higher pensions and severance pay, demonstrating that the effectiveness of this old tactic is not dead.[18]

The Polish Solidarity Movement also used the sitdown strike in 1980 to gain recognition from its employer, the Polish government.

Including the sitdown strike in a section titled "Alternatives To the Strike" may seem inappropriate, but the sitdown strike is not like ordinary strikes that allow the employer to easily bring scabs into the workplace and launch the strike-decertification scenario. Illegal and a serious threat to worker safety, the sitdown strike may be the only alternative in those situations where leaving the workplace subjects workers to the full force of the employer's power. U.S. workers in the 1930s and more recently in Oshawa, Ontario, and Poland used the sitdown strike for this very reason.[19]

CONCLUSION

Difficult as it is, a union must attempt to forecast the outcome of a strike, thereby equipping itself to avoid suicidal strikes and to choose between alternative actions. If a union does strike, the factor determining the strike's outcome over which it can exercise considerable control is the solidarity of the union's membership. This, then, is the first line of defense against "deunionization," whether the threat comes during a strike or at another time. Building union solidarity through internal organizing is the subject of the next chapter, "Staying Organized."

FOOTNOTES

[1] Edward Meadows, "The FAA Keeps Them Flying," *Fortune,* December 28, 1981, p. 51.

[2] Jonathan Alter, "Featherbedding in the Tower," *Washington Monthly,* October 1981, pp. 22–27.

[3] "The Economics of the Air Controllers' Strike," *Dollars & Sense,* October 1981, No. 70, pp. 6–8.

[4] Robert E. Poli, "A PATCO Post-Mortem—Why the Controllers' Strike Failed," *The New York Times,* January 17, 1982, p. 2F.

[5] Poli, "A PATCO Post-Mortem."

[6] John J. Oslund, "FAA Managers Blamed for PATCO Strike," *The Minneapolis Tribune,* August 1, 1982, p. 8D.

[7] John Oslund, "Expert Concludes FAA Should Rehire Controllers," *The Minneapolis Star and Tribune,* April 14, 1982, p. 7C.

[8] Oslund, "FAA Managers Blamed."

[9] Herbert E. Meyer, "The Decline of Strikes," *Fortune,* November 2, 1981, pp. 66–70.

[10] Meyer, "The Decline of Strikes," p. 70.

[11] The legal requirements are beyond the scope of this book. Refer to a labor law book like Feldacker's *Labor Guide to Labor Law* (Reston Publishing Company, 1980).

[12] Workers who engage in strikes that violate the no-strike provision in union contracts engage in illegal strikes and can be discharged or otherwise disciplined by the employer. So-called "wildcat" strikers would have no right to vote in a decertification election unless they are reinstated by the employer, an unlikely event when a decertification election is pending.

[13] Alfred T. De Maria, *The Process of Deunionization* (New York: Executive Enterprise Publications, 1979), p. 52.

[14] This section draws heavily upon *How to Win Strikes—A Union Strike Manual,* prepared by Teamsters Union Local No. 115 in 1979. This booklet has excellent material on strike preparedness and strategy. Contact Teamsters Union Local No. 115, 2833 Cottman Avenue, Philadelphia, Pa. 19149.

[15] Josephine Marcotty, "Bureau of Engraving Strike Settled," *Minneapolis Tribune,* June 26, 1982, pp. 1A and 4A.

[16] Dave Elsila, "Moog: The Saga of a Shop-Floor Victory," *UAW Solidarity,* June 1982, p. 12.

[17] Elsila, "Moog," pp. 12–16.

[18] "Strike Back: It Takes More Than a Picket Line," *American Labor,* No. 18, p. 2.

[19] A film, *Houdaille: Days of Courage, Days of Rage,* is available from UAW Education Department, 8000 East Jefferson, Detroit MI 48214.

8

Staying Organized

Teach courses to union activists for a number of years and without asking or even implying that you are interested, you will hear all sorts of complaints about their unions:

> "We haven't seen our business agent in six months. The only time we hear from the union office is when our per capita check is late."

> "We wait forever to get a response on grievances. When the business agent finally comes in, he wheels and deals with the boss on a whole bunch of old grievances. He wins some and loses some, but always tells us that without him we wouldn't get a thing. We're fed up."

> "We didn't vote for our business agent in the last election, so he doesn't do anything for us now."

> "Our international rep has so many contracts to negotiate that all he seems interested in is getting the contract settled. Our lousy contract shows that."

> "When we were trying to organize, the union couldn't do enough for us. Now that we're in the union, it's nearly impossible to get them to come over."

> "The international disbanded our local and a bunch of other small locals and threw us together into one big local. Supposedly, this is more efficient. Hell, we got better service with a part-time business agent! We also had control of our union."

"We have meetings of the amalgamated local and we feel left out. A couple of big units dominate the meetings and spend all of the time talking about their problems."

"We never had shop stewards until three months ago. Our contract called for a union shop but it wasn't enforced. Only two out of 46 people joined the union. Our contract expired over a year ago and we're still negotiating. The employer doesn't want to give us a union shop now. Our business agent has 75 shops to cover. The only good thing is that our local is being merged with a 20 shop local with one business agent. We'll have two business agents for 95 shops, rather than one for 75 shops."

Most of these complaints are from workers in small units of less than fifty members, precisely the size unit which is most likely to decertify.[1] This is not surprising. The units the activists represent are often amalgamated into local unions comprised of many small units. In other unions, each small unit is designated as a "local" and is affiliated with a regional or district office of the international union. Regardless of the union structure, each small unit is highly dependent upon one or more business agents or international union representatives who travel from unit to unit providing collective bargaining and contract administration services.

Too often, it is physically impossible for one man or woman in the role of union business agent or international representative to adequately tend to all of the units placed under his or her jurisdiction. The problem of having too many units to service is aggravated when the units are spread out over large geographic regions. It is not uncommon for one full-time union staff person to be responsible for all of the small units that the union represents in one state. The situation is aggravated further because, regardless of whether business agents or international representatives are elected or appointed, too often they are insecure and fearful of sharing their authority with the people they represent. They may have attained their present position by challenging the performance of a previous representative. Allowing members of the various small units to exercise authority so that the overall effectiveness of the union improves is viewed as risky, because challengers to the union representative's position might arise. The "supreme commander" approach to union leadership is bound to fail with the ultimate demonstration of its failure being decertification of the union.

In a previous chapter, we saw the importance of Saul Alinsky's "Iron Rule" of organizing—"never do for others what they can do for themselves"—and how to apply this rule to organizing unorganized workers. Alinsky's "Iron Rule" is equally important and more difficult to apply in the process of internal organizing. The outside organizer has limited access to groups of unorganized workers and, therefore, more incentive to follow the "Iron Rule" than the internal organizer who has greater access to organized workers and must overcome his or her fear of relinquishing control.

Internal organizing provides answers to the question, "What am I getting in return for my union dues?" Internal organizing demonstrates that the choice of union representation is an efficient expenditure of money, time, and effort. Internal organizing is a continuous process which should begin the moment a union achieves certification as the exclusive bargaining agent for a group of workers. Internal organizing is based upon the premise that through the demonstration of the union's effectiveness at solving workplace issues, nonmembers and apathetic members will be motivated to join and to actively support the union. Recall the two primary reasons why workers form unions. They expect the union to improve wages and fringe benefits, and they expect the union to give them a fair shake at the workplace through a grievance procedure and seniority system. Internal organizing is important for all unions, particularly those whose collective bargaining power is limited so that they are unable to demonstrate significant wage and fringe benefit plans. In this era of recurring high inflation and low economic growth, many unions find themselves in this unfortunate position. Every workplace, however, has issues that the union can use as a vehicle for demonstrating its effectiveness.

When organizing a group of unorganized workers, the union can promise improved wages and working conditions as a result of union representation. Too often, it is precisely the exaggerated promises of what the union will do after winning an organizing drive that sow the seeds for a decertification. Promises will not win an internal organizing drive. The union has established a track record. The track record may not be very good in the view of a substantial portion of the bargaining unit. Internal organizing seeks to improve the union's performance or at least the manner in which its performance is viewed by the workers it represents.

It is no coincidence that the unions that devote considerable attention to internal organizing around issues other than wages and fringe benefits are in the public sector. They are too often denied the right to bargain over wages and fringe benefits by law. Instead, they are restricted to lobbying government legislative bodies for wage and benefit increases. These efforts are not always successful. Where they are successful, it is often difficult for union members and "free riders" to see the connection between the unions' lobbying efforts and wage and benefit improvements. Furthermore, public sector unions are too often denied the right to negotiate union shop provisions and the right to strike. Public sector union activists have on numerous occasions told me that the most frequent retort they get from "free riders" when asking them to join the union is "When we can strike, I'll join." On reflection, this response should not be too surprising. The media give a disproportionate amount of attention to the relatively small number of strikes that occur each year. Peaceful settlements, often for better contract terms, do not receive as much publicity. To an uninformed public, union power is too often equated with strikes. Internal organizing demonstrates that the union can exert power without striking and in areas of vital concern to workers other than wages and benefits.

Does this mean that unions that represent large bargaining units and that are effective at contract negotiations and contract administration should not be concerned with internal organizing? No! Even if a union decertification seems implausible, internal organizing is important for all unions. Internal organizing seeks to improve the solidarity of the union which should make it even more effective at contract negotiations and contract administration.

STEWARDS AND INTERNAL ORGANIZING

The internal organizing process relies upon the union representatives who are closest to members of the bargaining unit on a day-to-day basis. Usually, they have the title of "steward" or "shop steward." Sometimes they are called "building representative," "unit representative," "griever," or "grievance handler." They are not full-time union staff; their major daily activity is working for the employer. The steward's primary union activity is involvement at the first or second step of the grievance procedure.

If a union does not have a steward system which gives bargaining unit members face-to-face access to union representatives on a daily basis, then it must activate one. Just as union avoidance consultants cannot prevent union organization without utilizing foremen or other first-line supervisors, there is no way that full-time union staff can accomplish the task of internal organizing without relying on the direct involvement of union stewards. Some unions, which did not have stewards at workplaces comprised of small numbers of workers and which relied upon full-time business agents to provide service by traveling among workplaces, have eliminated business agent positions. The money previously spent on business agent salaries and expenses was used to train and support stewards at each workplace. The unions' presence was felt at each workplace on a daily basis. Service improved. The unions' dismal record with decertifications was reversed. Other unions have kept all of their business agents and added stewards to each workplace. Similar improvements in service have occurred. Decertifications have stopped. "Don't do for others what they can do for themselves."

Employers require foremen and other first-line supervisors to participate in union avoidance activities as a part of their jobs. In addition, management personnel are provided with the time and the training to conduct union avoidance activities. Many stewards are not as fortunate. They receive little or no training. Their contracts may allow them to take time off the job for union business, but often this is confined to grievance handling. Too often, a steward is responsible for too large of a unit to service adequately on grievances let alone internal organizing. The steward system becomes solely a defensive apparatus of the union. Rarely do the stewards go on the offensive on behalf of their unions as internal organizers.

A union that makes the commitment to internal organizing must emphasize internal organizing activities as a major function of stewardship to all who accept the position. More important, it must take the necessary steps to enable stewards to function as internal organizers. There are two steps that need to be taken. The union must provide stewards with the TIME to organize and the TRAINING to be internal organizers.

Providing stewards with the time for internal organizing may be accomplished by negotiating a release time for union business clause in the contract where one does not exist or by liberalizing the present clause. However, the cost in terms of what must be traded-off in collective bargaining in order to get the provision may be too great. There is an obvious alternative. If internal organizing cannot be accomplished "on the clock," then it may be accomplished "off the clock." However, internal organizing "off the clock" requires more stewards or other union representatives than "on the clock" organizing.

How many union representatives engaged in internal organizing are necessary for a workplace? Every workplace is different, so that no ratio of bargaining unit members to internal organizers can be specified. Let us examine employer policy for guidance. No employer would maintain a ratio of supervisors to workers that did not allow supervisors to have face-to-face contact or, at least, oral contact over the telephone with each of his or her subordinates on a daily basis. This policy acknowledges that the most effective type of communication is oral communication, preferably face-to-face. This daily communication between supervisors and workers is an important aspect of "deunionization" campaigns.

For the union, however, daily contact is not necessary and may even be self-defeating, if bargaining unit members perceive frequent contact initiated by stewards as intrusive and annoying. Union representatives should at least have the capability of face-to-face communication with every bargaining unit member on a weekly basis. The length of time necessary for each conversation need not be long; a few minutes should suffice. Because workers gather in small groups during rest periods and lunch breaks, stewards or other union representatives may be able to communicate with a number of workers simultaneously.

Achieving the capability of face-to-face communication with each member of the bargaining unit on a weekly basis requires no change for many unions. Unions without stewards which rely on business agents to provide service do not meet this guideline. Some unions with stewards and even some with release time for union business clauses in their contracts do not meet this guideline either, because there are simply too many bargaining unit members for stewards to adequately service. The best way to determine whether the union has a sufficient number of representatives to meet the guideline is to test the union's internal organizing communications system. Communicate a message not directly related to internal organizing. For example, each bargaining unit member could be invited personally to attend the next union meeting. Or each worker could be asked to support labor-endorsed candidates in an upcoming political election. Ask each steward to convey the information through face-to-face communication with the workers they represent. Determine whether stewards are able to communicate the message through "on the clock" or "off the clock" conversations with bargaining unit members. Stewards should not jeopardize their work records with the employer through on the clock conversations which violate the contract or work rules established by the employer. Likewise, the internal organizing activity should not impede stewards from performing their grievance handling function.

If a union finds that it does not pass the test of being able to communicate face-to-face with each bargaining unit member in a week, then it must increase the number of its union representatives. Some contracts limit the number of stewards. Even where the number of stewards may be increased rather easily, the union may believe that the grievance handling function is adequately covered. In either case, if the union is to engage in internal organizing it must create a position that provides the union with face-to-face communication with each bargaining unit member on a weekly basis. The position could be titled "assistant steward," "assistant griever," or "internal organizer." Ideally, it should be an elected position whose only function is to supplement the steward system so that effective internal organizing can be conducted.

Either the union's executive board or a special committee should be established to direct the internal organizing campaign. Their primary function is to train stewards and other union representatives to conduct internal organizing activities and to coordinate these activities on a continuous basis. The necessary training is not complicated and does not require a great deal of time. It is, however, crucial. The easiest way to accomplish the training is to have stewards and other internal organizers read this chapter. Then have a meeting to discuss the material, to add, delete, and otherwise adapt the suggestions made in the chapter to fit the particular circumstances of your union, and to practice some of the exercises suggested in the chapter. Through this "group think" process, the union should be able to develop an internal organizing mechanism with which it is comfortable and which is, above all, effective.

DEVELOPING A UNION SURVEY

For a union to rely on the warning signs enumerated in chapter 6 is a very passive approach to combating decertifications. The old saying that the best defense is a good offense applies to internal organizing. Rather than waiting for the employer to tip its hand, it is better for the union to take the initiative and determine just how likely is a successful decertification.

The first step in the internal organizing process is for the union to conduct a thorough self-examination. This is often difficult—not because it is necessarily very time consuming, but because union leaders tend to be very skeptical about the process of examining the performance of the union. To some, the process alone is very threatening. It is almost as if "in ignorance, there is bliss." Some typical objections to self-examination and repudiations of the objections follow:

> Examining the objections to the union's performance can play into management's hands. If management gets a hold of this information, they will use it to bust the union.

In chapter 3, the tactics of union avoidance consultants were examined. Management does not need to be fed inside information from the union to find out what objections members of the bargaining unit have to the union's performance. Employers often pay hundreds and even thousands of dollars per day to consultants to have them identify the union's weaknesses. Even if the union is filled with management spies, it will not be divulging information to the employer that it cannot find out itself. To believe that management does not know about union avoidance consultants and the service they offer is totally naive.

> You are never going to please all of the people in the bargaining unit regardless of what you do.

True! Internal organizing and its component of self-examination of the union are not intended to please all of the members of the bargaining unit. This is impossible. What is sought, however, is to make the union more responsive to more members of the bargaining unit than before so that allegiance to the union increases.

> We have regular membership meetings once a month, special meetings at contract time, a lot of grievances being filed, and a union newsletter sent to our members' homes to get our views

across. The union leadership has little opposition at election time or contract ratification time. The union must be supported by the membership.

Not necessarily true! A substantial portion of the membership may be apathetic, afraid to speak out, or may believe that challenging the union leadership is fruitless. A decertification campaign may provide the spark that brings dissatisfaction to the surface. The union should not take membership support for granted.

If we ask the membership how the union is doing, we are bound to hear all sorts of farfetched complaints. Even if everything is okay, they are sure to give us bad ratings just to keep us on our toes.

This apprehension must occur to employers when they follow the advice of union avoidance consultants and conduct surveys of their employees in an attempt to identify areas for improvement, whose correction will help defeat union organization. There are bound to be some workers who will exaggerate their complaints, just as there are bound to be some workers who will not reveal their complaints probably out of fear that their individual responses will somehow be attributable to them and some form of retribution will be taken against them. The premise behind attitude surveys is that only a small minority of workers hide their true beliefs so that a rather accurate picture of the beliefs of the group is depicted.

The act of asking in and by itself is a demonstration of the union's responsiveness to its members. If management asks, it is demonstrating its responsiveness to workers. It is better for the union, the organization charged with the mandate of representing the interests of workers, to do the asking. If the union does not ask the question, "What is wrong with *us*?", management will surely ask the question, "What is wrong with *them*?"

The self-examination begins with the development of a questionnaire by the union's executive board or a special committee established for the purpose of internal organizing. The questionnaire technique is borrowed from union avoidance consultants. The questionnaire will be distributed to all members of the bargaining unit and attempts to provide answers to the following three questions:

1. **Overall, do bargaining unit members view the union as effectively servicing their needs at the workplace?**

At this stage, the self-examination should not focus on specific work-related issues. The greatest dissatisfaction over the union's performance may be its inability to negotiate an end to mandatory overtime or a cost-of-living adjustment or to improve ventilation in the plant or office. And the best way to improve its image might be to resolve these specific workplace issues. The internal organizing process will focus upon specific workplace issues at a later stage. For now, the self-examination should focus on how workers view the *overall* performance of the union relative to what workers would expect if there was no union. By determining whether or not workers view themselves as better off with the union than without it, the union can determine whether a union decertification is likely and the extent to which it must alter its performance.

Examine questions 1, 2, 3, and 4 on the Union Survey (Exhibit 8–1). These questions attempt to gauge the views that bargaining unit members hold of the union's overall performance. If bargaining unit members believe that their wages and benefits are no better because of the union and that union representation in the grievance procedure is not helpful, there is little reason for them to continue union representation. If young workers comprise a large portion of the bargaining unit and they are dissatisfied with the seniority system, there is reason for concern.

These questions may not be appropriate for your union; other questions may be more appropriate. The objective, however, remains the same. The views of bargaining unit members on the union's overall performance should be measured in order to determine the likelihood of a union decertification effort and the extent to which the union must change its performance.

2. **Do bargaining unit members believe that they participate in the decision-making process of the union?**

Recent studies of auto workers and telephone company employees indicate that employee job satisfaction depends more on factors that give workers an opportunity to participate in decision-making than on wages, fringe benefits, job training, and relationships with co-workers. Among the behavior traits of management that brought employee approval and job satisfaction were giving employees ad-

EXHIBIT 8–1. Union Survey

This survey is being distributed to all members of the bargaining unit during lunch periods. Your union would like to know your views on how well it is representing your interests and what it can do to improve. Please take a few minutes to answer the questions. Do *not* sign the survey. Place the completed survey in the envelope provided to you, seal the envelope, and place it in the collection box maintained by your union representative. All responses are *confidential*.

1. Would you trust management to give you a fair deal on grievances, if there was no union?
    Yes _____   No _____

2. While the union does not always win, do you believe that it tries hard to represent you and your interests on grievances?
    Yes _____   No _____

3. Would you trust management to make fair decisions regarding promotions and layoffs without the seniority clause in the union contract?
    Yes _____   No _____

4. Do you believe that the union has been able to raise your wages and fringe benefits to a higher level than they would be without the union?
    Yes _____   No _____

5. Do you believe that you can express your views on union matters?
    Yes _____   No _____

6. Do you believe that you have the opportunity to run for union office?
    Yes _____   No _____

7. Do you believe that the union is run democratically, meaning that union members control the union?
    Yes _____   No _____

8. If a majority of union members voted to strike, would you join the strike?
    Yes _____   No _____

9. Union meetings are currently held at 8 p.m. on the first Tuesday of every month. Would you be more interested in attending union meetings if they were held immediately after work?
    Yes _____   No _____

10. How much of the union newsletter do you read?
    Almost all ___
    Some _____
    Very little _____

11. What are your major gripes about the union?

EXHIBIT 8–1. (Continued)

12.   What can the union do to improve?

13.   Please indicate your years of seniority:
      _____ 1 month to 2 years
      _____ 3 to 10 years
      _____ Over 10 years

14.   Please indicate your job classification:
      _____ Production
      _____ Maintenance

---

vance notice of changes, showing interest in employees' feelings about their work, dealing with employees in a straightforward manner, and taking workers' suggestions seriously.[2]

The same general factors may determine worker satisfaction with their unions. A survey of 1,515 union members in 1977 disclosed that they are generally satisfied with their unions' performance. The greatest dissatisfaction was expressed over "'internal union administration', . . . grievance handling, more say in the union, more feedback from the union." The need for improvement expressed over these areas was greater than that expressed over wages and fringe benefits.[3] This finding indicates that union members may be more concerned about participating in the internal affairs of their unions than one might conclude from attendance at union meetings.

A key strategy of union avoidance consultants is to develop employment relationships with workers that appear to give employees a voice in how the workplace is managed. According to *The Non-Union Company,* published by a management consulting firm:

> Poor communications is perhaps the major single cause for employee unrest. Particularly the younger generation wants a piece of the action; they require a feeling of involvement, to be "in" on things . . . If management is clever about the thing, it can also make the employees feel they are involved in some of the decisions made affecting them even though the company had planned to do it all along.[4]

The consultants view worker participation in decision-making as important but acknowledge that management does not want to share its authority.

I too am skeptical about management in the United States relinquishing some of its control and allowing effective worker participation in the management decision-making process. As appealing as quality circles, worker participation, and job enrichment are they do not have the same feasibility in the United States as in Japan, Sweden, and West Germany, their major practitioners. In Japan, workers are virtually assured of lifetime employment by their employers; in Sweden, by the government. In West Germany, worker representation on company boards of directors is required by law. A similar social contract between labor, capital, and government in the United States is not likely.

If participation is as important as the management consultants say, unions are at a distinct advantage relative to management. Unions by their very nature are supposed to involve workers in the decision-making process of the union. However, when they do not satisfy this objective, unions are in violation of the law and can be forced to involve workers in the decision-making process. There is no law in the United States requiring management to share decision-making with workers, except to the extent required by the laws of collective bargaining.

The Labor-Management Reporting and Disclosure Act of 1959, commonly known as the Landrum-Griffin Act, gives members of private sector unions a so-called "Bill of Rights." Union members have equal rights, the right of free speech, the right to pass on dues increases, the right to sue the union, the right of due process in the event of disciplinary measures imposed by the union, and the right to inspect the books and records of their unions upon showing cause. While the administration of the law by the U.S. Department of Labor has been lackluster, some important changes in the way unions handle their internal affairs have come about under Landrum-Griffin. There are lawyers and an organization titled the Association for Union Democracy that advocate strong labor unions. They will assist union members who find themselves prevented from participating in the internal affairs of their unions to remedy the conditions through the courts. Those who oppose strong labor unions also stand ready to pay the legal expenses of union members whose right to participation is infringed upon. The National Right to Work Committee has established a so-called "Legal Defense Fund" to assist union members. Unions that do not provide their members with the right of participation find it increasingly difficult to maintain this condition.

In addition to the potential futility of unions obstructing membership participation, there is an even more compelling reason for unions to involve members in the decision-making process. By involving members in the union's decision-making process, the likelihood of a decertification is lessened. Employer charges of "outsiders" and "union bosses" are empty when workers believe that they control their unions.

Examine questions 5, 6, 7, and 8 on the Union Survey (Exhibit 8–1). If union members do not believe that they can criticize the union or run for union office, they certainly do not believe that they have an opportunity to participate in the decision-making process of the union. Likewise, if they do not believe that the union is run democratically, they will feel divorced from the union. If a significant portion of the bargaining unit indicates that it would not support an authorized strike, this is a reflection on both the union's overall performance and the extent to which members believe that they participate in the union's decision-making process.

Again, the questions on the Union Survey suggest questions that may be appropriate for your union. The objective is the same regardless of the specific questions asked. The extent to which members of the bargaining unit believe that they have the opportunity to participate in the union's decision-making process should be measured.

3. What can be done to improve the union's performance in the view of bargaining unit members?

In developing questions for this part of the survey, it is important for the executive board or special internal organizing committee to brainstorm for ideas that might improve the union's performance. The executive board or internal organizing committee should also meet with stewards and incorporate their suggestions into the questionnaire. Two suggestions might be to change the time for union meetings and to stop relying on the union newsletter as the primary means for communicating with members. These suggestions are the basis for questions 9 and 10 on the Union Survey (Exhibit 8–1). Questions 11 and 12 are open-ended, meaning that they do not require a simple "Yes" or "No" answer and provide bargaining unit members with the opportunity to express their views on problems with the union and their suggestions for improvement.

In most bargaining units, there are significant differences between the workers who comprise the unit. Some workers have many years of seniority, while others have been at the workplace only a year or two. The type of work performed and wage rates also vary significantly. In addition to examining the views of the bargaining unit as a whole, the union can find it very useful to know the views of the various groups within the bargaining unit. Therefore, the Union Survey (Exhibit 8–1) contains two questions that endeavor to identify the views of different groups of workers within the bargaining unit.

Question 13 on the Union Survey asks about the seniority classification of the worker. The three classifications are derived from the seniority list. There are seventy-five workers within the bargaining unit represented by Local 100. Each seniority classification should represent one third of the workers. Therefore, twenty-five workers are in each of the three classifications. Starting with the most recently hired member of the bargaining unit, twenty-five workers were counted. Their seniority ranged from one month to two years. The next twenty-five workers counted had a seniority range of three to ten years. One third of the workers had over ten years of seniority.

There are two general job classifications within the bargaining unit represented by Local 100—production and maintenance. In other bargaining units, different job classifications are appropriate. Clerical and secretarial or straight-time wage and incentive might describe the job differences in your unit. Question 14 on the Union Survey asks workers to identify their job classification.

The questionnaire should be short. Ideally, it should fit on one page. The longer the questionnaire, the less likely bargaining unit members will respond.

DISTRIBUTING THE UNION SURVEY

Before distributing the survey, the union should mail a letter to each bargaining unit member's home. An example of such a letter is shown in Exhibit 8–2. The letter expresses the union's concern over the activities of union avoidance consultants, the poor image of organized labor projected by the media, the low level of participation at union

EXHIBIT 8–2. Letter to Union Member

UNITED WORKERS OF AMERICA — LOCAL 100

October 2, 1980

Mr. Olaf Olafson
32 Lutefisk Lane
Bloomingdales, MN 55499

Dear Olaf:

I am writing to you on behalf of the officers of Local 100. As the union enters its 28th anniversary year, we are very concerned about some recent developments and want to share our concerns with you.

So-called "union avoidance consultants" have become very active in Minnesota. In May, a two-day seminar on "Making Unions Unnecessary" was held in Minneapolis. Employers paid $500 to attend. Tax deductible, of course! The seminar was really a sales meeting. The consultants want to sign long-term contracts with employers and charge thousands of dollars per day to assist management in breaking unions. Are we going to be challenged by a bunch of high-priced lawyers hired by management to break this union?

During the past year, the TV and other news media have featured stories about a small number of unions which work against the interests of their members. These stories give all labor unions a bad image. The United Workers of America—Local 100 has represented the employees of J. J. Good since 1952. The people who helped form this union are retired. We are not sure that the people who have joined J. J. Good since 1952 really know why the union was formed and what it has accomplished.

As you know, the union has regular membership meetings every month. Like all other labor unions in the United States, we find that except for special contract ratification meetings, only a small percentage of the membership attends meetings. We would like to improve communication with the membership. We want to know how the members feel about the union and what the union can do to improve.

Next payday, you will receive a short questionnaire distributed during lunch period. Your appraisal of the union is requested. Replies are confidential and for the use of the union only. The questionnaire will take only a few minutes to complete. Please fill it out and turn it in.

Remember that the elected officers are not the union. You are the union! Fill out the questionnaire on payday and give your ideas on how the union is doing and what it can do to improve.

Yours truly,

Erik Erikson
President, Local 100

meetings, and the absence of the founders of the union from the bargaining unit. Plans for the distribution of the survey are announced and the cooperation of bargaining unit members is sought. Although it is basically a form letter, it should have some personal touches, such as addressing the recipient by his or her first name. A good premise for the letter is the anniversary of the founding of the union. While the letter does not expressly state that the union has made mistakes in the past, this may be inferred by some readers. Above all, the union conveys that the union is concerned and is willing to make an effort to improve.

The questionnaire can be distributed to bargaining unit members in two ways. One way leaves the union in the dark regarding the views of a substantial portion of the bargaining unit. The other has a greater likelihood of achieving a response from all members of the unit. The questionnaire can be passed out to workers as they leave or enter the workplace or mailed to their home. Workers must then fill out the questionnaires on their own time and either give the completed surveys to union representatives, drop them in collection boxes, or mail them to the union. Because the time between distribution and collection is long, many workers will put off answering the questions and returning the surveys. The union will be lucky to get responses from half the members of the unit. Apathetic union members and free riders, the persons most likely to support a decertification and to cross a union picket line, are the least likely to complete and return the questionnaires. The union is left in the dark.

Similarly, unions that do not use questionnaires and that rely solely upon discussions with stewards and other union activists to provide answers to the questions raised by the surveys receive only partial information on the views of the bargaining unit. Some bargaining unit members may not want to provide information. Others may be less than honest because they fear repercussion if their beliefs are known and can be attributed to them.

The other method for distributing and collecting the questionnaires is an adaptation of the tactic used by union avoidance consultants. They take workers off the job, gather them in a cafeteria or other large meeting place, and distribute their questionnaires. Workers are compelled to respond. Unions are not likely to get the permission of employers to conduct union surveys during work hours. If such permission would be forthcoming, however, unions should be cautious about accepting the opportunity lest the impression be given that the employer is collaborating with the union on the survey. The union does have other alternatives.

Under the Labor-Management Relations Act, unions have the right to distribute literature at the workplace during nonwork hours such as rest breaks and lunch periods. A request to complete a short, one-page questionnaire is a small imposition upon the free time of bargaining unit members. If workers customarily eat their lunches in a single cafeteria, at vending machine areas dispersed throughout the workplace, or at their workstations, the distribution and collection of the questionnaires by union stewards is relatively easy. If bargaining unit members leave the workplace and disperse during lunch periods, distribution and collection is more difficult but not impossible. Stewards can distribute surveys over the span of a few days as workers leave the job and collect the questionnaires upon their return. Everyone will not cooperate, but the union will obtain survey results for a larger proportion of the bargaining unit than by sending the surveys to workers' homes or by merely distributing and collecting questionnaires in mass.

The union should assure the confidentiality of responses. Sealable envelopes in which surveys can be placed should be provided. The appearance of confidentiality will be enhanced if stewards maintain collection boxes in which the surveys in sealed envelopes are placed. See the instructions to respondents at the beginning of the Union Survey (Exhibit 8–1).

CHANGING DIRECTIONS

After bargaining unit members respond to the union survey, the next step is to compile the results. This is a relatively simple task. The only complications may occur with large bargaining units because of the large number of surveys to be counted. If there is room in the union treasury for such an expenditure, a data processing service can be employed. There is an aura of scientific accuracy to computer print-outs, but the results are no different whether the survey responses are counted by hand or by computer. Large units choosing not to use a data processing service should divide the task of counting the survey responses among many union activists.

Regardless of whether the survey of bargaining unit members indicates that the union's performance is "excellent," the results of the survey should be released in order to substantiate confidence in the process. Unions with poor ratings on the survey must examine their policies and procedures and make changes. Unions with good ratings should look for ways to improve. This section contains a number of suggestions which should improve performance and membership satisfaction.

1. **If bargaining unit members doubt that the union's affairs are conducted democratically, the union should attempt to increase the participation of union members in the election of union officers.**

Leadership positions in some unions are hotly contested, and the vast majority of members vote in elections. Other unions never have a majority of members vote in elections of officers.

Unions can increase the role members play in governing the union by changing election procedures. If the union currently requires members to come to the union hall in order to vote, participation may increase by sending mail-in ballots to the homes of union members. Even more effective is voting at the workplace during time off the job in a manner similar to that recommended for the distribution of the union surveys.

Too often, issues presented by candidates in union elections are about on a par with those presented in elections to a high school student council. Name calling and promises with no rational explanations of how to achieve them are characteristic of many campaigns. To some union members, union elections are a joke, no more than a popularity contest. Of course, the same can be said about many elections for political office. Unions are in a position to upgrade the quality of rhetoric in campaigns for union office. Why not borrow from the tactic used by the League of Women Voters? Ask candidates to describe what they plan to accomplish through election to union office and how they propose to achieve their platforms. Limit them to a one-page response. Duplicate the positions of all candidates and distribute to union members.

Regardless of whether the union's elections are totally honest, cynics will claim that unions are incapable of policing themselves and will point to instances of union election fraud reported by the media to substantiate the claim. The union with honest elections may need to improve the image it conveys to its members. The appointment of election overseers comprised of respected members of the community may be the answer. Clergy, leaders of charitable organizations, and others who have established a reputation of honesty and integrity in the community should be willing to monitor union elections and lend credence to the honesty of elections.

2. **If the union receives low ratings on the survey for its ability to influence wages and fringe benefits, the union must investigate whether the perception of bargaining unit members is accurate.**

In recent years, most wage rates have not kept up with increases in the Consumer Price Index. This disparity is usually the reason for dissatisfaction over wages. However, a fairer test of the union's influence over wages is how the wages paid to bargaining unit members compare with those paid to workers in similar occupations employed elsewhere in the geographic region where the union is located. The Bureau of Labor Statistics of the U.S. Department of Labor conducts "Area Wage Surveys" which contain this information. The surveys provide information for both organized and unorganized employers. If the wage rates in the collective bargaining agreement exceed the rates for comparable occupations in the "Area Wage Survey," this information should be conveyed to bargaining unit members.

Pensions, health insurance, and other fringe benefits tend to be better at organized workplaces than at unorganized workplaces. The union should gather information on fringe benefits provided by other employers in their geographic area and provide this comparative information to bargaining unit members, if fringe benefit provisions in the contract exceed those of other employers.

The union can also demonstrate its accomplishments by distributing a one-page flyer comparing employment conditions prior to its organization with those in the current contract (see Exhibit 8–3).

Participation in the affairs of the union, and perhaps even the perception that bargaining unit members have of the union's performance in collective bargaining, can be improved by increasing the opportunities members have to formulate the union's contract demands. Nearly all unions conduct meetings at which members propose contract demands. Where these meetings are not well attended, some unions have developed alternative strategies for improving membership participation.

Some unions set up a telephone line with a device to record

EXHIBIT 8–3. Welcome to a New Member

Welcome to Local _____of the _____Union. We want you to know what your union has accomplished since it was organized in 19___. Be an active member, attend the local union meetings, and take part in all our activities. Help to make the organization a better one. Because of the support of the membership, here is what your union has won since it was organized.

	(Year Organized)	(Current Year)
WAGES		
FRINGE BENEFITS		
JOB SECURITY		
WORKING CONDITIONS		

If you have any questions concerning your rights, contact your steward, _____. Attend your membership meeting at _____Street. Date _____, Time _____.

---

incoming calls. They publicize the number and invite union members to call in suggestions for the union's collective bargaining agenda.

Other unions distribute questionnaires on the union's bargaining demands. The questionnaire may take the form of listing all the items suggested at the open meeting on negotiation demands. For each item, bargaining unit members are asked to indicate whether they view the item as "very important," "important," "somewhat important," or "unimportant." Suggestions for additional bargaining agenda items might also be requested. Not only does the union increase membership participation in its internal affairs, it is better prepared to negotiate and is more likely to achieve a contract ratification.

If the union surveys bargaining unit members prior to contract negotiations in order to determine the union's priorities in bargaining, it should consider releasing this information to management. Whether the union negotiators can get a contract ratification is always a concern of management. The closer the unratified settlement approaches the survey results, the better the odds for ratification.

3. **If the union received poor ratings on the survey of bargaining unit members for its handling of grievances, the union should attempt to identify the reasons.**

The test of the union's internal organizing communications system may indicate that there is an insufficient number of stewards or other union representatives to adequately service the bargaining unit. By increasing the number of stewards, the union may be able to improve its performance on grievance handling. It sounds simple, but it is not.

Some unions find it difficult to find union members to run for election to steward positions. Uncontested elections and no candidates at all for elections are common. Many unions find it difficult to retain stewards. The average career of the steward may be as low as two or three years—too short a time to learn the job because no training is provided for the stewards. Waiving union dues and small yearly stipends help unions retain stewards. Super-seniority for stewards during layoff and overtime periods help unions to make steward positions more desirable. Escape from the humdrum of the job, provided by the contract clause allowing release time for union business, also promotes interest in steward positions. However, for many unions these incentives do not solve the problem of attracting and retaining stewards.

Dissatisfaction with the steward position comes from a lack of training and a lack of authority. Untrained stewards are unable to deal with management and with the bargaining unit members they represent. Management makes them look bad on the grievances they file. Chronic complainers within the bargaining unit harass them with gripes, which untrained stewards find—the hard way—cannot be solved under the contract. The authority of stewards is undermined by the management policy of not allowing first-line supervisors to settle grievances with stewards at the first or second steps of the procedure and by union officers above the steward level who encourage bargaining unit members to by-pass stewards.

Unions receiving poor ratings on the survey for grievance handling but with little difficulty attracting and retaining stewards should examine the quality of the service they deliver. Stewards and other union officers involved in the grievance procedure may be simply outclassed by management. Experience is a great teacher, but it can also be the source of bad habits which reduce the effectiveness of the union at grievance handling.

The AFL-CIO, many international unions, and colleges and universities with labor education programs provide training on grievance handling. The best place to start when attempting to locate a program is your international union. Next, try the AFL-CIO's Department of Education. Compared to the cost of education in general, these programs are not expensive. But for local unions with small treasuries, it may be impossible for all stewards to attend. The union should send one or two stewards or other union officers to the course and have them train the other stewards. Printed materials are provided to participants in union and university grievance handling courses. Training for all of the local's stewards and other union officers can take the form of having everyone read the materials and meet to discuss the materials, with the people who attended the course leading the discussion.

Management's policy of not allowing first-line supervisors to settle grievances with stewards at the first or second step is not formally announced to the union. The union becomes aware of the policy through its day-to-day relationship with management. Some union officials encourage the practice. They do not trust their untrained stewards to settle grievances adequately and do not want to share their authority with others lest challengers to their positions emerge within the union. They remove decision-making from the shop or office floor, discourage stewards, prolong the settlement of grievances, and encourage bureaucratization of the union—precisely what promotes decertifications. If the union determines that it wants decision-making returned to stewards and management resists, the union is in a tough position. It must push and pull and otherwise cajole management to change its position. The issue should be brought to management's attention prior to and during contract negotiations. If the union's bargaining power permits, the union should be able to reverse management's policy. If not, the union leadership will, at least, convey to stewards that their abilities are respected.

No valid excuse exists for by-passing trained stewards. The union's executive board must make a commitment to following the lines of authority within the union and impose sanctions upon those who violate the principle. Maintenance of an effective steward system is too important an objective to be set aside in order to support the egos and insecurities of those who violate the principle.

4.   **The union should adopt a policy of having stewards seek out new employees and orient them to the union.**

Employers often hold orientation meetings for new employees. A member of the personnel department enumerates "employer provided" benefits such as vacations, hospitalization, and pensions and rules pertaining to matters such as promotions, absences, and work standards. If there is a union shop provision in the contract, new employees will be told that they are "required" to join the union. Rarely will the function of the union in collective bargaining and the grievance procedure be explained. If the contract does not have a union shop provision, the presence of the union may not even be mentioned, or the optional nature of the decision to join may be stressed. Criticisms of the union may be made. Some collective bargaining agreements provide unions with the opportunity to participate in new employee orientations. Most do not.

Regardless of whether a union shop provision exists, stewards should arrange to meet with new employees before work, during lunch periods, rest periods, or after work to orient them to the union. New employees should be given a copy of the union's constitution and bylaws and a copy of the current contract. These documents are not light reading and are not likely to be read thoroughly by most new members, but the documents should impress new members that the union is an organization of substance with written rules and regulations governing the conduct of its internal affairs and the conduct of the employer and bargaining unit members at the workplace. Contrary to the image projected by the media, unions and organized workplaces are not governed by the whims of union bosses but by rules and regulations developed by union members.

The union's executive board or internal organizing committee, in conjunction with stewards, should select key sections of the constitution, the bylaws, and the contract for discussion with new members. My selections from the constitution and bylaws would include procedures for electing union officers, formulating contract demands, ratifying contracts, calling strikes, and safeguarding union funds.

These aspects of the constitution and bylaws are selected because they project the image of the union as an honest, democratic organization. The union is controlled by the members for benefit of the members and not by "outsiders" and has procedures for accomplishing these objectives. Stewards should prepare a brief, informal presentation and be prepared to answer questions regarding these and other aspects of the constitution and bylaws.

From the contract, I would select (1) the grievance procedure and stress arbitration as a provision giving workers a better chance for a fair shake than at unorganized workplaces; (2) the seniority system with emphasis on management abuses prior to the union being organized; (3) wages and selected fringe benefits in comparison with their levels prior to the union; (4) the union shop clause, if applicable, and the reasons why the union needs dues money to cover collective bargaining costs and contract administration costs, primarily the cost of arbitration. If there is no union shop clause, reasons for supporting the union should be stressed.

If the survey of bargaining unit members indicates that workers with low seniority are more critical of the union's performance than workers with high seniority, the union should extend the orientation program for new employees to include low seniority workers.

The history of a union local is a useful tool for demonstrating the accomplishments of the union to new and recent members. As the founders of a local union retire, the bargaining unit loses sight of the reasons why the union was formed. The union's history need not be presented in a long, dull format. It can take the form of a short narrative with testimonials from the union's founders on the changes they have witnessed. Some union members are history buffs. They might be interested in putting together a short, snappy history for the local primarily by interviewing the union's founders. If not, contact a local college or university's history department. A teacher or student might be willing to take on the project.

If the union implements any of these suggestions or makes other changes in policy or procedures, bargaining unit members should be informed. Conveying the message through a union newsletter or leaflet is fine, but the importance of these changes as a demonstration of the union's responsiveness to bargaining unit members is too great to be left to the printed word. The union should communicate the changes through face-to-face conversation between stewards or other union representatives and bargaining unit members.

After the changes have been instituted and sufficient time has elapsed for bargaining unit members to feel their impact, the union should re-survey bargaining unit members. Additional changes may be necessary.

STAYING ON COURSE

The procedures outlined in this section are designed to make internal organizing as regular an activity of the union as the monthly membership meeting. In a nutshell, the process consists of identifying the concerns bargaining unit members have about the workplace, working to resolve these issues, and informing members of the union's efforts to resolve the issues.

The executive board or special internal organizing committee should work with stewards and other union representatives to develop a list of the bargaining unit members for whom each internal organizer will be responsible. The internal organizing communications system should be tested by following the procedure described above in order to determine whether there are a sufficient number of internal organizers. Adjustments of responsibilities indicated by the test should be made.

The executive board or internal organizing committee should supply internal organizers with a sufficient number of file cards in order that one may be maintained for each bargaining unit member. The cards should be preprinted in a manner similar to Exhibit 8–4. Space is provided for the name, department, job classification, the workplace concerns of the individual bargaining unit member, and the resolution of the issue. If there is no union shop clause, space is provided for indicating whether the individual is a union member.

Maintenance of the file cards has many purposes. The union is assured that all bargaining unit members are targeted for internal organizing. Continuity of the internal organizing activity can be attained when the people who hold steward and other internal organizer positions turn over. Most important, the information recorded on the cards assists the union in developing internal organizing strategies.

Information on the workplace concerns of bargaining unit members is gathered through very informal discussions during rest periods, lunch breaks, and before and after work. Internal organizers should not take notes while conversing with bargaining unit members. Information should be recorded privately at a later time.

There is no scientific recipe on how to frame one's conversation with bargaining unit members. Discussions with university professors who teach "Persuasive Communications" courses lead me to conclude two things. First, internal organizers must be comfortable dur-

---

EXHIBIT 8–4. Card for Maintaining Data on Bargaining Unit Members

Name _____ Union Member _____

Department _____

Job Classification _____

Workplace Issue:

Resolution:

Workplace Issue:

Resolution:

---

ing the conversations. They are not actors and should not try to follow a script. Be honest. Do not make incredible promises. Just straight talk. Be yourself!

Second, internal organizers should be good listeners. Listening means learning. Learning the views of bargaining unit members on the workplace and the union is vital to persuading them to support the union. Listening to someone demonstrates that he or she is important. Unions that demonstrate that bargaining unit members are important reduce the odds of being decertified and improve the odds of maintaining membership solidarity. The following are some hints on how to listen effectively while engaged in internal organizing:

1. **Stop Talking.** You can't listen while you are talking.

2. **Empathize with the Other Person.** Try to put yourself into the other person's place so that you can understand what the individual *is trying to say*.

3. **Ask Questions.** When you don't understand, when you need further clarification, when you want the person to like you, when you want to show that you are listening. Don't ask questions that will embarrass or belittle.

4. **Don't Interrupt.** Give the other person time to say what has to be said.

5. **Concentrate on What is Being Said.** Actively focus your attention on the words, ideas, and feelings that are being expressed about the union.

6. **Look at the Other Person.** The face, the mouth, the eyes, and

the hands will all help that person to communicate with you. Eye contact is most important. It helps you to concentrate, too. This makes the person feel that you are listening.

7. **Leave Your Emotions Behind** (if you can). Try to push your worries, your fears, your problems outside of the meeting room. "Personal hang-ups" may prevent you from listening well.

8. **Control Your Anger.** Try not to get angry at what a person says; your anger may prevent you from understanding the person's words or their true meaning.

9. **Get Rid of Distractions.** Put down any papers, buttons, pens, etc., that you may have in your hands; they may distract your attention.

10. **Get the Main Points.** Concentrate on the main ideas and not on side issues. Examine the side issues only to see if they prove, support, or define the main idea.

11. **Share Responsibility for Communication.** Only part of the responsibility rests with the speaker; you as the listener should ask for clarification when you don't understand a point.

12. **React to Ideas, Not to the Person.** Don't allow your reactions to the personality to influence your interpretation of what is being said. The ideas may be good even though you don't like the individual as a person or care for his or her looks.

13. **Don't Argue Mentally.** When you are trying to understand the other non-union worker, it is a handicap to argue mentally with each spoken word. This sets up a barrier to the communications between you and the nonmember.

14. **Use the Difference in Rate.** Speech rate is about 100 to 150 words per minute; thinking, 400 to 600 words per minute. Therefore, use this rate difference to your advantage; stay on track; anticipate, think over, and evaluate what has been said.

15. **Listen for What Is Not Said.** Sometimes you can learn just as much by determining what the other person leaves out or avoids in talking with you, as you can by listening to what is being said.

16. **Listen to How Something Is Said.** We frequently concentrate so hard on *what* is being said that we miss the importance of the reactions and attitudes related to what is said. The speaker's

attitudes and emotional reactions may be more important than *what* is actually said in words.

17. **Don't Antagonize the Non-Union Person.** You may cause the other person to conceal their ideas, emotions, and attitudes through antagonism in the following ways: arguing, criticizing, taking notes, sometimes not taking notes, asking questions, not asking questions, etc. Try to judge and be aware of the effect that you are having on the other person. *Adapt* to the individual.

18. **Listen for the Personality.** One of the best ways of finding out information about a person is to listen; as the person talks, the speech pattern will reveal likes and dislikes, motivations, value systems, thinking patterns, and how that person ticks.[6]

The conversations with bargaining unit members identify the issues of the internal organizing campaign. If the union is able to resolve workplace issues or at least demonstrate that it is able to exert some influence on the resolution of the issues, it can vividly answer the question "What am I getting in return for my union dues?"

Internal organizing relies on the three C's: *conflict, confrontation,* and *communication.* Workplace *conflicts* abound. A supervisor harasses workers. The amount of production required of workers increases without assistance in achieving the higher standards. Workers receive last-minute notices of overtime work. Workers are subject to unhealthy and unsafe working conditions. The list of potential conflicts is endless.

The need for talking to workers in order to identify workplace issues will not at all be clear to many stewards and other union representatives. They may already talk to all of the workers they represent about workplace conflicts. Or they may believe that if workers have problems, they do not hesitate to approach their union representatives. The worker who is shy, the worker who does not understand the role of the union, the worker who does not understand the union contract, and the worker who is afraid of filing a grievance lest he or she be branded a "troublemaker" by management do not approach their stewards. Criminal justice system experts estimate that at least half of the crimes committed in the United States go unreported. Is the workplace different? I doubt it. Consider that OSHA inspectors usually find health and safety violations, some of them being very serious, when they conduct inspections of union-organized workplaces. The union is often unaware of many of these violations until the inspection occurs.

Unions regularly use *confrontation* to resolve conflicts. Most confrontations occur through the grievance procedure. If a workplace issue is covered by a provision of the collective bargaining agreement, the union files a grievance in an attempt to resolve the conflict. If the union loses the grievance or the issue is beyond the scope of the contract, it may attempt to resolve the conflict through another type of confrontation, collective bargaining. The strike and threat of strike are integral parts of collective bargaining where allowed by law and sometimes where prohibited by law.

Grievances, collective bargaining, and strikes are not the only confrontation tactics available to unions, particularly in regard to "gripes." The most fundamental distinction stewards must make is between "grievances" and "gripes." Grievances are work-related conflicts that are covered in the contract. Gripes are work-related conflicts *not* covered in the contract. Thus, a conflict such as the employer requiring increased production from workers is a grievance for some unions, because the contract gives the union a role in determining production standards, and a gripe for other unions, because the contract gives management exclusive power in setting production standards. The conflict is the same for both unions, but the confrontation for settling the conflict is different. Ultimately, the union for which the conflict is a gripe may attempt to negotiate a provision in its contract giving it a role in setting production standards.

What does the union do in the meantime? The conflict does not go away. Other confrontation tactics are appropriate.

In some states, public employees do not have the right to engage in collective bargaining. In other states public employees are granted collective bargaining, but the right to strike is withheld. They must use other confrontation tactics. Where collective bargaining exists in the public sector, what do unions do when conflicts over wages, production standards, and other matters are prohibited by law from being mandatory subjects for negotiations? Other confrontation tactics must be used to turn gripes into demonstrations of union strength or, at least, demonstrations of the union's commitment to advance and protect the interests of workers.

In addition to grievances, collective bargaining, and strikes, the confrontation tactics available to unions include the following:

A Petition protesting a condition at the workplace, signed by all or a large proportion of the bargaining unit, may be an effective tactic. The petition very likely will not cause management to reverse its decision. Top management may be far removed from the realities of the shop or office floor. A petition does, however, make management aware of the condition and of the fact that the union can rally the support of the bargaining unit in protesting the situation. The petition also lets management know that the union will hold the support of workers in a decertification effort and that it will demonstrate solidarity in the event of a strike.

Petitions are most appropriate as a protest against gripes which cannot be confronted through the grievance procedure. However, petitions need not be limited to gripes. A grievance can be turned into a petition by having all or a large proportion of the bargaining unit sign it.

A petition is not only a demonstration of the union's support, it is a test of the union's strength. Choose the issue to be protested carefully. A petition signed by a small percentage of the bargaining unit makes the union look weak.

Unions that are effective at internal organizing do not pick the wrong issue. From their informal discussions with workers and their maintenance of file cards, issues are selected that the vast majority of workers view as important.

Signing a petition is an act of courage. The old adage of "safety in numbers" applies. When circulating the petition, first ask those whom the informal discussions indicate are the most likely to sign. Then approach those who might be reluctant.

Informational Picketing and Demonstrations are more dramatic than petitions but have the same objectives as petitions. Management will be informed of workplace conflicts and the union will demonstrate its solidarity.

Informational picketing and demonstrations can be more effective than petitions, but they also are more difficult to successfully deliver. They require more effort and require bargaining unit members to stick their necks out even further than the act of signing a petition. A poorly attended demonstration makes the union look bad. A poor turnout indicates that the union leadership is not in touch with the membership. Do not hold a parade that no one attends. An effective internal organizing network will allow a union to know in advance whether the picketing or rally will succeed.

Job Actions such as sick-outs, slowdowns, and wildcat strikes can be effective ways of pressuring employers and promoting union solidarity. However, job actions must be used very cautiously. Bargaining unit members and the union itself may be subject to severe penalties. These range from suspension and discharge to fines and imprisonment depending upon the job action and the state or federal government statute being violated. Before engaging in job actions, the union must be aware of all the penalties which could be imposed upon it. Private sector unions should check with the NLRB, and public sector unions should check with the appropriate state or federal government agency.

The union must then assess its bargaining power in order to determine whether the job action is likely to achieve its objective and whether penalties are likely to be imposed. The union must answer the following questions: Are all bargaining unit members likely to participate in the job action? Can the employer easily replace participants in the job action? Is the product or service provided by labor vital to customers or the public so that pressure will be exerted upon the employer to settle on the union's terms? Particularly in the case of public employees, is the community supportive of the union's demands?

If the likelihood of success is good and the union decides to proceed with the job action, the internal organizing communications system is used to inform bargaining unit members of the tactic and to assure their participation.

The End-Run involves by-passing management with whom the union deals on a day-to-day basis and taking the conflict to another body in an attempt to settle the issue on the union's terms. Unions regularly use the end-run by lobbying legislators and other government officials in an attempt to achieve objectives that they are unable to achieve through collective bargaining. Many international unions have full-time lobbyists. The major function of the AFL-CIO at the state and national levels is lobbying for laws and administrative agency policies favorable to unions.

Unions attempt to influence the public through news releases, press conferences, and advertising in the media. Consumer boycotts of J.P. Stevens and PPG products and non-union lettuce and grapes are examples of going beyond collective bargaining to achieve union objectives.

Also, unions by-pass managers with whom they have daily contact and bring conflicts to the attention of their superiors at agency or corporate headquarters. Local managers dislike the end-run, because they fear looking bad in the view of their superiors. Sometimes, threatening the end-run is all that is necessary to bring management around to the union's position. Petitions, demonstrations, and job actions are ways of making an end-run around local management.

The National Education Association represents teachers in all fifty states. In some states it has the right of collective bargaining. In other states, collective bargaining for public employees is not legally sanctioned, and every workplace conflict is a "gripe" and not a "grievance." The work of the director of a suburban Des Moines UniServ cluster illustrates how organizing around issues can be used effectively in the following case history of how one NEA chapter confronted a gripe:

> A school system superintendent became very upset over an incident in which football players from the local high school team and an opposing team damaged a school bus following a game. The superintendent called in the coaches of the local team and told them he was developing a policy proposal for presentation to the school board which would require that coaches pay for any damages to school property by football players out of their paychecks.
>
> The coaches reported this to the association president, who also had received issue organizing training. The president called in the UniServ director. The director met the following day with a small cadre of association officers and coaches to map out strategy. (In this case, no search for real leaders was needed.) The group decided the issue was hot, and that it would seek a written vote of support from the high school faculty to proceed to resolve the issue. The president and two other members were appointed to seek a meeting with the superintendent.
>
> Next day the signatures of all faculty members were obtained on a document of support and the president met with the superintendent. The latter reacted angrily, refused to meet with association leaders and said it was none of their business. Later

in the day, the superintendent called the president out of her class for a 60-minute lecture which was overheard by teachers and students and which infuriated the faculty.

The following day, an Iowa State Education Association staff member joined the UniServ director in an effort to obtain a meeting with the superintendent. The superintendent refused.

A school board meeting had been scheduled for several days later, so the association used the intervening time to contact board members about the matter and to develop a statement to be read at the meeting. Faculties of other schools in the system and the local media were informed of the high school teachers' plans and their determination to deal with the issue.

At the school board meeting, the president and the UniServ director were greeted cooly by the board, but allowed to make their presentations. The president stated the association's opposition to any policy which would violate the coaches' contracts. The school board president said there must be some misunderstanding because neither the board nor the superintendent were considering any such policy.

The next morning's newspaper carried a story on the whole matter and quoted the superintendent as saying, "I don't like the strong-arm tactics of the union."[6]

After the union has confronted a workplace conflict through collective bargaining, the grievance procedure, a petition, a demonstration, a job action, or an end-run, it must *communicate* the outcome of the confrontation to bargaining unit members. Ideally, of course, the union has resolved the conflict favorably. Nothing beats a victory. If the contract does not have a union shop clause, now is the time to approach nonmembers about joining the union.

If the confrontation has not resolved the conflict, this must be communicated. The reasons why the confrontation failed to resolve the issue and the next step, if any, planned by the union must be given. Usually, the next step will be to resurrect the issue during the next contract negotiation. If there is good reason for optimism, be optimistic. If it is a lost cause, convey that the union did its best and will continue to confront management. The union is demonstrating to bargaining unit members that it is working diligently to serve their needs. That is what internal organizing and staying organized are all about.

CASE STUDIES

Try your hand at developing confrontation tactics for dealing with workplace conflicts. The six case studies that follow are based upon actual workplace conflicts. In each case, the union had an opportunity to organize internally. You can too. Approach each case from the particular circumstances of your union. For example, you will probably approach Case Study 1 differently if your union represents workers in the public sector rather than workers in the private sector. Be creative! There is no law that restricts the confrontation tactics of unions to contract negotiations and the grievance procedure. In some situations, even they are denied. (The actual union responses to the conflicts follow the case studies.)

CASE STUDY 1

John Williams, a supervisor, has called each worker in the department at home and asked them to make "a suggested contribution of $30" to a political organization to which he belongs. Williams has a reputation among workers as "pretty good as far as supervisors go except that he sometimes plays favorites." A union member tells you that some of the workers felt intimidated and "made contributions just to be safe." There is no law prohibiting Williams's action. It is common practice for workers to sell raffle tickets for charitable organizations at work, but this is the first time that political contributions have been solicited.

CASE STUDY 2

Three years ago a clerical department employed sixty workers. Through attrition and failure to replace, fifty workers are now employed. The amount of work performed has remained constant. Frequent overtime has been required. The employer finds it cheaper to pay time and a half for overtime than to hire additional workers because of the savings made on fringe benefits. At first, most workers welcomed the extra money. Now, many find the heavy mandatory overtime to be burdensome. The contract treats overtime as solely the employer's prerogative.

CASE STUDY 3

Under the contract workers are allowed ten days paid sick leave per year. A note from a doctor is required for absences for medical reasons exceeding two days. Mary LaFever, a supervisor, approaches all workers who take one or two days of sick leave and interrogates them about their illnesses. She often tells workers that she does not believe they were ill and that they are abusing the sick leave "privilege." Also, she regularly calls workers at home and asks work-related questions during the afternoons of days when they are on sick leave. Workers feel intimidated, but no one has told Mary, as she is quick to tell you—a shop steward—when you confront her about the matter.

You speak with Mary's supervisor. She says that there is nothing in the contract prohibiting Mary's actions. The amount of paid sick leave days taken has increased dramatically since they were increased from five days to ten days in the last contract, so Mary is merely doing her job.

In talking to other stewards, you find that Mary's actions are not unique. Other supervisors do the same thing, but workers are afraid to complain because recommendations from supervisors are an important consideration in promotions.

CASE STUDY 4

Normally, the doors to the kitchen are open because of the heat. Food was reported stolen, so management ordered the doors to be closed. Kitchen workers complained to their supervisor who told them that under the contract, management has the right to maintain security and that he checked with a government agency responsible for health and safety. The temperature in the kitchen is no hotter than that in a foundry, and therefore, within approved limits. He concluded with "You know the old saying. If you can't stand the heat, . . ."[7]

CASE STUDY 5

A new management policy is announced: "Because of the energy crisis we will henceforth encourage all employees to form car pools or use mass transit for commuting to and from work by charging $1 per day for parking."

The contract does not contain any reference to the free parking previously provided by the employer. However, the new policy is a unilateral change in the terms and conditions of employment.

CASE STUDY 6

The contract treats the setting of production standards as solely a management right. Two months ago, management announced increased production standards for most jobs. Nearly all of the workers affected by the change have failed to meet the new standards. Supervisors continually remind workers of their failure to meet production. No one has been disciplined or threatened with disciplinary action, but some workers are becoming very anxious about the situation. You notice that workers in your unit are more irritable than before the production standards were raised. A worker confides that he is having trouble sleeping because of the pressure applied by his supervisor.

UNION RESPONSES TO CONFLICTS PRESENTED IN CASE STUDIES

1. The public employee union in a state not providing collective bargaining rights used the end-run. A friendly legislator was contacted by the union, who in turn contacted the director of the agency. The supervisor was reprimanded and the union publicized its resolution of the problem in its newsletter.

2. A steward of this private sector union conveyed the concern of the membership to management which did not change its stand on heavy compulsory overtime. The steward informed each member of her effort with management at a lunch-time meeting. The members decided that they should tell supervisors that they object to working overtime and want additional workers hired whenever instructed to work overtime in order to keep the issue alive. In addition, a noon-time rally was planned for the following week. The media would be invited. The theme of the rally was "excessive overtime, during high unemployment." Because of its downtown location, the rally was highly visible and gained media attention. Management agreed to discuss the matter with the union and eventually increased the workforce, cutting overtime to a more acceptable level.

3. A grievance under the general category of "harassment" was filed. Virtually, all members of the bargaining unit signed the grievance which was won at the third step of the procedure. The union publicized the victory in its newsletter.

4. The union posted an informational picket line at this public sector facility. Management rescinded its order and union members and non-members alike quickly learned of the victory.

5. A grievance was filed and was won at the second step of the procedure. The public employee union distributed money in thousand dollar denominations with the inscription "Union Dividend." Coupled with an intensive face-to-face solicitation of non-members, about ten percent of the "free-riders" agreed to join the union.

6.   The union distributed leaflets charging management with a "speed-up" and "harassment." Three times a week, for a month, informational pickets greeted members on their way to work with the same theme. By the end of the month, scrap production and maintenance of equipment reached high proportions. A rumor circulated among the workforce that "there's more than one way to skin a cat." Supervisors eased up and the picketing was stopped.

FOOTNOTES

[1] John C. Anderson, Gloria Busman, and Charles A. O'Reilly III, "The Decertification Process: Evidence from California," *Industrial Relations,* Vol. 21, No. 2, Spring 1982, p. 178.

[2] "The Workplace," *The Minneapolis Star,* May 22, 1981, p. 2D.

[3] "How Important Is Union Democracy?" *Union Democracy Review,* No. 16, p. 3.

[4] Steven Lagerfeld, "To Break a Union," *Harpers,* May 1981, p. 18.

[5] American Federation of Government Employees. *Internal Organizing.* Mimeo, n.d., pp. 15–16.

[6] National Education Association, *Issue Organizing.* Offset, Worksheet No. 3, 1976, p. 2.

[7] Adapted from the American Federation of State, County, and Municipal Employee's "Internal Organizing" sound-filmstrip presentation, n.d.

Labor's Prospects For Growth

In 1982, *Fortune* magazine gathered six economists together to discuss the future of organized labor in the United States. Their predictions ranged from the mildly optimistic to the pessimistic and approached the proverbial twelve opinions from six economists.[1] As this last chapter will demonstrate, the uncertainty of the six economists is justified. To deny that unions have suffered setbacks and face an uphill fight is unrealistic, but there are glimmers of evidence that organized labor may reverse the decline in the proportion of the labor force it represents.

LABOR AND POLITICS

Labor's ability to organize is limited by the legal constraints placed upon it and the lack of constraints placed upon the anti-union behavior of employers. Al Bilik succinctly appraises the legal environment in which unions organize:

> Companies small and large, north and south, are now convinced that it pays to violate, even if found guilty by the NLRB. They measure the cost of violating against the cost of collective bargaining and coldly opt for the former. Given the weapons available to employers and their growing willingness to use them, it is surprising that so many workers today actually do vote for union representation.[2]

Bilik may be labeled as a labor union advocate, but union advocates are not alone in their appraisal of the law's regulation of union organizing. The U.S. General Accounting Office (GAO) confirms this view. The GAO studied 368 union representation elections held during 1979 and found that employer unfair labor practices have a "chilling effect on the free exercise of employee rights to select the union."[3]

Since the passage of Taft-Hartley in the mid-1940s, organized labor has railed and rallied against the law to no avail. The exclusion of supervisors from the law's protections, the prohibition of the secondary boycott, so-called "right to work" laws, and the absence of effective sanctions against employers who discharge union supporters and refuse to bargain are legislative acts away from changing dramatically the future of organized labor.

Failure to secure passage of common situs picketing and labor law reform during the Carter administration—despite the financial and organizational assistance that labor contributed to Carter's 1976 campaign and the defeat of labor candidates in 1980 through the support of union members—prompted organized labor to reexamine its political activities.

The political strategy as of this writing is for the AFL-CIO to determine whether there is sufficient consensus among its affiliates to endorse a candidate for the Democratic Party's presidential nomination well before the primary elections are held in 1984. This plan represents a significant departure from the AFL-CIO's traditional strategy of keeping a distance from either party in order to preserve its leverage on both parties and to avoid choosing sides in Democratic Party primary fights. The strategy is not without its risks. If a consensus is reached among AFL-CIO affiliates and an endorsement is made, labor's candidate could lose in the primaries, which would weaken labor's influence with the Party's eventual candidate.

In addition to strengthening its ties to the Democratic Party, the AFL-CIO is polling rank and file union members in an effort to influence political candidates, engaging in direct mail campaigns, assisting state AFL-CIO's with legislation affecting their members, and organizing "grass-roots" committees made up of rank and filers who lobby legislators in key congressional districts. Plans have also been made to increase public relations expenditures so as to improve organized labor's public image and promote its legislative platform.[4] These changes in technique imitate the tactics used successfully by conservative interest groups in the 1980s and should enable organized labor to offset the impact of these organizations.

ORGANIZING IN THE SOUTH

American industry is expanding in the region of the country where organized labor has traditionally been the weakest—the South—with the consequence of diminishing the influence of unions in that region even further, as evidenced by the decline in the organized portion of the South's labor force from 17.6 percent in 1970 to 14.1 percent in 1980.[5] Failure to increase the likelihood that employers will not escape unionization by moving South jeopardizes the future of organized labor by providing an increasingly attractive incentive to employers to run away to a safe haven.

Organized labor is attempting to stem the tide. In 1981 and 1982, the AFL-CIO launched concerted organizing drives in Houston and Atlanta respectively, the South's two largest industrial centers. Over twenty international unions are participating in each campaign with the budget for the Houston drive set at over $1 million per year. The Houston campaign may involve as many as 200 organizers simultaneously. These multi-union organizing drives coordinated by the AFL-CIO represent somewhat of a departure from the policies of the late George Meany who preferred that organizing be conducted by individual affiliates, although multi-union drives are not entirely new.[6] AFL-CIO President Lane Kirkland views these multi-union organizing drives in the South as a long-term commitment, vowing "We're here for the long pull."[7]

The outcome of these multi-union drives is difficult to predict, because the Industrial Union Department (IUD) of the AFL-CIO has conducted multi-union drives in the South for years and experienced mixed results. During the 1960s, the IUD and its participating international unions spent $13 million and organized just 93,000 Southern workers.[8] Yet the IUD and its participating affiliates can take much of the credit for the increase between 1970 and 1980 in the proportion of union members in Mississippi, the nation's poorest state, by winning sixty-three of ninety-four authorization elections held between 1974 and 1981.[9] An AFL-CIO coordinated drive in Los Angeles is credited with organizing 400,000 workers into unions between 1962 and 1982.[10]

Unions have been able to weaken the resistance of some organized employers who have expanded their productive capacity in the South. As part of its 1982 contract settlement, General Motors agreed to recognize the United Auto Workers without NLRB elections and on the basis of a majority of authorization card signatories demonstrating interest. Within a few months, 415 workers at a GM plant in Meridian, Mississippi, 300 workers in Fitzgerald, Georgia, and 1,700 workers in Decatur, Alabama, were organized.[11] The impact of the boycott against Coor's beer by the AFL-CIO and by women's and gays' organizations was probably a factor in the decision of the Miller Brewing Company not to resist the organization of its North Carolina plant.[12] At the bargaining table and through boycotts and other actions, unions can make the South more conducive to organizing.

Ultimately, the fate of organized labor in the South does not depend upon the immediate success of the Houston and Atlanta campaigns as much as upon the commitment to continue the effort. If in fact organized labor is in the South "for the long pull," it has a good chance of making the runaway shop a risky venture. If the campaigns fail and organized labor reduces its organizing efforts correspondingly, the fate of unions in the South is likely to be sealed. A commitment to organizing the South should be likened to the long-run union avoidance strategy of employers, a campaign of continuous pressure.

ORGANIZING THE SERVICE INDUSTRIES AND WHITE-COLLAR OCCUPATIONS

Highly organized manufacturing industries like autos, steel, and rubber are losing market share to foreign competition and are automating at a rate that insures a permanent displacement of labor. As a result, observers say that the United States is on its way to becoming a "postindustrial society" dominated by high-technology, service, and information industries with jobs in such fields as computers, accounting, banking, engineering, economics, physics, law, and health care. Between 1950 and 1982, blue-collar employment fell from 40 percent to 30 percent of the U.S. labor force while white-collar employment grew from 36 percent to 54 percent. The growth of industries and occupations in which unions have traditionally been weak will continue.[13]

As in the South, unions are attempting to organize workers in the growth industries and occupations. District 65 of the Auto Workers, the Service Employees, the Food and Commercial Workers, the Office and Professional Employees, and the Communication Workers are among the unions attempting to keep up with the changing economy and are experiencing some success. Betweeen 1977 and 1980, the U.S. Bureau of Labor statistics reported that the number of organized white-collar workers increased from 7.3 million to 8.5 million, a 16 percent increase in three years.

About 20 million women are employed in clerical jobs with only a small proportion organized into unions. Despite increased participation by women in jobs traditionally dominated by men, most new female job market entrants through the 1980s will secure jobs in occupations already dominated by women.[14] Female-dominated occupations are low paying and are often supervised by men and in some cases by women, who treat workers as indentured servants, as was vividly portrayed in the film *9 to 5*. Recognizing the special problems of female clerical workers, the Service Employees International Union recently entered into a joint organizing effort with Working Women, a 10,000-member organization dedicated to uplift the pay and dignity of women office workers through means other than collective bargaining.[15] Because black civil rights organizations and unions have worked together successfully during organizing drives, particularly in the South, coalitions of unions and women's rights organizations are very promising.

Workers in traditionally unorganized industries and occupations seem to be motivated to join unions for the same reasons as workers in industries with high degrees of unionization—inadequate wages and benefits and arbitrary treatment being the most prevalent reasons.[16] While non-union employers are reluctant to release information on their employees' attitudes, there is evidence that all is not well in the traditionally unorganized sectors. A survey by the American Management Association discloses that of 2,600 executives questioned, most said that advancement at their companies is the result of "largely subjective evaluation or arbitrary decision." More than half of the salaried employees surveyed at Ford Motor Company believe that there is little consistency in the standards used to rate job performance and that improved job performance would not help their chances for promotion.[17]

The arbitrary treatment that these surveys show, along with the changing demographic characteristics of the labor force, indicate that conditions for unionization may improve substantially. There will be a dramatic increase in the number of college educated persons in the twenty-five to forty-four age group over the next few years, reaching 50 percent of the labor force by 1990. This development is the result of the post-World War II baby boom, a significant increase in the years of formal education received by this segment of the population, and increased labor force participation by women. There will be more competition for jobs and promotions, slower advancement to high paying jobs, and lower wages in the 1990s than if this surplus in the labor market did not occur.[18,19] Unionization provides workers with a way to exercise some control over these conditions in the 1980s and 1990s, just as they did in the 1930s. Professor Oscar Ornati predicts:

> Probably in the next decade there will be unionization in areas that we don't even think of—banking, financial services. The people who work in these areas are becoming the factory workers of today.[20]

LABOR'S NEW ORGANIZING TECHNIQUES

The sophisticated rhetorical, psychological, and organizational techniques of employers—the short-run and long-run union avoidance strategies—are a major reason why unions find organizing difficult. Organized labor is responding to this challenge with the development of its own sophisticated organizing techniques. The AFL-CIO Department of Organization and Field Services is formally committed to intensifying its "development of training projects and teaching materials for organizers" and "to develop creative methods to combat union-busters."[21]

Changes are occurring in the way organizing targets are selected. Rather than simply targeting a workplace because it is handy or has a large number of workers or is a runaway shop, some unions are expending considerable effort to determine whether potential targets can be organized and whether a contract can be negotiated that represents an improvement in the terms and conditions of employment. By surveying workers at potential targets before launching a drive, organizers determine whether conditions are ripe for organizing. If workers are generally satisfied with their jobs, the expense of launching a campaign is avoided.[22]

Unions are also using new ways to convey their message. Because of the strong influence of television, the AFL-CIO has videotaped messages by Screen Actor's Guild President Ed Asner and other union members, which organizers can play when making housecalls on workers. In its Houston campaign, the AFL-CIO has instituted a computerized mailing system. In its Atlanta campaign, it is attempting to recruit rank and file union members to participate as volunteers in organizing drives.[23]

Unions are also using new ways to improve their public image. In Tupelo, Mississippi, the AFL-CIO sponsors a free social-service center assisting low income people at obtaining government benefits and providing counseling on legal matters and family problems.[24] This tactic is likely to be used in other organizing campaigns in the South because of the notoriously poor social services generally provided in the region.[25] Radio and television advertisements are part of the Houston campaign and are being used increasingly by unions in other parts of the country, particularly in the consumer-sensitive food and beverage trades.

Some unions are devoting more time to educating workers at organizing targets on the flexibility of unions and collective bargaining. For example, professionals who enjoy great latitude in the work they perform are often under the misconception that union representation means strict job classifications restricting the work that individuals can perform. Also, when organizing office workers and professionals, greater care is taken to select organizers who match the education and work experience of workers at organizing targets so that organizers and targeted workers can relate to one another on a common basis. Likewise, rather than being part of an amalgamated local union which includes workers of different occupations, and therefore different workplace concerns, greater effort is being made to grant local union autonomy to workers along occupational lines.[26]

Organized labor is also shining the light of publicity upon union avoidance consultants. Through its periodic RUB Sheets (*Report on Union Busters*), the AFL-CIO Department of Organization identifies the consultants, their clients, their campaign tactics, and operating procedures. This information can be valuable to union organizers involved in campaigns engineered by consultants. On occasion, unions have set up informational picket lines at facilities where union avoidance seminars are conducted.[27] Picketing may result in seminars being canceled and may be useful in demonstrating to union members the necessity of committing financial resources to organizing new members.

Recently, some unions have headlined in their newspapers the need to intensify organizing efforts as the primary reason for dues increases. However, an examination of the fine print indicates that, in some cases, the need to organize is used as a smokescreen to convince the membership of the need for a dues increase with the bulk of the increase in both absolute and relative terms earmarked for the general fund and the allocation for organizing only sufficient to keep pace with inflation. In other cases, a sincere effort to intensify organizing activity is made. The Graphic Arts International Union, for example, increased its full-time organizing staff from four to ten and improved the services its research department provides to organizers so as "to eliminate organizers spending, hours, days, and weeks in libraries deciding which companies to target for organizing."[28]

The AFL-CIO-funded George Meany Center for Labor Studies offers organizer training programs on a regular basis. However, labor education-studies programs at public colleges and universities have not played a significant role in conducting research or classes designed to improve the effectiveness of unions at organizing. Instead of providing the stimulus for innovation which schools of agriculture, medicine, business, and engineering provide for their respective constituencies, labor education-studies programs have virtually ignored organized labor's growth process for reasons that solidify the traditional antipathy of organized labor in the United States toward intellectuals.

Many of these programs were established in the immediate post-World War II period in the environment that fostered the passage of Taft-Hartley as adjuncts of industrial and labor relations centers whose mission was to promote "industrial peace," "objective scholarship," and "neutrality in all areas of dispute between labor and capital."[29] Despite the indisputable legality of union organizing, research and teaching that assist union organizing have not generally been perceived as "objective and neutral." While the shield of "academic freedom" would presumably protect this research and teaching, it does not shield those who fear that employers would retaliate and cut the budgets of their personal fiefdoms. Nor does "academic freedom" protect the "new entrepreneurs" whose business it is to promote "neutrality" and their pocketbooks as arbitrators and mediators of labor-management disputes,[30] because employers might perceive those connected with an institution promoting union organization as incapable of "neutrality." All the while, industrial and labor relations programs train legions of personnel specialists for industry and at least implicitly promote the strategy of "making unions unnecessary."

Changes have occurred in recent years. Usually from a very cautious beginning, some programs openly offer regular classes on organizing and staying organized. Sometimes the change comes from within, because it is difficult to ignore one of the major problems confronting organized labor. In other cases, change comes from the prodding of union activists who see no reason to lobby state legislatures for the funding of unresponsive programs. Union activists who take their roles as advisors to labor education-studies programs seriously can make these programs approach parity with the employer interests served by industrial and labor relations centers.

Unions could improve their organizing potential by keeping track of workers who were once members of bargaining units, because they offer the best testimony to union effectiveness and, therefore, are good inside contacts at unorganized workplaces. A way of keeping track of these workers would be to offer them a form of inactive membership. In return for nominal dues, they might receive group insurance, prepaid legal services, or educational benefits. "The basic principle is simple: once a worker is part of the labor movement, he or she should always be a part of it."[31]

The Communication Workers are targeting skilled microelectronics workers for organization. Because these workers tend to be mobile between firms in the booming electronics industry, part of the union's strategy is to have workers maintain their union memberships when they change employers.[32] With labor turnover in the U.S. economy averaging about 30 percent each year, the concept of lifetime union membership offers tremendous potential.

The seventeen-year campaign by the Amalgamated Clothing and Textile Workers Union to gain union recognition and secure a contract from J.P. Stevens & Company was finally won in 1980, because the union developed a "corporate strategy" which isolated the company from the corporate community. The union studied the relationships that J.P. Stevens had with other corporations and found that officers of Avon Products and Hanover Trust Company served on its board of directors. By publicizing these relationships and at least implicitly threatening that a consumer boycott of the two firms might occur because of their relationships with Stevens, the two outside directors resigned from the Stevens board. Likewise, the president of Stevens resigned from the boards of Hanover Trust and the New York Life Insurance Company. These resignations probably could have been tolerated by Stevens, but the union's next move broke its resistance.

In September 1980, the union mounted a campaign against Metropolitan Life Insurance Company, which was Stevens' biggest lender with $97 million in loans. The union announced plans to nominate two directors to the insurance company's board of directors. Under New York state law all 23 million of Metropolitan Life's policy holders would have to be sent ballots so that they could vote in the contested election. The cost to Metropolitan Life was estimated at more than $9 million. Within a month, a contract was reached between the ACTWU and Stevens, including an agreement by the union to drop its plan to contest the Metropolitan Life election.[33]

Ray Rogers, who engineered the ACTWU's "corporate campaign" against J.P. Stevens, formed a company called Corporate Campaign, Inc., a consulting firm dedicated to assisting unions rather than working against them. By putting pressure on the institutions tied through loans, stockholdings, and interlocking directorates to the corporations with which unions have disputes, Rogers hopes to replicate the success of the Stevens campaign and to demonstrate how organized labor can obtain the power to beat large corporations.[34]

The AFL-CIO Food and Beverage Trades Department conducts seminars on the "corporate campaign" and has developed an excellent booklet on the topic.[35] An example of the corporate campaign in an organizing drive is the Food and Beverage Trades Department's effort to organize Beverly Enterprises, the largest nursing home chain in the country with 39,000 employees, about 10 percent of whom are organized. On two occasions, the FBTD has unsuccessfully sponsored candidates for the board of directors of the company.[36] In the District of Columbia, the FNTD has challenged the granting of a license to Beverly to operate a nursing home on the grounds that it did not provide adequate patient care.[37] On June 10 and 11, 1982, five FBTD members, including its president, Robert Harbrant, staged a thirty-hour sit-in at Beverly's Pasadena, California, headquarters, because Beverly blocked FBTD's attempt to ask questions at its shareholders' meeting about its labor law violations and the company's patient care. The sit-in and supporting demonstration outside the building, which included members of the National Council of Senior Citizens and the Gray Panthers, was halted after the company agreed to answer questions about its operations.[38]

While the "corporate campaign" is certainly annoying to organizing targets, it is not effective in all situations. Instantaneous results cannot be expected, so that a long-term commitment is required of the union, the costs can be high, and, above all, many employers are not as vulnerable as J.P. Stevens ultimately proved to be. Campaigns against Texaco and New York Air failed for at least one of these reasons.[39] Yet it is encouraging that organized labor has developed a new organizing tactic which is likely to succeed in some situations.

The most thought-provoking book in many years on how organized labor might improve its power in the corporate environment within which organizing occurs is Jeremy Rifkin's and Randy Barber's *The North Will Rise Again—Pensions, Politics, and Power in the 1980s.*[40] The essence of Rifkin's and Barber's strategy is that pension funds are the largest single source of investment capital in the United States, with a significant portion of these pension funds negotiated by unions. Yet unions exercise little control over the investment of pension funds, because their management is usually turned over to banks, insurance companies, and other financial intermediaries. Because of this lack of union control, union-negotiated pension funds are often invested in companies that are stridently opposed to the unionization of their employees. By exercising control, unions could make the corporate environment more conducive to organizing.

Organized labor has been influenced by Rifkin's and Barber's strategy. In 1981, the AFL-CIO Executive Council passed a resolution urging affiliates to implement programs that use union-negotiated pension funds to advance the interests of organized labor. Concurrent with this resolution, the Industrial Union Department of the AFL-CIO issues a monthly newsletter titled *Labor & Investments*, which reports progress at implementing the strategy.

An example of how the strategy can be implemented is the action taken by the United Steelworkers against Procter and Gamble.

Over a year after winning authorization to represent 500 workers at Procter and Gamble's Kansas City soap plant and failing to reach agreement on a first contract, the Steelworkers launched a consumer boycott against the company's soap products in November 1981. To strengthen its position, the union advised security analysts and institutional investors attending a Procter and Gamble forecast meeting in March 1982 that union-negotiated pension plans are the company's largest stockholder group and that the union would exert pressure on the company until it changed its anti-union policies.[41]

The threat to withhold investments by union-negotiated pension plans from anti-union companies is easier said than done in 1982, but this may not be the case in 1992 if unions are serious about implementing the Rifkin and Barber strategy. The framers of the Taft-Hartley Act had great foresight to prohibit union control of pension funds in 1947 at a time when few unions had negotiated retirement benefits. It was not until 1949 that the U.S. Supreme Court made pensions a mandatory subject for collective bargaining, and all that unions could negotiate because of Taft-Hartley was joint control with management over pension fund investments. The first large-scale pension plans were negotiated in the post-World War II years by the United Auto Workers. Rather than determining (or more appropriately, negotiating) with management the investment of each dollar of pension fund contributions, UAW President Walter Reuther chose to turn this responsibility over to financial intermediaries, because, according to long-time UAW insiders, he feared that even partial control would subject union officials to the temptation of making investments that advanced their personal fortunes. Most other unions followed the UAW example and the record of the Teamster's Central States Pension Fund lends credence to Reuther's prognosis.

The banking and insurance company lobbies are powerful and must be reckoned with if organized labor is to exercise even partial control (or obtain negotiating rights) over pension plan investments. Organized labor must proceed on at least two fronts: (1) it must, through collective bargaining, negotiate joint labor-management control of pension funds and (2) it must fend off the vested interests in the political arena which seek to maintain the status quo. Because the primary purpose of pension fund investments is to insure benefits to retirees, organized labor should anticipate a major objection to joint control by establishing an ethical practices committee comprised of labor, management, and neutral public interest groups which would oversee pension fund investments. Given the poor return on investment records of most pension plans in the 1970s and 1980s and the crystal ball gazing involved, "prudent" investments that also improve the organizing climate should not be difficult to identify.

The day when the results of pension plan investment negotiations are as eagerly anticipated by the media as major contract negotiations is a long way off. But with sufficient determination, the organizing climate in 1992 can be vastly different from that in 1982 where the threat to withhold union-negotiated pension plan investments from anti-union companies is largely empty.

CONCLUSION

Former Secretary of Labor John Dunlop draws an analogy between social movements and waves eating away at a cliff: nothing seems to happen for a long time, until one day the cliff falls in. Likewise, unions have grown in spurts.[42] Twenty years ago, few people would have predicted that the majority of nonsupervisory government employees would be represented by unions as they are today, or that supervisors in the public sector of the state of Minnesota would have collective bargaining rights, or that major league baseball and football players would organize into unions and call strikes. Also, it is easy to forget that the long-established unions of today were not organized overnight. Efforts to organize the steel industry, for example, began in the nineteenth century and did not succeed until the late 1930s.

A 1982 poll on the attitudes of unorganized workers toward unionization disclosed that 51 percent of unorganized workers said that they would join a union if they were working on a job where they could. This response is significantly higher than in previous polls on the issue.[43] The increased receptivity toward unionization may be a reflection of the state of the economy. Real wage gains in the 1980s are at their lowest levels since the 1930s, when organized labor experienced its greatest growth.

Organizing the unorganized, however, is not inevitable; it will not just happen. Unions must make it happen. Through intensified organizing efforts in the South and among workers in white-collar occupations and the service industries, by altering its political strategies, and by developing organizing tactics attuned to the sophisticated hostility of employers, organized labor shows signs of life.

Battered and pronounced dead, organized labor, like the legendary Joe Hill, is still alive as long as it does not neglect Hill's last word: "Organize!"

FOOTNOTES

[1] "Are Unions Dead or Just Sleeping?" *Fortune,* September 20, 1982, p. 100.

[2] Al Bilik, "Corrupt, Crusty, or Neither? The Poll-ish View of American Unions," *Labor Law Journal,* Vol. 30, 1979, p. 329.

[3] "Study Bears Out Need for NLRA Reform," *AFL-CIO News,* July 17, 1982, p. 4.

[4] "Lane Kirkland's Catch-Up Game," *Business Week,* June 28, 1982, pp. 75 and 79.

[5] "Unions Still Find South a Tough Row to Hoe," *U.S. News & World Report,* June 21, 1982, pp. 62–63.

[6] "Labor's New Campaign to Crack the Sunbelt," *Business Week,* October 19, 1981, pp. 43–44.

[7] "Unions Still Find South," p. 63.

[8] "Unions in the Sunbelt," *Business Week,* May 17, 1976.

[9] "Unions Still Find South," p. 62.

[10] "20 Years of Success Hailed in L.A. Organizing Project," *AFL-CIO News,* September 25, 1981, p. 5.

[11] "UAW Organizes 1,700 at GM's Alabama Plant," *Labor World,* September 9, 1982, p. 8.

[12] "Unions in the South," *Business Week,* April 18, 1979, p. 66.

[13] "Jobs: A Million That Will Never Come Back," *U.S. News & World Report,* September 13, 1982, pp. 53–56.

[14] "U.S. Business Trends That Shape the Future," *U.S. News & World Report,* October 4, 1982, pp. 65–66.

[15] Phillip Shabecoff, "New Union Hopes to Quash Indignities of '9 to 5' Work," *Minneapolis Tribune,* April 5, 1981, p. 6D.

[16] Kenneth S. Warner et al, "Motives for Unionization Among State Social Service Employees," *Public Personnel Journal,* May–June 1978, pp. 181–191.

[17] Michael Ver Muelen, "How To Take Your Boss to Court and Win," *Prime Time,* June 1980.

[18] Myron Roomkin and Hervey Juris, "The Changing Character of Unionism in Traditionally Organized Sectors," *Monthly Labor Review,* February 1979, p. 37.

[19] John Hoerr, "A Warning that Worker Discontent Is Rising," *Business Week,* June 4, 1979, p. 152.

[20] "Labor's Downbeat Labor Day," *Time,* September 13, 1982, p. 76.

[21] "Houston Campaign Hailed as Model for Coordinated Organizing Effort," *AFL-CIO News*, November 28, 1981, p. 14.

[22] "Unions Still Find South," p. 63.

[23] "Laborious Task: Union Organizer Faces Harder Than Ever in Recession-Hit South," *New York Times*, August 8, 1982.

[24] "Unions Still Find South," p. 63.

[25] "Labor's New Campaign," p. 44.

[26] "Unions Move Into the Office," *Business Week*, January 25, 1982, p. 92.

[27] "Seminar on Dealing with Unions Called Off after Picketing," *The Seattle Times*, November 29, 1979.

[28] "New Involvement by Locals Stressed as Key to Organizing," *Union Tabloid*, p. 5.

[29] Richard E. Dwyer, Miles E. Galvin, and Simeon Larson, "Labor Studies: In Quest of Industrial Justice," *Labor Studies Journal*, Vol. 2, No. 2, Fall 1977, p. 106.

[30] Dwyer, Galvin, & Larson, "Labor Studies," p. 112.

[31] Steve Early, "How Labor Can Play with a Full Deck," *Working Papers*, January-February 1982, pp. 10–12.

[32] "Labor's Downbeat Labor Day," p. 76.

[33] "The Ripples Spreading from the Stevens Pact," *Business Week*, November 3, 1980, pp. 67.

[34] "An Interview with Ray Rogers," *Working Papers*, January-February, 1982, pp. 48–57.

[35] Obtain a copy of the *Manual of Corporate Investigation* from Food and Beverage Trades Department, AFL-CIO, 815 16th St., N.W., Washington, D.C. 20005, Telephone 202/347-2640. The cost is $15.

[36] "Beverly's Proxy War Against Unionization," *Business Week*, May 31, 1982, pp. 32 and 34.

[37] *The Food and Beverage Trades Dept. AFL-CIO Presents Organizing in the 80's, Reducing the Delay.* Offset, n.d., pp. 93–132.

[38] "Sit-In Persuades Firm to Union Queries," *AFL-CIO News*, June 26, 1982, p. 6.

[39] "Pros Who Try to Help Unions Win," *Business Week*, August 23, 1982, pp. 96 and 100.

[40] Boston: Beacon Press, 1978.

[41] "Steelworker's New Strategy Focuses on P & G Investors," *AFL-CIO News*, March 6, 1982, p. 6.

[42] "Are Unions Dead," p. 100.

[43] "Poll Finds Love for Labor, Hate for Its Leaders," *The Minneapolis Star*, February 8, 1982, p. 16A.

Index

301